Xi'an, Sha
and the
Terracotta Army

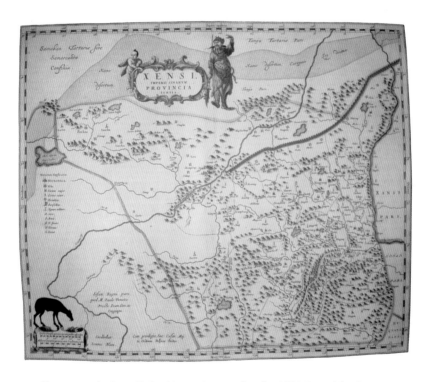

*Shaanxi map by Jesuit Father Martino Martini, from his 1655 Novus Atlas Sinensis,
the first published atlas of China's provinces.*

ODYSSEY BOOKS & GUIDES

Distributed in the USA by
W.W. Norton & Company, Inc.,
500 Fifth Avenue, New York, NY 10110, USA
Tel: 800-233-4830; Fax: 800-458-6515
www.wwnorton.com

Distributed in the UK and Europe by
Cordee Books and Maps,
3a De Montfort Street, Leicester, LE1 7HD, UK,
Tel: 0116-254-3579; Fax: 0116-247-1176
www.cordee.co.uk

Xi'an, Shaanxi and the Terracotta Army © 2005 Airphoto International Ltd.
Odyssey Books & Guides is a division of Airphoto International Ltd.
903 Seaview Commercial Building, 21–24 Connaught Road West, Sheung Wan, Hong Kong
Tel: (852)2856 3896; Fax: (852)2565 8004; E-mail: sales@odysseypublications.com

ISBN: 962-217-729-8   Library of Congress Catalog Card Number has been requested.

Grateful acknowledgement is made to the authors and publishers for permissions granted:
China Photo Archives, Beijing Aeronautical & Space University for *In Memory of Mao Zedong* © 1992 Central Party Literature Publishing House ; Faber and Faber Limited for *Journey to a War* by W H Auden and Christopher Isherwood © revised edition 1991 W H Auden and Christopher Isherwood; Foreign Languages Press, Beijing for *Tu Fu: Selected Poems* compiled by Feng Chih and translated by Rewi Alley; Gillette, Maris Boyd for the map of the Muslim Quarter in Xi'an from *Between Mecca and Beijing*, Copyright © 2000 by the Board of Trustees of the Leland Stanford Junior University; Kodansha International Ltd for *Lou-lan and Other Stories* by Yasushi Inoue translated by Edward Seidensticker © 1979 Kodansha International Ltd; Hodder and Stoughton for *Alone on the Great Wall* by William Lindesay © Hodder & Stoughton; William Heinemann Limited for *Behind the Wall* by Colin Thubron © 1987 Colin Thubron; Century Publishing Co, London for *China's Sorrow* by Lynn Pan © 1985 Lynn Pan; API Press Ltd for *Saturday Night Fever* by John Colling © 1991, John Colling; Zhang Zhonghui for *Mao Zedong: Historical Images and Classical Posters* © Subculture Ltd 1994.

Managing Editor: Helen Northey
Cover Design: Au Yeung Chui Kwai
Design: Aubrey Tse

Map Design: Mark Stroud, Aubrey Tse
Map Consultant: Professor Bai Yiliang

This guide is based upon an earlier work written for Odyssey Guides by Simon Holledge (revised by Kevin Bishop) entitled *Xi'an—China's Ancient Capital*, © Odyssey Publications 2000.

Front cover photography by Xia Juxian
Photography courtesy of API Ltd 294, 302, 304; Christoph Baumer 188; Guo Baofa (and staff of the Preservation Department of the Museum of Terracotta Warriors and Horses of Qin Shihuangdi) 77, 90, 92, 104, 105, 114, 120, 122; Kevin Bishop 238, 305; China Guide Series 316, 320; Dragonair 19; Harvard University, Lattimore Foundation/The Chinese Century 300; Simon Holledge 206; Hong Kong China Photo Tourism Library 58–59, 132, 136–137, 156, 207; William Lindesay 1, 8–9, 45, 250–251, 275, 276; Luo Zhongmin 83, 86–87, 96, 116 (bottom), 202–203, 209 (bottom); Mao Ling Museum 157 (bottom); Catherine Maudsley 145, 157 (top), 198, 220, 221; Paul Mooney 32, 33, 36, 37, 41, 209 (top), 234, 235, 246, 247, 257, 258, 264, 268, 285, 288, 289, 292, 301; Ingrid Morejohn 40; Rare Birds of China represented by Kennedy Fine Arts of London and the Altfield Gallery of Hong Kong 48; Raynor Shaw 51, 63, 189, 255; Wong How Man 227, 266–267; Qiu Ziyu © The National Museum of Shaanxi History 81, 149, 165, 167, 168, 169, 171, 172, 173, 174, 175, 176, 177, 178, 180, 181, 182, 183, 184, 185, 186, 187, 199, 212–213, 224, 230-231, 243; Xia Juxian 4–5, 16–17, 89, 94, 97, 98, 102, 103, 106, 107, 108, 109, 110, 111, 112, 113, 115, 116 (top), 117, 118, 119, 121, 124, 125, 127, 128–129, 141; Yang Ling Mausoleum Archaeological Team 160, 161,162–163, 164; Jacky Yip 64–65, 100, 194–195, 216, 242, 254, 262, 296, 312; Yu Shijun 68–69; Zhang Xuede 80.

Production and printing by Twin Age Limited, Hong Kong
E-mail: twinage@netvigator.com
Manufactured in Hong Kong

Xi'an, Shaanxi and the Terracotta Army

by
Paul Mooney
Catherine Maudsley
Gerald Hatherly

Acknowledgements

We would like to thank Professor Wang Baoping, Yang Ling Museum; Professor Wang Zhijie, Director of Mao Ling Museum; Professor Zhou Zhenxi of the Yaozhou Kilns Museum; Professor Wang Xueli; Mr. Zhang Xueli, Director of Operations, English Division, of China International Travel Service, Xian Branch (CITS), and Mr Zhao Licheng, Deputy Manager, English Department of Xi'an CITS, for their valuable assistance in updating this guidebook. The assistance of the Management and Staff of the Shangri-la Golden Flower Hotel and Abercombie and Kent (Hong Kong) Ltd is also greatly appreciated. Many thanks also to Eileen Wen Mooney for help in researching and checking many of the details in this book.

Contents

(Preceding pages) *Qin Shihuangdi burial mound, marking the position of his tomb at Lintong, east of Xi'an.*

Sian-fu
View from the drum-tower

View across 1920s Sian-fu (Xi'an) from the Drum Tower to the Bell Tower.

INTRODUCTION—Gerald Hatherly

On frosty morn floats the wanderer's parting song,
Accompanying you across the river all along,
Can you bear the sad strains of wild geese flying past,
When, grieved in clouded mountains, you must travel fast?

Yellow leaves around the pass hear winter's call,
The Royal Park at dusk resounds to all,
Do not take Chang'an for a capital of pleasure,
Wherein to idle time away but for a fleeting treasure.
(Li Qi, 690–754)

Written over 1,300 years ago Li Qi's melancholy sonnet hints at the cultural and material wealth of Chang'an (today Xi'an), once the greatest city, not only in China, but also on earth. Its rich history spans some 6,000 years from the Neolithic to its present role as capital of China's Shaanxi Province. Often called China's "cultural cradle" and "birthplace of Han civilization", Xi'an is, indeed, a city of great antiquity and history.

Over the past 20 years I have travelled to Xi'an more than 100 times and through my visits have become well acquainted with its marvelous historic sites and many of the people involved in archaeological research. One comment that has stayed with me, and which I constantly tell friends who plan to visit the Xi'an region, was related by an esteemed archaeologist who told me that if you were to take a compass and draw a circle on a map of the Xi'an region with a circumference of 100 kilometres and then began to dig—in any direction within the 100 kilometre radius—you would inevitably make some discovery. Turn your mind across 6,000 years of history—Chinese History—and imagine. From the deepest depths come the distinctive artefacts of the Yangshao culture, whose burnt red pottery with striking black paint geometric patterns heralded the first flowering of early civilization in the region. Move forward to the semi-mythical time of the Xia and Shang periods (21st–16th centuries BCE) and note the rise of the Zhou culture and kingdom, at first a vassal to Shang, and ultimately, by the 10th century BCE, the heart of a Yellow River regional kingdom. The rulers of Zhou adopted the concept of the "Mandate of Heaven", which was an enduring pillar of legitimacy for the imperial system of rule. Travel another 700 years forward and marvel at the rise of Qin, the most powerful of the Warring States that ultimately, under the rule of Yingzheng (the infamous Qin Shihuangdi), conquered and absorbed the remaining six rival states to found the first united empire of China (220 BCE) from which we, in the West, devised the name "China".

Moving ever forward to the present, Xi'an's history continued to enrich and enthrall—the founding of the Han dynasty in 206 BCE (with the fall of Qin) ushers in China's first true Golden Age, a span of some 400 years (206 BCE–220 CE) that, more or less, is marked by peace and prosperity. Chang'an (as Xi'an was then called) became the nucleus of an ever-expanding empire driven by trade, alliance and conquest that reached into present day Central Asia in the west, the rich taiga forests of southern Siberia in the north, and south into the Red River Delta of northern Vietnam.

This expansion into new lands also spurred the growth of trade—both commercial and cultural—that resulted in the creation of the fabled "Silk Road", the historic caravan routes that linked the worlds of imperial China to imperial Rome via the kingdoms of Central Asia and the Middle East. It is truly amazing to think that during the 1st century BCE the demand for Chinese silks almost bankrupted the treasury of Rome. But beyond the commercial there is the cultural, and it was during the Han and into later periods that the cultural riches of different regions moved beyond regional borders.

This remarkable cultural exchange is best exemplified in China's far west in the ancient Buddhist Caves of Kezil and Kumtara. Carved and painted some 1,700 years ago, the vivid wall murals tell a tale of more than just Buddhism; they bring together celestial visions that include Apollo mounted in his flaming chariot racing across the heavens while Persian and Indian influences are present as well.

Han culture, with Chang'an as its showcase, marked a stunning evolution in Chinese art from the utilitarian to the creation of art for its aesthetic value. An unparalleled period of stability (at least to that point in history) and a marked growth in material wealth at all levels of society provided the impetus for this artistic revolution.

The fall of the Han in 220 CE and the subsequent era of instability and chaos that ensued across China north of the Yangzi River set the stage for Xi'an's most glorious historic period, the Tang dynasty (618–907), the culmination of history to that point. The period prior to the founding of the Tang dynasty, while marked by invasion, depopulation and periods of hardship, was crucial for the establishment of Buddhism within China. Having reached the Han court during the 1st century CE, Buddhism did not, initially, appeal to the general population of China. But the chaos, which marked the period immediately after the fall of the Han, proved fertile ground for the flowering of Buddhist philosophy. With the constant threat of invasion, imminent death and declining living standards many turned to the hope of salvation offered through reincarnation and the path taken to the ultimate goal of Nirvana. Buddhism took root and by the time of the Tang, the ruling families became increasingly aligned with the ever more powerful Buddhist clergy. Under the reign of China's only true female emperor, Wu Zetian (690–705), Buddhism was elevated to the position of de facto state religion.

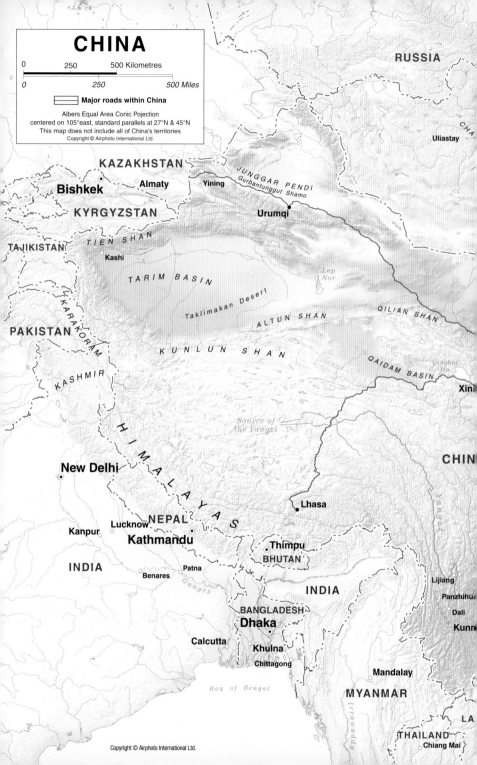

CHINA

RUSSIA

CHA

Uliastay

KAZAKHSTAN

Bishkek   Almaty   Yining   JUNGGAR PENDI
                                            Gurbantunggut Shamo

KYRGYZSTAN   Urumqi

TAJIKISTAN   TIEN SHAN

                  Kashi   Lop
                                             Nor
                  TARIM BASIN

                        Taklimakan Desert

KARAKORAM   ALTUN SHAN   QILIAN SHAN

PAKISTAN   KUNLUN SHAN

                                                  QAIDAM BASIN   Qinghai
KASHMIR   Hu

                                                                     Xin

        H I M A L A Y A S   Source of
                                 the Yangzi

New Delhi   CHIN

                                              Lhasa

Kanpur   Lucknow   NEPAL
                     Kathmandu   Thimpu   Lijiang
INDIA   BHUTAN   Panzhihua
        Benares   Patna   Dali
                          Ganges   INDIA   Kunn

                     BANGLADESH
                     Dhaka

Calcutta   Khulna

        Chittagong

                                                   Mandalay

                Bay of Bengal   MYANMAR   LA

                                              THAILAND
                                              Chiang Mai

Imperial Tang China, with its capital at Chang'an, became a beacon of civilization and diversity never before seen in China. Through commercial and cultural exchanges with Asian kingdoms and the Mediterranean world, the city was the dazzling epicentre of the Tang dynasty. Within her walls lived communities of traders, scholars and emissaries from Japan, Korea, India, Vietnam, the Middle East and the Eastern Roman Empire. Royal tomb murals from period tombs depict, in delightful detail, the rapturous life of Tang China. Games of polo, hunting parties, court ladies at leisure—a world now lost to time but ever present in these glorious images painted more than 1,300 years past.

The fall of the Tang in the 10th century marked the beginning of a significant shift in Chinese political power. The ruling court moved eastward while the once dominant overland trade began to decline. The 1453 sacking of Constantinople by the Ottoman Turks closed the overland trade routes spurring the search for a sea route to China. Chang'an, renamed as Xi'an during the Ming dynasty (1368–1644), became a regional centre of influence and administrative power but never again assumed its status as the greatest city in China.

Since the founding of the People's Republic of China in 1949 Xi'an has grown into its role as the capital of Shaanxi province and the designated gateway to China's "great northwest". It is often called the city that leads to the west, even though it is geographically situated in the eastern third of the country. While cities like Beijing, Shanghai and Guangzhou steal the spotlight in today's fast developing China, Xi'an remains an important urban centre and one of China's five most visited cities. As a provincial capital it is noted as a centre of education with some outstanding universities and research facilities. It is gathering strength as a regional manufacturing hub for the central valley of the Huang He (Yellow River) with some high tech and sophisticated manufacturing. And with the central government's "Go West" campaign—a commercial movement to attract overseas investment to inland areas— Xi'an has become an important centre for the commercial development of the vast frontier regions of western China.

But it is the wonderful tableaux of history and culture that is so deeply rooted in Xi'an that is its single most attractive feature, and it is precisely this that continues to make the city a wonderful travel magnet. Few, if any, visitors will extol the virtues of modern Xi'an's architecture, or speak rapturously of its modern amenities. Instead, it is the staggering wealth of history that makes this such an irresistible visit. Scattered within and around the modern city—behind and hidden by its rather unimpressive and pedestrian modern buildings—are a series of historic sites that are virtual sign posts of China's remarkable longevity as a civilization.

At Banpo Village the Neolithic findings of the Yangshao culture are on display— an early 1950s accidental discovery by construction workers opened up a conduit leading back more than 6,000 years past into the region's early settlement. The striking and stylized ziggurat shape of the Dayan Ta (Big Wild Goose Pagoda) is a beacon to the glories of Tang civilization, while the stately majesty of the Ming period city wall marks the city's third major city wall construction (the other two being the 1st century BCE Han period city wall found outside the city and the 8th century Tang period city wall remains, which can still be seen in the southern sections of the city).

But these are merely the beginning. Walk the old city quarter to the Da Qingzhen Si, or the Great Mosque, and experience a little known footnote of Silk Road history: the presence of Islam within the heart of China. The mosque was completed in 742, signaling the beginning of a strong and vibrant Muslim community that today numbers over 70,000 within the city proper, and over 200,000 in Shaanxi province. The present mosque, a beautiful melding of traditional Chinese temple design embellished with Middle Eastern flourishes, was constructed in the early Ming dynasty under the royal patronage of the Emperor Hong Wu. You can also take in the fine collection of stone carved stele at Beilin (The Forest of Stone Tablets Museum) that was originally the Shaanxi Provincial Museum and, before that, the Confucian Temple, which was first constructed in the Song dynasty, over 800 years ago. And as you hurry about the city you will pass the Drum and Bell Towers, lovely Ming period structures, the Little Wild Goose Pagoda and a number of smaller temples, just superficial remnants of a much greater and ancient history.

Driving outside the city brings you into contact with the royal ruins that begin with the Zhou and end with the Tang—some 72 imperial tombs and a staggering number of lesser tombs that number in the tens of thousands. There are the Han period tombs highlighted by the ongoing excavation at Yang Ling (where, at last count, archaeologists have confirmed some 5,000 tombs present), the Tang tombs at Qian Ling, the most impressive of all, and the vast funerary site of Qin Shihuangdi in Lingtong County. This World Heritage Site is the single most popular tourist attraction in the Xi'an area, and one of the five most important sites in all China. It is also considered the largest ancient tomb site on earth, covering 56 square kilometres.

Xi'an is a city of tremendous history and, as China moves forward, an increasingly important centre for development as the prosperity now engulfing the coastal regions of the nation washes inland.

But Xi'an is also a starting point for Shaanxi province which, along with its neighbour to the east, Shanxi, forms a wondrous historic and cultural cradle of Chinese civilization. Shaanxi lies to the west of the great bend in the Yellow River and its loess hills and dusty plains are testament to its antiquity. For as long as the Chinese have referred to the "huang tu", or yellow earth, that has blown across the pages of its history, Shaanxi has been a foundation for civilization in the area. The annual

A dismounted cavalryman and his horse, excavated from Pit Number Two.
Cavalrymen wore simple headgear tied under their chins to prevent blowing off while riding.
The hole on the horse's side was an essential design feature during the moulding and baking
process to allow hot air to escape and prevent cracking of the mould.
Warriors' torsos are also hollow.

deposition of fine loess soil—mineral rich and easily drained—ongoing for millions of years, and the presence of no less than eight tributary rivers of the Yellow River, provided the initial ingredients in the rise of civilization. To travel throughout Shaanxi is to also experience the unfolding saga of early Chinese civilization.

Spanning a north to south divide of some eight degrees of latitude (from 31 degrees North in the south to 39 degrees North in the north) that includes the northern loess plateau, the central Guanzhong Plain and the southern Qin-Ba Mountains, with their subtropical valleys, Shaanxi is also a rich kaleidoscope of land. Its present population of approximately 37 million (last available census projection) ranks it in the middle of China's provinces and autonomous regions. More than 50% of the people live on the Guanzhong Plain, a statistic that has been accelerating since the early 1990s. Prior to 1996 more people were classified as being rural farmers than urban residents, but within less than 10 years the population balance has swung the other way with the urban to rural population now being 24 million to 13 million.

Shaanxi is rich in mineral resources and holds the largest exploitable fields of natural gas in China. It ranks third in coal production and has more than 80 types of commercially viable mineral resources. In the mountainous south there are large and potentially useable areas of water resources (for hydro power generation) while the central Guanzhong Plain is the agricultural centre for the province. These encouraging statistics are, however, challenged by the disproportionate distribution of the population and a serious decline in available water for irrigation.

For travellers Shaanxi offers many historic and culturally significant sites outside of Xi'an. Baoji and the towns lying to the west of Xi'an on the main rail and road lines to Gansu province are rich in ancient historic sites. To the north is Yan'an, the legendary terminus of the Long March and the World War II base for the Communist guerilla fighters under the leadership of the late Chairman Mao Zedong (1893–1976). Today Yan'an has become a place of pilgrimage for all—the journey back to the source where the purest and most noble truths of the communist movement took root.

In November 2004, excavations began on a new group of tombs found in two caves on Fenghuang Mountain, near the Duke of Zhou Temple in Qishan county. The tombs, believed to date back to the Zhou dynasty, were found in March 2004 after two caves were discovered to contain oracle bones. Inscriptions on the bones are said to have provided important information that will help unravel mysteries about the dynasty.

Xi'an and Shaanxi—a city steeped in legendary history and the vast provincial hinterland that surrounds it. For the visitor this area offers a fascinating and rewarding journey through time to the very roots of Chinese cultural civilization. As you explore the pages of this guidebook remember the words of the archaeologist and his compass—take a turn and explore China's greatest cultural cradle.

Facts for the Traveller

Getting to Xi'an

Before the Second World War the few foreigners who made the arduous journey to Xi'an considered themselves adventurers rather than tourists. To reach their destination they had to travel to the end of the railway line in the neighbouring province of Henan, and then transfer to bumpy carts and boats for a further journey through 'bandit infested' country. When the famous writer Lu Xun made the trip in 1924, he left Beijing on 7 July, and did not arrive in Xi'an until seven days later. The boat journey along the Wei and Yellow Rivers was somewhat dangerous, but apparently did not faze this experienced boat traveller. The journey became easier when the railway reached Xi'an in 1934. A new station was built only in 1986. Today Xi'an has become the main communications centre for the northwest region of China.

BY AIR

Dragonair, the Hong Kong-based airline, operates a round-trip service to Xi'an on Mondays and Fridays: departing Hong Kong 7:45 am, arriving 10:35 am; departing Xi'an 11:30 am, arriving 14:20 pm. (www.dragonair. com) China Eastern Xibei Airlines,

offers a service to and from Hong Kong six times a week, Monday through Saturday: departing Xi'an 14:30 pm, arriving 17:00 pm; departing Hong Kong 18:00 pm, arriving 21:15 pm. (www.ce-air.com) There are also daily flights that connect with all major cities in China, as well as regular flights to capital cities of other Southeast Asian countries. Bangkok Airways also offers services Bangkok—Xi'an twice a week. (www.bangkokair.com)

Xi'an's airport is located in the neighbouring city of Xianyang, about 45 kilometres away. The most convenient way to reach Xi'an from Xianyang Airport is to take a taxi. Although the driver may try to negotiate the fare before departure, all taxis are fitted with meters and you should insist that this be used. As at the beginning of 2005, the fare into Xi'an was around Rmb 150 depending on the exact destination. Journey time on the expressway is around one hour—most of the time can be spent sitting in the notoriously bad traffic once in the city itself. A cheaper, slower and probably less convenient alternative is the airport bus. This makes various scheduled stops in town before terminating at the China Northwest Airlines Booking Office at Xishaomen, outside the western gate of the city (see Useful Addresses, page 323).

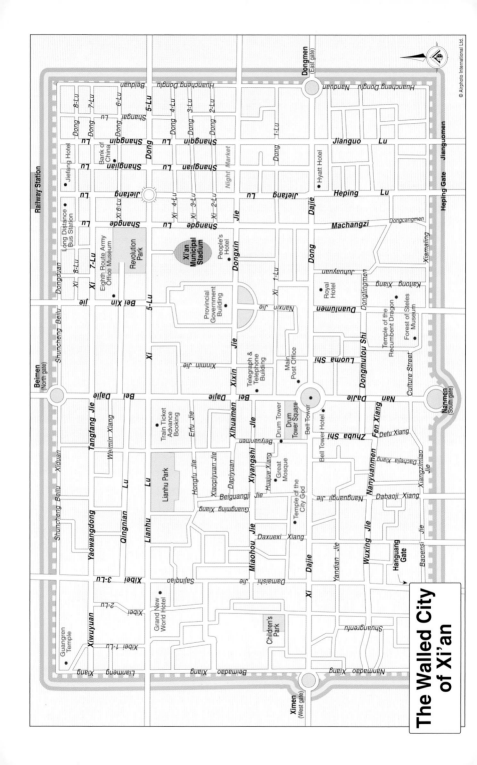

The Walled City of Xi'an

By Rail

Xi'an is on the main east-west railway that goes all the way from Shanghai to the Alataw Pass on the Xinjiang Autonomous Region border with Kazakhstan. A Eurasian railway continues to Almati, and then through several CIS republics before eventually ending up in Rotterdam.

Express trains arrive daily from Beijing (taking about 12 hours), and also from Shanghai, Chengdu, Chongqing, Guangzhou, Lanzhou, Luoyang, Nanjing, Qingdao, Taiyuan, Urumqi, and Zhengzhou. There are also numerous services to other destinations throughout China.

Hard and soft sleeper tickets can be bought in advance on the second floor of Xi'an Railway Station Ticket Office. A sign in English points the way to the special window serving foreigners, thus avoiding the need to stand in long queues with the locals downstairs. However, depending on the season it can be extremely difficult to purchase tickets, particularly during the Spring Festival (the Lunar New Year holiday) and the week-long holidays around May 1 and October 1. To avoid potential problems, and for convenience, it is recommended you purchase your rail tickets through a travel service, such as CITS (see page 323). They can also provide you with accurate information on schedules.

Visas

Everyone must get a visa to go to China, but this is usually an easy, trouble-free process. Tourists travelling in a group enter China on a group visa—a single document listing all members of the group. The visa is obtained by the tour operator on behalf of the clients, and individual passports will not be stamped unless specifically requested.

Tourist visas for individual travellers can be obtained directly through Chinese embassies and consulates. Certain travel agents and tour operators around the world can also arrange individual visas. It is simplest in Hong Kong, where visas can be obtained directly from the Chinese Ministry of Foreign Affairs visa office located on the ground floor of China Resources Building, Wanchai. Just one passport photograph and a completed application form are necessary. However, they keep strict office hours and only open from Monday to Friday. A more convenient alternative is the large number of travel agents handling visa applications, or from the offices of CITS or CTS, which charge a reasonable handling fee.

Visa fees vary considerably, depending on the source of the visa, and on the time taken to get it. One of the most reliable and reasonable visa services is offered by Forever Bright Travel Service to be found at Room 707, 7th floor, New Mandarin Plaza, 14 Science Museum Road, Tsim Sha Tsui East, Kowloon, tel. 2369-3188, fax 2312-2989. A single-entry tourist visa costs HK$720 for US passport holders;

HK$480 for UK passports; 6 months multiple tourist entries HK$1200 for US passports; HK$970 for UK passports. The mechanics of getting a business visa are much more flexible than in the past, particularly in Hong Kong. The applicant should have either an invitation from the appropriate Foreign Trade Corporation (several now have permanent representatives abroad), or from the organizers of a special trade fair or seminar. In Hong Kong, all that is needed is a letter from the applicant's company confirming that s/he wishes to travel to China on business. Some travel agencies in Hong Kong and China can also provide six-month multiple entry business visas with no letters or documents required.

Visas can normally be extended by designated Public Security Bureaus dealing with the entry and exit of aliens. Extensions are normally granted without too much trouble for a maximum of one month, usually on no more than one occasion. The Division of Aliens and Exit-Entry Administration of the Xi'an Municipal Public Security Bureau is located close to the Bell Tower, at 138 Xi Dajie (see Useful Addresses, page 323).

Customs

The ordinary visitor is no longer required to complete a customs declaration form on arrival. There is no limit on the amount of foreign currency that can be brought into China. Visitors carrying goods or samples for business purposes and those with unaccompanied baggage should also make a declaration. Customs forms should be kept safely and handed in on departure.

One-and-a-half litres of alcohol over 12 percent proof, 400 cigarettes or 100 cigars, unlimited film and medicines for personal use may be brought into the country.

When buying antiques one must remember that the only items made after the reign of the Jiaqing Emperor (1820) may be legally exported, and all must bear a red wax seal affixed by the Bureau of Cultural Relics. Receipts for these and gold and silver goods should be kept in case inspection is required on departure.

Money

Chinese Currency

The People's Currency, or Renminbi (Rmb) as it is known, is the common form of exchange in China. The basic unit of currency is the yuan, or kuai as it is commonly referred to in spoken Chinese. The yuan is divided into 10 jiao, colloquially called mao. Each jiao is, in turn, divided into 10 fen. There are larger notes for 100, 50, 10, 5, 2 and 1 yuan, small notes for 5, 2 and 1 jiao, and coins for 5, 2 and 1 fen.

Hard currencies can be conveniently exchanged into Renminbi at hotels, large stores and branches of the Bank of China. All major European, American and Japanese traveller's cheques are accepted, and these are changed at a slightly better rate than cash. Renminbi can be obtained via credit card at some banks, though a hefty surcharge is levied. Renminbi can be obtained using your credit or ATM card at cash machines around China, but not all machines accept international bank cards. Look for signs on the machines listing the bank cards that are accepted. Bank of China and the Industrial and Commercial Bank of China ATM machines normally accept international cards, but availability is limited in smaller cities.

Up to 50 percent of the total amount of Renminbi obtained may be reconverted to hard currency on leaving China, providing exchange receipts covering the amount are shown. For those travelling to Hong Kong, Renminbi can easily be converted to Hong Kong dollars at numerous banks and money changers without the need for receipts.

FOREIGN CURRENCY

If more cash is needed during your stay, it is possible to have money wired in your name to the local main branch of the Bank of China. The remittance will arrive in four to six working days. Alternatively a substantial cash advance on your credit card can be drawn at any branch of the Bank of China. American Express cardholders many cash personal cheques up to US$1,000 (green/corporate card) or US$ 5,000 (gold card) every 21 days on payment of a service charge.

TRAVELLER'S CHEQUES AND CREDIT CARDS

All the usual American, European and Japanese traveller's cheques are accepted by the Bank of China and are changed at a slightly better rate than cash.

China is experiencing a credit card boom, a development that should widen the use of international credit cards at retail outlets. At present international credit cards are widely accepted at designated tourist restaurants and stores as well as at most tourist hotels. However, they are of little value for most main street shopping, though they are usually accepted at the new breed of luxury stores, international boutiques and emporiums that are opening up in all the major Chinese cities.

TIPPING

Although tipping is, in theory, forbidden it has become an accepted and expected practice in many sectors of the hospitality industry. Tipping has become particularly routine in hotels for bell boys. For group tourists tipping of drivers and guides is an obligatory practice. Tipping waiters and taxi drivers is not necessary unless some exceptional service is provided.

(Following page) *Damaged members of the terracotta army.*

XI'AN CHINA INTERNATIONAL TRAVEL SERVICE CO. LTD.

Xi'an China International Travel Service (CITS) was founded in 1956. It is now the largest travel service among the mainland cities of China. Xi'an CITS is mainly engaged in travel industry sales and marketing promotion and in the organisation of world visitors to China. It has over 300 well-trained and professional guides fluent in various languages including English, Japanese, French, German, Spanish and Italian.

As the first agent for IATA in northwest China, Xi'an CITS also provides a complete range of services for international air-ticketing.

Since 1978 it has hosted over three million international tourists and in recent years has handled up to 300,000 visitors annually from around the globe—over 50 percent of the total number of international visitors to Shaanxi Province.

Xi'an CITS has played host to various dignitaries including the former Prime Minister of Canada Mr Pierre Trudeau and head of Microsoft Mr Bill Gates. In 1998, the company provided guides and arranged the visit of US President Mr Bill Clinton and his family to Xi'an.

The FIT (Foreign Individual Traveller) Service Centre is one of the most important departments in Xi'an CITS. The centre offers a complete and comprehensive service for individual travellers or families, organising and customising all travel arrangements to suit their specific needs.

Xi'an CITS is also experienced in organising special interest tours in such fields as calligraphy, archaeology, culture, science and technology.

Everywhere in Xi'an the visitor will find the company motto becoming a reality:
At home you are your own boss, in China your Aladdin's Lamp is CITS.

Main Office:
48 Chang'an Road, Xi'an, China 710061
Tel. (86-29) 85262066
Fax. (86-29) 85261453; 85261558
www.citsxa.com

Sales and Marketing Centre:
Tel. (86-29) 85255401
Fax. (86-29) 85261453

FIT Department:
Tel. (86-29) 85261454
Fax. (86-29) 85261454

Travel Agencies and Tour Operators

There are a number of State-owned corporations which handle foreign visitors to China. The largest is China International Travel Service (CITS) (www.citsxa.com), see page 323. Other large organizations providing similar services are China Travel Service (CTS), China Youth Travel Service (CYTS) and Overseas Travel Corporation (OTC).

These agencies offer a comprehensive service covering accommodation, transport, food, sightseeing, interpreters, in addition to special visits to schools, hospitals, factories and other places foreigners might be interested in seeing.

Abercrombie & Kent (Hong Kong) Ltd. has been working in the People's Republic of China since 1983. They operate both set brochure tours of China (published out of London, England and the United States) as well as handle personally tailored China itineraries for both groups and individual travellers. They have built up a strong network of contacts within China (including Xi'an) which can result in arrangements not always possible to the individual traveller or group tours operated by other companies. This includes a good working relationship with the Cultural Relics Bureau and the archaeology authorities of Shaanxi province. With a regional office in Hong Kong, Abercombie & Kent offers personal on-site service to Xi'an and other areas of China. (For contact details see Travel Arrangements on page 326)

Local Time

Amazingly for a country measuring some 4,300 kilometres (over 2,500 miles) from east to west, the whole of China operates within one time zone, eight hours ahead of GMT and 13 hours ahead of EST. There is no daylight saving time in China.

Communications

Direct Dialling for calls within China and International Direct Dialling is available in nearly all tourist hotels. The same hotels also have business centres providing photocopying, telex and facsimile services. Internet and e-mailing services are fast becoming common as well. Public phones on the streets of large cities are increasingly becoming card operated—phone cards can be purchased from your hotel or from numerous small general shops and stalls. Be aware that phone charges begin when the phone rings and not when it is answered, so payment must still be made even if there is no answer.

China's own English-language newspaper, *China Daily*, is available at most hotels, and the larger joint-venture hotels usually have available a selection of international papers such as the *International Herald Tribune*, *Asian Wall Street Journal*, *USA Today* and the *South China Morning Post*, although these will obviously be a day or two late.

Packing Checklist

As well as bringing along any prescription medicines you may need, it is a good idea to pack a supply of common cold and stomach remedies. While it is not necessary to pack toilet paper these days, it is advisable to take some with you when going out sightseeing, as public toilets do not always provide it. Bring plenty of film for your camera and batteries for this and any other accessories you may be carrying. Although both are widely available, they could be old stock or of dubious quality. Comfortable, non-slip shoes for walking are a must.

The electricity supply is 220 volts and hotels have a wide variety of socket types. Although many hotels provide adaptors for British and American plugs, it is a good idea to bring along your own adaptors.

If you wear glasses or contact lenses bring your prescription and a spare pair, and ensure you are well-stocked with essential fluids and solutions.

Health

There are no mandatory vaccination requirements. However, you may be advised by your doctor to take certain precautions. In recent years the US Consulate in Hong Kong has recommended inoculations against hepatitis A and B, Japanese encephalitis B, tetanus, polio, cholera and malaria. The risk of contracting any of these diseases is small, although it increases during the summer months and in rural areas. A hepatitis A inoculation is highly recommended. To minimize risks, remember to drink only mineral or boiled water—the former is sold almost everywhere and the latter is provided in flasks in all hotel rooms and from carriage attendants on board trains. Make sure food is freshly cooked and peel all fruit.

A word of caution, too, for those suffering from asthma or other respiratory problems: as China continues to industrialise at a rapid pace, and the improved average standard of living means that the bicycle is now increasingly outnumbered on the streets of major cities by the motorbike, private car and taxi, the quality of air in places like Xi'an can sometimes be quite poor. This can of course vary with the weather conditions, but in the dry autumn months, particularly when farmers burn off their fields after the harvest, air pollution can be considerable.

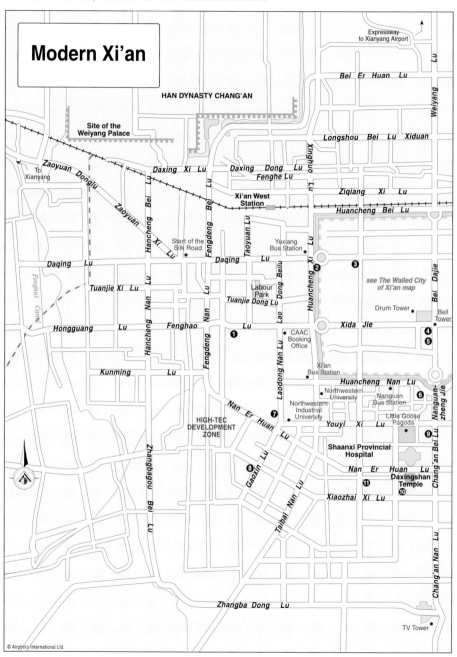

Modern Xi'an

HAN DYNASTY CHANG'AN

Site of the
Weiyang Palace

Expressway
to Xianyang Airport

Bei Er Huan Lu

Longshou Bei Lu Xiduan

Zaoyuan Donglu

To
Xianyang

Daxing Xi Lu

Daxing Dong Lu
Fenghe Lu

Xi'an West
Station

Ziqiang Xi Lu

Huancheng Bei Lu

Zaoyuan

Hancheng Bei Lu

Fengdeng Bei Lu

Taoyuan Lu

Start of the
Silk Road

Yuxiang
Bus Station

Huancheng Xi Lu

Daqing Lu

Daqing Lu

Lao Dong Beilu

see The Walled City
of Xi'an map

Tuanjie Xi Lu

Hancheng Nan Lu

Fengdeng Nan Lu

Labour
Park

Tuanjie Dong Lu

Drum Tower

Bei Dajie

Bell
Tower

Hongguang Lu

Fenghao Lu

Xida Jie

CAAC
Booking
Office

Kunming Lu

Xi'an
Bus Station

Huancheng Nan Lu

Nan Er Huan Lu

Laodong Nan Lu

Northwestern
University

Nanguan
Bus Station

Northwestern
Industrial
University

Youyi Xi Lu

Little Goose
Pagoda

HIGH-TEC
DEVELOPMENT
ZONE

Shaanxi Provincial
Hospital

Nan Er Huan Lu

Daxingshan
Temple

Zhangbagou Bei Lu

Gaoxin Lu

Taibai Nan Lu

Xiaozhai Xi Lu

Chang'an Bei Lu

Chang'an Nan Lu

Zhangba Dong Lu

TV Tower

Fenghui Canal

© Airphoto International Ltd.

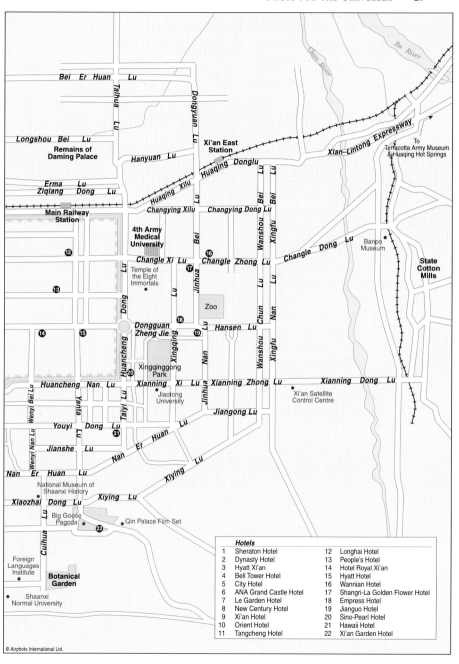

Bei   Er   Huan   Lu
Taihua Lu
Dongyuan Lu
Longshou   Bei   Lu
Remains of
Daming Palace
Hanyuan Lu
Xi'an East
Station
Huaqing Donglu
Xian–Lintong Expressway
To
Terracotta Army Museum
& Huaqing Hot Springs
Chan River
Ba River

Erma   Lu
Ziqiang   Dong   Lu
Huaqing Xilu
Changying Xilu
Changying Dong Lu
Bei
Bei
Wanshou
Xingfu

Main Railway
Station
4th Army
Medical
University
Changle Xi Lu
Changle   Zhong   Lu
Changle   Dong   Lu
Banpo
Museum
State
Cotton
Mills

Temple of
the Eight
Immortals
Lu
Lu
Chun
Nan

Zoo
Dongguan
Zheng Jie
Hansen   Lu
Wanshou
Xingfu

Huancheng   Dong   Lu
Xingqinggong
Park
Xinning   Xi   Lu   Xianning   Zhong   Lu
Xianning   Dong   Lu

Huancheng   Nan   Lu   Xianning
Jiaotong
University
Xi'an Satellite
Control Centre

Wenyi Bei Lu
Yanta Lu
Taiyi Lu
Jinhua Lu
Nan
Youyi   Dong   Lu
Jiangong Lu

Wenyi Nan Lu
Jianshe   Lu
Nan   Er   Huan   Lu
Lu

Nan   Er   Huan   Lu
Xiying   Lu

National Museum of
Shaanxi History
Xiying   Lu
Xiaozhai   Dong   Lu
Big Goose
Pagoda
Qin Palace Film Set

Cuihua
Foreign
Languages
Institute
Botanical
Garden
Shaanxi
Normal University

	Hotels		
1	Sheraton Hotel	12	Longhai Hotel
2	Dynasty Hotel	13	People's Hotel
3	Hyatt Xi'an	14	Hotel Royal Xi'an
4	Bell Tower Hotel	15	Hyatt Hotel
5	City Hotel	16	Wannian Hotel
6	ANA Grand Castle Hotel	17	Shangri-La Golden Flower Hotel
7	Le Garden Hotel	18	Empress Hotel
8	New Century Hotel	19	Jianguo Hotel
9	Xi'an Hotel	20	Sino-Pearl Hotel
10	Orient Hotel	21	Hawaii Hotel
11	Tangcheng Hotel	22	Xi'an Garden Hotel

© Airphoto International Ltd.

Holidays

In contrast to the long calendar of traditional Chinese festivals, modern China now has only four official holidays: New Year's Day (1st January); Labour Day (1st May); National Day, marking the foundation of the People's Republic of China (1st October); and Chinese New Year, usually called Spring Festival in China itself, which comes at the lunar new year, usually around the end of January or in February.

Climate and Clothing

Xi'an's climate is much drier and cooler than that of southwest or southeast China, and less extreme than that of Beijing. The Qin Mountains to the south of the Wei River valley shield Xi'an from the southeastern monsoon, which brings much rain and considerable humidity to the neighbouring province of Sichuan. Annual precipitation is only 530–600 millimetres (21–24 inches). Most of the rainfall occurs in July, August and September.

Spring is usually the best season, with the city at its most beautiful under relatively clear skies. Summer begins in May, and is usually fine and sunny. The hottest month is July, when noon temperatures may reach over 38°C (100°F). Late summer and early autumn is cooler and can be overcast. Late autumn is usually fine, and winter is dry and cold with a little snow. At night during winter temperatures usually drop well below 0°C (32°F).

In mid-summer only the lightest clothing is necessary. In mid-winter thermal underwear and multi-layered clothing add to comfort.

XI'AN TEMPERATURES

	Average	High	Low		Average	High	Low
Jan	−1.3°C (29°F)	5.1°C (41°F)	−5.5°C (22°F)	Jul	26.7°C (80°F)	34.0°C (93°F)	22.5°C (72°F)
Feb	2.1°C (36°F)	8.0°C (46°F)	−2.4°C (28°F)	Aug	25.4°C (78°F)	31.5°C (89°F)	20.9°C (70°F)
Mar	8.0°C (46°F)	14.7°C (58°F)	2.7°C (37°F)	Sep	19.4°C (67°F)	25.0°C (77°F)	15.5°C (60°F)
Apr	14.0°C (57°F)	21.5°C (70°F)	8.6°C (47°F)	Oct	13.6°C (56°F)	20.0°C (68°F)	8.9°C (48°F)
May	19.2°C (67°F)	27.7°C (82°F)	13.8°C (57°F)	Nov	6.5°C (44°F)	12.4°C (54°F)	2.3°C (36°F)
Jun	25.3°C (78°F)	32.8°C (91°F)	19.0°C (66°F)	Dec	0.6°C (33°F)	6.2°C (43°F)	−3.9°C (25°F)

Getting around Xi'an

There are some fascinating areas within the city walls which are well worth exploring on foot. Particularly attractive for their old buildings are the streets around the Drum Tower and the Great Mosque as well as those near the South and West Gates and north and west of the Beilin Museum. Dong Dajie, the main shopping area, is another good place to stroll, with its large department stores and wide sidewalks. Xi Dajie is more compact and has dozens of small shops with a variety of intriguing items.

Public transport is cheap but could prove difficult unless you have your destination written in Chinese or a basic knowledge of the language. If you plan to venture out independently, it is always a good idea to ask your hotel receptionist to write the names of the places you intend to visit in Chinese characters to assist in using public transport or just asking directions on the street.

There are numerous bus routes around the city, some of which extend into the newly developed urban areas. Buses can be an interesting way to get around, but are often comparatively slow and very crowded. Excellent maps of Xi'an are available from hotel shops and from hawkers at the railway station, bus stations and most sightseeing spots, and these clearly show all bus routes, the bus numbers and where they terminate. These are very useful and although most of them are in Chinese, some are printed with names in English as well.

Taxis are available at hotels, can be hailed in the streets, and usually wait at all the major places of interest to tourists. Green and white taxis crowd the streets of Xi'an, and one only has to stand on the second-floor balcony of the Bell Tower at the centre of town to appreciate just how many. They have a 6 yuan flag fall and charge 1.20 yuan per kilometre thereafter, thereby making them a convenient and affordable means of getting around town. All taxis are fitted with meters and drivers generally use them without having to be asked (the airport is perhaps the only exception to this).

If you prefer to cycle around Xi'an, you can rent a bicycle from one of the bicycle rental shops in the city centre. One convenient location is near the gate of the People's Hotel, where there are a few small shops.

Many of Xi'an's major sights are a long way from the city, but travel agencies offer tours by comfortable air-conditioned buses to most of these places. Tours can also be easily arranged at all major hotels. Public buses go to most sightseeing places as well.

Those who prefer to arrange their own itinerary can hire a taxi for the day, or customized tour through the FITS department of CITS (see page 323). With your own transport and an early start it is possible to visit Famen Temple, the Baoji Bronze Culture Museum and the tombs of Qian Ling in a single day trip. Another worthwhile day trip can take in the Xianyang museum, and the tombs of Mao Ling and Zhao Ling.

THE PEASANT PAINTERS OF HUXIAN

—Ann Dewi Mooney

In 1955, a young artist cum cadre, Ding Jitang, was sent to Huxian County on the outskirts of Xi'an to be a primary school teacher. Ding went everywhere with his brush and paints in his pocket and drawing board slung over his shoulder, painting whenever he felt moved by the scenes of country life. Some of the local peasants were inspired to paint as well, and soon they began to follow in Ding's footsteps, carrying their own drawing materials wherever they went.

A year after Ding arrived in Huxian, he was appointed by the Communist Party to lead the Mass Art Movement, a campaign to mass-produce propaganda posters. Ding organized classes and the peasants began to learn how to paint from him. Black and white photos on Ding's work desk show peasants bent over easels in front of their houses or groups of people sitting on stools, painting in the fields. In 1942, Mao Zedong gave a speech in Yan'an, insisting that literature and art should be used for the sole purpose of reflecting the views of peasants, workers and soldiers. This Mass Art Movement was a continuation of this idea that art should serve the people.

Peasant women such as Li Fenglan (see photograph on page 235), a first generation peasant painter and a student of Ding's, grew up learning different folk arts. She started doing paper cutting when she was eight, and her mother taught her how to embroider when she was seventeen. The style and colours

Peasant painting: Farmers harvesting sorghum.

they used in the paintings were drawn from their tradition of paper cutting and embroidery. "We used our emotions to paint", she says. "We wanted to reflect the new society".

This "new society" was represented in the pictures exhibiting hardy workers building a dam, peasants squatting in rice fields planting seeds or feeding chickens. They were encouraged to portray the concept of *haoren, haoshi*, or good people doing good deeds, people working selflessly for the future of the nation. Soon, these peasant paintings could be found on doors, walls and notice boards all over the county.

During the Anti-Rightist Campaign, the purpose of the paintings changed from simply encouraging a hard work ethic to criticizing enemies of the state, primarily intellectuals. When the Great Leap Forward began in 1958 the political posters began to cater specifically to Mao's new plan to accelerate economic development. He believed that with the will power of humans alone, despite the lack of modern technology, China's economic situation could surpass countries such as England. Ding says, "The styles of the paintings [at that time] were exaggerated and very romanticized, and people felt happy when they saw them." The paintings of bumper harvests, yards full of healthy livestock and smiling workers represented a brighter future that people wanted to believe in.

Apprentice learning the colourful art of peasant painting.

Later, during the Cultural Revolution, the Gang of Four, decided to use the peasant paintings for even more personal purposes, manipulating the paintings by adding slogans to criticize their opponents, a trend that upset Ding. "The political slogans ruined beautiful paintings", he says, "but you cannot blame the artists. It was the social environment of that period."

Peasant painting became more widely known in 1973 when the first exhibition of these paintings was held at the Great Hall of the People in Beijing. But it was not until the economic reforms of the early 1980s that the Huxian peasant paintings blossomed. The peasants were no longer bound by political obligations, and for the first time they could let their brushes flow freely and paint what they desired. Besides subjects such as hard working farmers, the painters began to pick new subjects such as wedding ceremonies, children playing with firecrackers during the New Year, or simply a countryside snow scene.

Ding says that the peasants' works started as a combination of realism and romanticism. While the themes show the backbreaking work of farmers, the colours are vibrant and uplifting. Chinese farm life, particularly in the past, is grim; any realistic artist would paint such dusty and muddy scenes with shades of grays and browns. However, the peasant paintings use pinks, bright reds, sky blues and deep greens to reflect their belief of the future in store.

What had started as propaganda paintings, has evolved into what we call "peasant paintings" today. Peasant paintings have been exhibited and sold in galleries in and out of China for the past thirty years. There was a time when they were worth hundreds to thousands of dollars. However, due to the popularity of the paintings, counterfeit copies have emerged on the market and many artists have turned to mass production. Therefore, the value of these paintings has dropped significantly.

On the other hand, peasant paintings began as propaganda posters, made by not just one individual, but by a whole group of people who needed to mass produce art. In a sense, this has always been an art that was mass-produced and the posters were rarely or never signed by the individual artist. In Huxian today, peasant paintings are sold for as cheap as twenty dollars. The buyers do not have to be preoccupied with the authenticity of the painting. If a vibrant painting of a woman sitting in her yard, husking corn pleases your eye, why not look at it as a nice souvenir or piece of decorative art to remind you of your pleasant visit to Shaanxi?

Shopping

Earlier this century Xi'an was known for its curio shops stocked with antiquities of the city. Today, however, you would be lucky to find anything very old; most antiques in these shops date from the Qing and Republican periods, or are reproductions.

Shaanxi's folk crafts are thriving with the rapid increase of tourism in Xi'an. Hawkers cluster round every site visited by tourists, selling brightly coloured patchwork waistcoats and shoulder bags, embroidered children's shoes, hats and toys, shadow puppets, and amusing painted clay ornaments decorated in brilliant primary colours. Buying in the free markets can be much more fun than in the established arts and crafts shops, but be prepared for some fierce bargaining, and even then you may not be assured of a good deal. It always pays to shop around—many is the occasion that the unwary tourist has returned with their purchase only to find the same item on sale in the hotel gift shop for considerably less.

Embroidery is one of Shaanxi's richest traditional skills that is gaining recognition elsewhere; some of the more distinctive items crop up in hotel souvenir shops in other parts of China. There are children's patchwork waistcoats, predominantly red, and decorated with some, or all, of the 'five poisonous creatures'—toad, snake, centipede, lizard, scorpion—in the belief that the process of sewing the forms onto the waistcoat will nullify the creatures' evil powers. Embroidered cylindrical cotton pillows, with an intricately decorated tiger's head at each end, are also common. These are favourite gifts for babies when the first month of life is celebrated. Tiger motifs often appear on other children's clothes and shoes, since the tiger can readily devour evil spirits. Its eyes are usually wide open and staring to help deflect evil influences away from the wearer.

Painted clay toys, originally from the nearby city of Fengxiang, in western Shaanxi province, were traditional gifts for festivals, weddings and birthdays. They can now be bought in many of the free markets and souvenir shops in the city. These toys are often in the form of tigers, sometimes covered with flowers or butterflies, and are predominantly red and green to symbolize prosperity and happiness. Other popular subjects are comical monkeys and chubby children.

Shadow puppets, cut out of semi-transparent hide and painted in bright colours, are another speciality of Xi'an. The puppet's flexible joints allow it—in skilled hands at least—to somersault expertly, or engage in armed combat. The characters depicted are usually from traditional folk tales.

Chinese stone rubbings are a very appropriate souvenir of China's former capital since Xi'an has the country's best collection of steles, or inscribed stone tables, most

Busy peasant family selling chicks—by Li Fenglan.

Rural scene in the fall—woodblock print by artist Ding Jitang.

Snow welcomes in the New Year—by Ding Jitang.

Cotton harvest—woodblock print by Shaanxi artist Ding Jitang.

of them in the Forest of Steles Museum (see page 237). The rubbings of memorials, calligraphy, pictures and even maps are produced by laying paper on top of a stele, and then pounding it with ball of tightly-wrapped ink-filled cloth. It is often possible to see this being done, either at the Forest of Steles or at a handicraft factory. An expert job from a famous stone can cost hundreds, even thousands, of yuan. Rubbings of all prices are on sale almost everywhere around the city.

You may find it interesting to visit the workshops and showrooms of some small handicraft enterprises. Quality varies; none of the factories are particularly old but some of the craft techniques are worth seeing, and you will always be given a warm welcome. The Jade Carving Factory of Xi'an is at 173 Xiyi Lu, and has a retail outlet. Some 300 workers carve jadeite, amethyst, crystal, many other semi-precious stones and petrified wood. Attached to the factory is a unit making rubbings from reproductions of stones in the Forest of Steles Museum.

The Xi'an Special Arts and Crafts Factory on Huancheng Xi Lu, just north of the West Gate, produces sculptures and collage pictures using sea-shells, feathers, silk and other material together with inlaid woodwork.

Other interesting items found most easily at the small shops surrounding major sights include local pottery for everyday use, basketware, paper cuts, and micro-carvings on minute pieces of ivory no bigger than a grain of rice.

Many tourist shops sell Chinese paintings and calligraphy. Most of the work is by mediocre local artists, of which there are literally scores. The city's most famous artists are Luo Guoshi and his son Luo Liangbi, who specialize in painting local scenic spots.

Another popular local art form is the colourful paintings of the peasant farmers of Huxian (see page 32). A good selection of these for sale can be found at the Little Goose Pagoda and the shop of the Tang Dynasty Arts Museum, just around the corner from the Big Goose Pagoda. The latter also has a good selection of shadow puppets. It's also possible to pay a visit to the galleries of peasant painters in Huxian, and to watch young students learning the trade.

Tourists or visitors planning to make serious purchases of local arts or crafts would be well advised to visit the Wenbaozhai Store on Yanta Zhong Lu. This is a Tourist Administration appointed store selling locally made silk carpets, jade, pottery, furniture and art. The store prides itself on its honesty and claims to be cheaper than anywhere else in town, promising to match any lower prices found elsewhere. Here buyers can be assured of purchasing the genuine article as all items come with a certificate of authenticity. The reproduction terracotta warriors on sale here are made in the only factory authorized to use the original Gaoling County clay. There are also some workshops for display only, where visitors can watch craftsmen and women carving jade and making pottery or carpets. The store can arrange for shipping and insurance and accepts all major currencies and credit cards. It is open daily from 8:30 am to 6:00 pm.

Replicas of the distinctive Banpo pottery can be bought at the Banpo Museum Retail Shop.

The main shopping street is Dong Dajie, particularly the section between Nanxin Jie and the Bell Tower. The principal department store, the Xi'an Kaiyuan Shopping Centre, is located opposite the Bell Tower on the south side of Dong Dajie. This state-owned store is one of the newest in Xi'an and seems to stock everything imaginable, from microwaves to washing machines and food to fashion. It is interesting to visit if only to see what is available to the newly-affluent middle class of China. On the opposite side of the Bell Tower, beneath the square on the north side of Xi Dajie, is the expensive Century Ginwa Department Store, stocking all the latest European fashion labels and a supermarket stocked with Chinese and international foods and beverages.

In complete contrast to these is the street market of Luoma Shi. This used to be where mules and horses were sold in ancient times, but the street has now become the biggest clothing market in Xi'an with cheap fashion from the export-orientated garment factories of the Special Economic Zones of Guangdong. A little farther along Dong Dajie are the Foreign Languages Bookshop and the Xinhua Bookshop (for publications in Chinese). There are also restaurants, snack-bars, coffee shops, and fruit and vegetable stalls.

Another important shopping area is around Jiefang Lu, within the northeast corner of the walled city.

On Xi Dajie, and of particular interest to visitors, are many small Chinese opera costume shops supplying the municipal and county opera troupes of Shaanxi Province with embroidered silk costumes, elaborate head-dresses, hats, false beards and whiskers and odd props.

A fascinating, Qing-dynasty style Ancient Culture Street located next to the Forest of Steles Museum, has many calligraphy and painting stores, cloisonné stores and folk art stores. Most items on sale tend to be cheap reproductions, but the street itself is interesting to see.

Food and Drink

Shaanxi province is the noodle capital of China and has the best freshly made noodles in the country. They come in all shapes and sizes; some are long and thread-like, others are square shaped and thick, and some are shaped like shells. The noodles are made with flour, wheat, buckwheat and even different kinds of beans. The ones made with beans are transparent after they're cooked.

One popular dish is knife-sliced noodle (*daoxiaomian*; 刀削面). The cook holds a ball of dough in one hand and with his other hand shaves slivers of dough right into a pot of boiling water. To prepare another variety of noodle (*jiumian*; 揪面), the dough is stretched by hand and then cut into square pieces. A flat and wide noodle (*chemian*; 扯面) is also worth sampling. These noodles tend to be thick and chewy and are usually served in a light beef or mutton broth, a hot and sour soup (*suanla*; 酸辣), or in a sauce made of fried bean sauce and minced meat (*zhajiang*; 炸酱) .

A noodle made of mung beans (*liangfen*; 凉粉) is light, transparent and slippery. It is often served as a cold dish in tahini. *Liangfen* can also be cut into chunks and stir-fried with soy sauce and spring onions.

Vinegar is a common condiment in Shaanxi cuisine. There is always a hint of vinegar in cold appetizer (*majiangliangpi*; 麻酱凉皮), (*mala liangfen*; 麻辣凉粉), and (*qiangban yinsi*; 炝拌银丝).

Another well-known and common staple is a Muslim, or Hui, specialty called *mo*. It is a flat round bread toasted in a big iron skillet until browned on both sides. *Mo* is used in two popular dishes. One dish is beef or mutton *paomo* (*yangrou/niurou paomo*; 羊肉/牛肉泡馍), . The *mo* is broken up into little pieces and then soaked in an aromatic mutton broth which has been simmered with spices such as aniseed star, cloves, bay leaves, cardamom, and cinnamon sticks, just to name a few. Another popular broth (*hulutou*; 葫芦头), where the cow and lamb innards are simmered with a variety of spices that remove the odour of the innards.

In the evening, lamb kebabs, (*kao yangrouchuan*; 烤羊肉串) are barbecued at almost every restaurant in the Muslim Quarter. You can order kebabs by the stick or you can try tasty lamb stuffed in the *mo* (*rou jiamo*; 肉夹馍). To make the vegetarian option (*cai jiamo*; 菜夹馍), the *mo* is stuffed with stir fried potatoes, green peppers, kelp and soy protein.

Shaanxi handicrafts on sale at Qin Ling.

Smiling vendor hands over a crystal rice cake, filled with crushed peanuts, sugar, and rose petals, to a buyer in the bustling Muslim Quarter.

Shaanxi province produces a variety of grains including millet (*xiaomi*), corn (*yumi*), mung beans (*ludou*), red beans (*hongdou*), and buckwheat (*qiaomai*), which is why Shaanxi is known for its *zaliang*, grains other than wheat and rice. Shaanxi is also known for its small dishes (*xiaochi*; 小吃), which are made from *zaliang*. They are famous for their green bean curd, made of mung bean; a combination of millet flour and glutinous flour, sprinkled with granulated sugar (*yougao*); a fried dough (*youmomo*) made from millet, and a steamed cake (*huangmo*) also made from millet.

Dumplings (*shuijiao*; 水饺), sometimes referred to as the Chinese ravioli, are also widely served in Shaanxi. The dough for the dumpling is made with flour and water, and the filling for the dumpling is usually made with beef or mutton mixed with chives. Vegetarian versions are filled with a mix of minced vermicelli, bean curd, chives, carrot and dried mushroom. The dough is rolled out into small circles, the filling is placed in the middle of the circle, and then the skin is folded so the edges of the skin meet and seal to form the shape of an ingot. Dumplings can either be boiled (*shuijiao*), steamed (*zhengjiao*) or fried (*jianjiao*). Locally, dumplings are served in a spicy and vinegary broth (*suanla shuijiao*) made of hot chili, tiny dried shrimp, and vinegar, and garnished with chopped cilantro and scallion.

Muslim restaurants are denoted by Arabic calligraphy or the characters 清真 *qingzhen*, Chinese for halal, or kosher. The narrow streets in the Muslim Quarter are full of vendors selling a myriad of sweet snacks and hundreds of small restaurants.

The people of Shaanxi also make a milky millet wine called *mijiu* (米酒) which is served hot to bring out the fragrance. The wine has a thick consistency, and the flavour is sweet and unique. The leading brand of liqueur is call 'Xifeng', a colourless spirit made in Liulin Village, near Fengxiang, about 145 kilometres (90 miles) west of Xi'an. Another local drink is the yellow Osmanthus Thick Wine (*Huanggui choujiu*). Both are said to owe their origin to alcoholic drinks of the Tang period. There are two main local bottled beers, Baoji and Hans. The latter is produced in a 'light' or 'dry' variety by the largest brewery in Xi'an—a joint-venture with a German company.

Entertainment and the Arts

Xi'an is the home of several professional performing arts organizations serving both the city and the countryside. The city also has its own Conservatory of Music (at Daxingshan Temple Park), a provincial Opera School attached to the Institute of Opera in Wenyi Lu, and its own film studio (see page 44) near the Big Goose Pagoda.

The Shaanxi Acrobatics Troupe, which includes conjurors, is very popular with local people. The Shaanxi Song and Dance Troupe is known for its vocal, orchestral and instrumental performances of both Chinese and Western music, including Western light classical, international folk and Chinese operatic pieces. The Xi'an Song and Dance Troupe concentrates on Western ballet and Chinese traditional dance. Like the Shaanxi Troupe, it has its own orchestra.

There are several big theatres in the city. The most important is the People's Theatre on Bei Dajie. This is mainly used for concerts, dancing and Beijing opera (performed by the Shaanxi Number One and Shaanxi Number Two Opera Companies).

China has over 300 forms of local theatre and the celebrated local Qinqiang opera of Shaanxi Province is one of the oldest, most vigorous and most influential of them all. It is almost certainly the original form of 'clapper opera', with which it is synonymous. In this style of Chinese opera, time is beaten with large wooden clap boards that look like oversize castanets.

The drama is performed in local Xi'an dialect, with its own characteristic, rather loud, vocal style, accompanied by string instruments. It has its own conventions of costumes and make-up. Individual operas are often three or four hours long with rapidly developing plots using all the dramatic devices found in Shakespearean comedies—abrupt changes in fortune, mistaken identities, men dressed as women, women dressed as men, both as animals (notably predatory, acrobatic tigers). Drag parts in which comedians take off vulgar, meddlesome old ladies are often star roles.

Unfortunately, in the fast-changing China of the 1990s, Qinqiang is losing its popularity, especially amongst young people. The two Qinqiang companies have been forced to spend most of their year touring the countryside, where the farming communities still enjoy live operas. If you are interested, you should ask your guide or hotel to check to find out when performances are scheduled in the city and if so, where you can buy tickets.

The Tang Dynasty is a theatre and restaurant that offers dinner followed by a one-hour performance by the Tang Dynasty Song and Dance Troupe, attempting to reproduce authentic music and dance of the ancient capital Chang'an. This colourful and lively performance features musical instruments usually seen only in museums and no longer used by modern-day orchestras. The theatre can seat up to 500 diners for the evening performance and booking is advisable. Dinner begins at 7:00 pm. During the peak season an earlier matinee performance without the meal begins at 5:45 pm. The theatre offers a lunchtime buffet but this is without the show. (See page 319 for more details.)

XI'AN FILM STUDIO —Paul Mooney

In the mid-1980s, a group of young graduates of the Beijing Film Academy, China's premier film school, began to look for an alternative to the stultifying atmosphere in the Chinese capital. These members of China's Fifth Generation of filmmakers, post-Cultural Revolution graduates of the film school, began turning to smaller studios around the country that they hoped would provide more space to practice their craft. They soon found what they were looking for at the Xi'an Film Studio. The studio, established in 1956, was under the direction of Wu Tianming, a progressive and accomplished filmmaker, who offered the filmmakers a creative space to experiment and produce films based on art rather than politics. The Xi'an Film Studio soon replaced the Beijing Film Academy as the "spiritual home" of the group of young directors.

In 1985, Wu Tianming, invited the cinematographer Zhang Yimou to work on his new film project, *Old Well*. Zhang had just finished work on *The Yellow Earth*, a Chinese classic directed by classmate Chen Kaige. The Shaanxi native agreed to take on the project, but asked Wu to support him in his own directorial debut. After completing *Old Well*, for which Zhang also picked up the Best Actor award at the Tokyo International Film Festival, he launched his directorial debut. *Red Sorghum*, a moving film shot in the Shandong countryside in the 1930s, uses minimal dialogue, rich cinematography, and evocative music to portray the story of a young woman who rises to the task of running her husband's winery after he passes away. The debut film won Zhang the Berlin Gold Bear and an Oscar nomination, propelling him into the ranks of leading international directors.

Mama, directed by Zhang Yuan and released in 1990 for distribution by the Xi'an Film Studio, marked a break from traditional cinema in China, and had a significant effect on Chinese filmmakers. The film, the first independent production since the Communists came to power in 1949, examined the lack of government assistance for families with mentally handicapped children. In shooting the film, Zhang Yuan wove together a combination of real documentary interviews filmed in colour with fiction shot in black-and-white 35 mm.

Several of the sensitive movies produced in Xi'an were banned in China after their release, but after long deliberation by Chinese censors were later approved for domestic or international release. These include *To Live*, based on a novella by writer Yu Hua and directed by Zhang Yimou; *River Without Buoys*, directed by Wu Tianming; *Wild Mountain*, directed by Yan Xueshu;

Big Parade, directed by Chen Kaige, with Zhang Yimou as cinematographer; and *The Black Cannon Incident*, directed by Huang Jianxin.

Zhang Yimou, who was born in Xi'an, has become Xi'an Film Studio's most famous son, making a series of movies which have attracted a great deal of attention from world cinema circles. After making his debut as a director with *Red Sorghum*, he directed *Judou*, *Raise the Red Lantern* and *The Story of Qiu Ju* (winner of the Golden Lion Award at the Venice Film Festival in 1992). Zhang added to these awards, winning a second Golden Lion at the 1999 Venice Film Festival with *Not One Less*. Part of the charm of this moving film, based on a true story about a 13-year-old primary school teacher, lies in the performances of its cast of non-professional children

Poster for the film Judou, *directed by Zhang Yimou.*

whose interactions with people on the streets were captured by hidden cameras. In 2002, Zhang returned to Xi'an to film *I Love You*, an intimate and realistic look at a young couple's disintegrating marriage. His most recent films, *Hero* (2003) and *House of Flying Daggers* (2004), were panned by local audiences unhappy with the storylines. However, the two films received international acclaim for their beautiful cinematography—*House of Flying Daggers* was nominated for a foreign film Oscar. Neither film was produced at the Xi'an Film Studio.

The controversial *Warriors of Heaven and Earth*, directed by He Ping, was co-produced by Xi'an Film Studio, Columbia Pictures Film Production Asia, was nominated for an Academy Award in 2004.

WEAVING A SPELL

Here was a kaleidoscope of colour beyond belief within a dusty desert place, as refreshingly different as discovering Van Gogh's 'Sunflowers' amongst the murky Manchester factories and figures of Lowry. A sword is brandished above a trailing satin sleeve, the fiery orange of dancing flames. Yellow silk of Sun and Earth is the Emperor's colour, embroidered with a red-tongued golden dragon. Mood is swiftly changed as these vivid silken robes shimmer in the hot caressing breeze, suddenly enlivened by the dramatic overtures of a white-bearded man toward a timid young maiden, as he rushed shrieking to left, to right. The musicians, accommodated at the side of the cast-concrete stage, produce a mixture of melody and sound-effects to fit the action, emotion and body language. The conflict of a sword is created by a rapid and voluminous thrashing of drum and cymbal; remorse and contemplation by the sad drone of the two-stringed erhu; gaiety by the bird-like chatter of the dizi bamboo flute; and tranquillity by the subtle plucking of the moon guitar. Exits are made to a flurried finale of everything that the orchestra can muster.

Backstage is the open-air dressing, make-up and green room rolled into one. The trunks of this travelling troupe lay open, overflowing with the finest embroidered silks. Masks, beards, bald heads and head-dresses lie strewn in apparent confusion. Oblivious to the crowd of peasants a young girl makes up as the Empress. She picks up colour from a tiny paintbox, guiding herself with the use of a palm-sized mirror. She pales her oriental complexion to eggshell smoothness. Her slender tapering eyes are accentuated. She pouts her lips to paint on their apex a slim scarlet rosebud, and rouges her cheeks to the subtle tint of a ripening apple. Only then does this girl allow her face to be dimpled by a smile of majestic beauty. Crowned with a head-dress of red silk and silver she enters the stage, followed by ladies of the court to a deafening fanfare.

William Lindesay, Alone on the Great Wall,
Colorado USA, Fulcrum Publishing, 1991

Flora and Fauna

During the Tang dynasty (618–907 CE) horticulture flourished in the capital Chang'an (present day Xi'an). One of its citizens was the most celebrated gardener of Chinese history, the hunchback 'Camel' Guo. He is supposed to have grown golden peaches and propagated lotus with deep blue flowers by soaking the seeds in indigo dye.

The inhabitants of the capital were especially proud of their tree peonies, which became something of a mania, and blooms were sold for huge sums in the Chang'an Flower Market. The most popular colours were pale pink and deep purple. Tree peonies had been cultivated from about the fifth century onwards, originally in either Shaanxi or Sichuan. (The plant did not reach Europe until 1789 when the first one was found a home in London's Kew Gardens). The best peony garden was at Da Cien Temple, the temple of the Big Goose Pagoda (see page 211). It is no longer there today, but the Xi'an Botanical Garden has a small display. While perhaps not worth a special trip, the Botanical Garden is an excellent place to escape the crowds that fill most tourist sights and is a short taxi ride from the Big Goose Pagoda or Daxingshan Temple. It has a good variety of trees and plants in peaceful surroundings and, depending on the season, can be quite pretty. It is located on Cuihua Lu, south of the city, and can be reached by bus number 27 or by taxi.

In the second century BCE, an envoy of Emperor Han Wudi (reigned 140–86 BCE), who was sent to central Asia, brought the pomegranate tree back to China. Today, during the months of May and June, the hillsides around Lintong County, including the slopes of the Mausoleum of the First Emperor of Qin, are covered with the red and white pomegranate flowers. The fruit grown in Xi'an and especially Lintong, 15 kilometres (9 miles) to the east, is considered the best in the country, giving rise to the Chinese saying that 'When you think of Lintong, you think of pomegranates.'

The first attempt to catalogue the animals, birds and reptiles of Shaanxi according to Western science was made in 1908–9. Robert Stirling Clark of New York led an expedition of 36 men, including the ornithologist Arthur de C Sowerby of the Smithsonian.

Among some of today's rarest birds recorded by Sowerby were the pink, grey and white 'Chinese' ibises. These wading birds, members of the stork family, are properly called Japanese ibis, though they are call *toki* in Japan. The long-beaked birds are distinguished by the bright red colouring on the side of the head and legs. The adult grows to a length of about 77 centimetres (2.5 feet) head to tail.

These ibises were formerly spread throughout east and northeast China, Korea and Japan, but environmental changes in the 20th century have been disastrous for the species. They declined in numbers and disappeared altogether after 1964. By

1980 there were only two known pairs left in the world. These were at the Toki Protection Centre on Japan's Sado Island. They had not reproduced for four years, and artificial incubation failed. Then, that same year, Chinese zoologists found two nesting pairs in Shaanxi, at Yangxian County in the Qin Mountains. Three young were hatched that year in what is now the Qinling Number One Ibis Colony.

By comparison with the ibis, the giant panda is not nearly so rare. There are still about 1,000 of these large black and white, high-altitude living, bamboo-munching 'cat-bears'. Most of them are in the neighbouring province of Sichuan; a few unlucky, if pampered, ones play star roles in world zoos. In Shaanxi Province there is one special nature reserve for them in Foping County, southwest of Xi'an and not far from the Qinling Ibis Colony.

The orange snub-nosed monkey, also known as the golden-haired monkey, is another inhabitant of the Qin Mountains. Found in birch forests and mountain gullies, at around 2,500–3,000 metres (about 8,000–10,000 feet), these very agile, acrobatic animals have bright yellow-orange fur, with white chests, long tails and distinctive blue circles around their eyes.

The so-called Reeves pheasant is the original proud possessor of the long, waving tail feathers worn by generals in Chinese opera. The tail of the male reaches to 100–140 centimetres (3.3–4.6 feet) in length. The bird is found in mountain forests, between 600-2,000 metres (about 2,000–5,000 feet) above sea level.

The Xi'an Zoo on Jinhua Beilu, not far from the Shangri-La Golden Flower Hotel, has examples of both giant and lesser pandas, together with what is said to be the only surviving brown panda in the world. There are also pheasants and orange snub-nosed monkeys as well as northeast China tigers, leopards, Sichuan parrots, wild donkeys and other animals indigenous to China. There are also a number of animals presented to the Xi'an Zoo by the Japanese cities of Kyoto and Nara, with which Xi'an has a formal as well as a historical relationship. The zoo was established in Revolution Park in 1956, but moved to its much larger present site to the east in 1976.

Until surveys are published of the complete fauna of southern Shaanxi there will not be a definitive inventory of species. The British traveller, Violet Cressy-Marcks, who interviewed Mao Zedong in Yan'an, recorded in 1938 that in an area 20 miles from the city she saw 'common jay, Chinese jay, blue magpie, golden eagle, pheasants, green woodpeckers, flocks of bustard, wild horned sheep and wild ducks and I was told there were leopards but I did not see any.' Near Xi'an 'there were many sulphur bellied rats, wood and field mice, also mallard, teal, wrens, redstarts, minks and goral'. At Lintong she saw 'geese, ducks, hares, snipe, bustard and mallard'. The wildlife of the Wei River plain is almost certainly much depleted now, in contrast to that of the mountains of the south.

(Left) *Impeyan pheasants, taken from a set of original paintings of rare and endangered species of Chinese birds by J Fenwick Lansdowne. The 32 paintings were completed with the cooperation of ornithologists in Beijing after the artist made field trips to Chengdu and the Wolong Nature Reserve, among other places in China.*

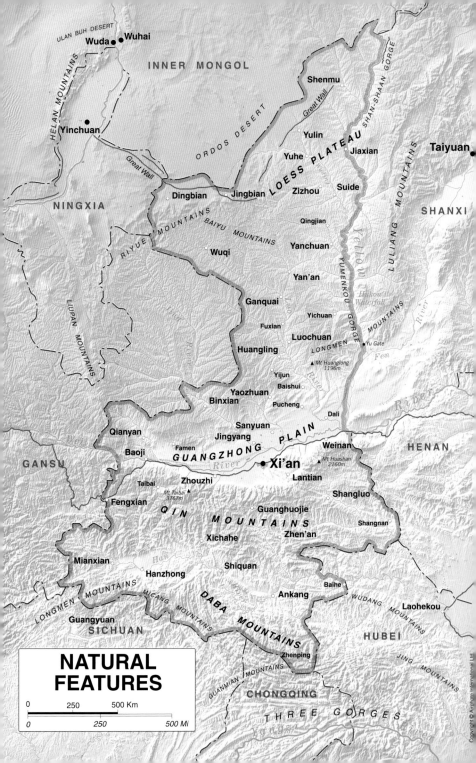

NATURAL FEATURES

```
0        250        500 Km
0        250        500 Mi
```

The Landscape and Environment of Shaanxi Province —Raynor Shaw

Shaanxi is a markedly elongated province that extends for about 1,000 kilometres from north to south, and ranges between about 150 and 500 kilometres wide. Located in the middle reaches of the Yellow River, the province covers an area of almost 206,000 square kilometres, and supports a population of approximately 35 million, comprising 44 ethnicities, of mostly rural peasants, the majority of whom live in the central and southern parts where the climate and soils are more hospitable. The province is widely held to be the cradle of the 5,000 year old Chinese civilization.

GEOGRAPHICAL SUBDIVISIONS

Geographically, the province comprises three distinctive zones (see map opposite). In the north is the vast Loess Plateau that ranges in elevation between 900 and 1,500 metres above sea level and occupies about 45% of the province. The lower lying Guangzhong Plain lies in the centre, occupying about 20% of the area of Shaanxi. Ranging in elevation from 320 to 800 metres above sea level, the plain is crossed from west to east by the Weihe River. Living conditions are generally more favourable than

The Yellow River at Longmen; view downstream to the road bridge at the southern end of Yumenkou Gorge.

in the north, with a milder climate and more fertile soils. Higher ground occurs to the south, with the Qin and Daba mountains forming a west to east oriented range of impressive peaks, fronted by steep rock faces, that rise to between 1,500 and 3,000 metres above sea level. This mountain range forms the watershed between the Yellow and Yangzi rivers, effectively dividing northern and southern China. Mount Taibai (3,767 metres), the highest peak of the Qin range, retains a snow cover until June. The sacred peak of Huashan (2,160 metres) is located on the northern edge of the range, 120 kilometres to the east of Xi'an (see page 263).

The Major Rivers

Broadly, the drainage system of northern Shaanxi province comprises three southward flowing dendritic systems, namely the Jingshui River in the west, the Luo River in the centre, and the main Yellow River in the east. Flowing from west to east along the steep northern margin of the Qin Mountains in the southern part of Shaanxi province is the Wei River, which occupies a rift valley (a down-faulted block or graben). The Wei River, a major right bank tributary of the Yellow River, (see map opposite) receives the Jingshui and Luo rivers as major north bank tributaries before joining the Yellow River near the sharp bend at Laotongguan. These three rivers all carry heavy silt loads to the Yellow River.

The Yellow River, the second longest river in China, enters Shaanxi province in the far north-east corner of the province at Hequ. There it enters the 700 kilometre long Shan-Shaan Gorge that forms the natural border between Shanxi and Shaanxi provinces. In this section, crossing the Loess Plateau, the river acquires almost 50% of its silt load. Within the Shan-Shaan Gorge, the channel becomes narrower, the gradient steeper, and the water faster flowing, making the river un-navigable. The channel bed falls from 900 metres above sea level at its northern end to 300 metres above sea level in the south at Yumenkou, where the river enters the Yumenkou Gorge through the Longmen Mountains. Near Yumenkou the channel narrows from over 400 metres wide to about 40 metres wide and plunges 50 metres over the horseshoe-shaped Hukou Waterfall, the second largest waterfall in China. Longmen (Dragon's Mouth or Yu Gate) marks the southern end of Yumenkou Gorge (see photograph page 51), where the river broadens from 40 metres wide to become a vast braided channel. The river makes a sharp eastward turn at Laotongguan, at the confluence with the Wei River. From there, navigation is again difficult until the river emerges from the Sanmen Gorge and widens dramatically to form a 15 kilometre-wide braided channel in the Fen-Wei Basin.

Wei Valley

100 Km
50
0

100 Mi
50
0

A BRIEF GEOLOGICAL HISTORY OF SHAANXI PROVINCE

Geology influences the landscape of an area in three important ways. Firstly, the landforms are directly controlled by the properties of the rock (limestone, granite, etc.) or sediment types (river alluvium, glacial deposits, etc.) that are exposed at the land surface. Secondly, the landscape is profoundly affected by current geological processes (shaken by volcanic eruptions, deformed by active mountain building, etc.). Thirdly, geology affects the climate of a location, which in turn determines the geological processes (glaciations, river erosion, tropical weathering, etc.) that are active. Evidence of these changes is recorded in the rocks, sediment, natural resources and scenery of a region.

The oldest geological evidence in Shaanxi Province is of the laying down of predominantly marine sediments, their folding, crumpling and alteration during Pre-Cambrian times (prior to 543 million years ago). These rocks form the geological basement of the North China Platform. This basement is overlain by a cover of several thousand metres of Cambrian to Middle Ordovician age rocks (543 to 458 million years old) that were deposited as marine sediments. Conditions changed during the Upper Ordovician to Early Carboniferous periods (458 to 323 million years ago) when the seas retreated and extensive erosion of the new landmass began. From the Late Carboniferous to the end of the Permian periods (323 to 248 million years ago), the area was again covered by sea. Fine-grained shales, sandstones and thin beds of coal and limestone were deposited in shallow, fluctuating marine conditions. Northern China emerged as a continent at the end of the Permian Period (about 248 million years ago). However, subsequent volcanic activity and related igneous intrusions (granite), with associated folding and faulting of the rocks, fundamentally altered the geological composition of the area.

Subsequent weathering and erosion have weakened and sculpted the exposed rocks, continually modifying the land surface to produce a landscape of wide, open plains that were later buried by loess deposits during the glaciations of the Quaternary Period (the last 1.6 million years, or fourth major period of geological time).

NATURAL RESOURCES

Below the surface of Shaanxi province, and the neighbouring Shanxi and Hunan provinces, lie great coalfields whose combined reserves were estimated (1965 figures) to be 40,000 million tones of anthracite and 160,000 million tones of bituminous coal. However, owing to the remoteness and lack of communications, these reserves have not been fully developed in Shaanxi province. The principal coal mines are situated to the east in neighbouring Shanxi province, around Datong and in the Taiyuan-Yangchuan area. Large iron and steel manufacturing industries are also located in Taiyuan. Oil reserves have been discovered in the north of Shaanxi province, and small-scale pumping can be seen in many areas.

THE LOESS PLATEAU

Fundamental to the character of the scenery of northern Shaanxi province, and to the development of the culture and economy, are the distinctive deposits of the Loess Plateau. The Loess Plateau covers a total area of 300,000 square kilometres in China, and accounts for 93,000 of the 206,000 square kilometres of Shaanxi province. Loess deposits are part of a belt of wind-borne dust that extends from Europe to China. They occur as isolated patches in France and Germany, become thicker and more extensive across Russia and Turkistan, and attain their maximum development in Shaanxi province (see the loess distribution map opposite). These distinctive accumulations of silt-sized particles were first described in 1824 by Professor Karl Caesar von Leonard (1779–1862) from a site at Haarlass, near Heidelberg in Germany. However, although von Leonard proposed the name loess (yellow silty loam), the aeolian (wind-blown) origin was only later recognised by Baron Ferdinand von Richthofen (1833–1905), which he described in his book *Travels in China*, published in 1886.

EXTENT AND SUBDIVISIONS

Loess covers about 10% of the land surface of the earth, and is concentrated in the temperate zones and semi-arid desert margins that today are commonly intensively agricultural, highly industrial, and densely populated. In China, loess covers an area of about 440,000 square kilometres. The thickest accumulations are concentrated over an area of about 300,000 square kilometres in the middle reaches of the Yellow River. The secondary loess covers an area of about 190,000 square kilometres, including the North China Plain. Although loess occupies only 10% of the area of China, it represents 20% of the tillable land and supports 20% of the population (about 200 million people).

The Loess Plateau begins at the southern edge of the Inner Mongolia Plateau (along the line of the Great Wall) in the north, and extends southwards to the Qin Mountains. Laterally, the plateau is bounded by the Riyue Mountains in the west, and the Taihang Mountains in the east. Former rocky peaks, such as the Liupan and Luliang mountains, emerge like islands from the surrounding loess cover. The upper altitudinal limit of the loess, the "loess line", varies across the plateau, reaching about 1,000 metres above sea level against the Luliang Mountains, and rising to 1,800 metres on the eastern flanks of the Liupan Mountains and to nearly 3,000 metres on their western flanks.

Loess forms a thick and fertile blanket that, except for the emergent mountain peaks, completely buries the original landscape, which consisted of an extensive plain traversed by a network of river valleys. The average thickness of this loess cover is between 30 to 60 metres, although it reaches about 200 metres thick in certain

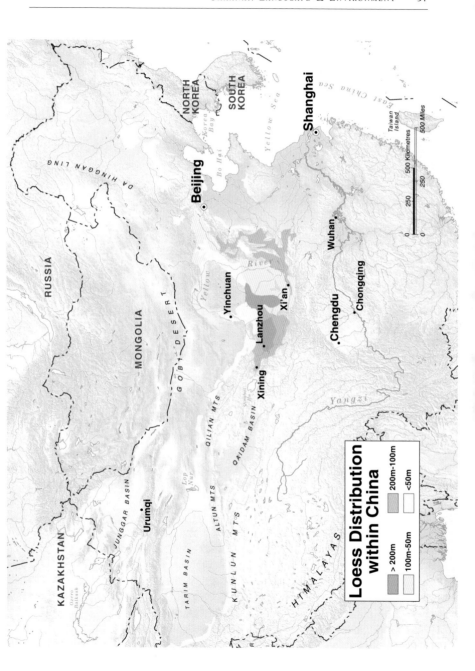

Loess Distribution within China

> 200m
100m-50m
200m-100m
<50m

localities. Wide valleys have been filled, transforming them into broad, high plains that stand as a dissected plateau between 600 metres and 1,050 metres above sea level. Maps, aerial photographs or views from an aircraft window clearly reveal that the drainage density of the Loess Plateau is unusually high, that is the stream channels and tributaries are very closely spaced giving a fine-textured, frond-like appearance to the channel network.

Several distinctive landforms occur within the Loess Plateau. Depending upon the degree of erosion, loess landforms are classified into three major types. *Yuan* are relatively large and flat plateaus, *Liang* are elongate, upstanding ridges, and *Mao* are dome-shaped hills. The sequence reflects stages of erosion of the plateau, from a flat plain, to channel divides, to remnant mounds.

Regionally, three major subdivisions of the Loess Plateau are recognised, each characterized by a distinctive scenery. In the north is a landscape of loess hills and gullies, predominantly comprising low ridges (*Liang*) with gentle side slopes that have been dissected into a rugged topography. The loess grains are coarser in the north than the south, constituting the so-called sandy loess. Soil erosion in this area is severe, with deep ravines flanked by steep and unstable cliffs, and scattered *Mao*. Overall, there is a need to restore the grass cover and enforce other soil conservation measures. The area supports pasture, farming and forestry. The central region consists of extensive, flat, high level loess plains (*Yuan*) traversed by a network of well-developed erosional gullies that are up to 100 metres deep. Farming and pasture are the main activities. Transport across the northern and central areas is difficult, particularly transverse to the drainage channels. However, constant traffic along the existing unsurfaced roads has worn them down to 3 metres, or even 6 metres (10 to 20 feet), below the surrounding land. The southern region is dominated by the broad Wei River Valley, which comprises a broad river flood plain and three adjacent, elevated river terraces. The loess is finer and thinner than in the north, constituting the clayey loess. This is a sub-region of intensive farming, and is an especially important grain producing area.

ORIGIN OF THE LOESS

Geological evidence indicates that the loess has two primary origins, glacial grinding or desert weathering. During the Quaternary glacial periods, great ice sheets spread out from the northern latitudes eroding the rocks over which they slid, grinding the surface to produce a fine rock flour. This fine debris was either washed out from the margins of the ice sheets by seasonal meltwaters and deposited as fluvio-glacial outwash plains, or plastered on to the base of the glacier near its margins, to be exposed when the ice sheet began to melt. Cold northerly winds blowing across these unvegetated outwash plains winnowed-out the finer rock and mineral particles and

(Preceding pages) *Landscape of the Loess (Yellow Earth) Plateau, northern Shaanxi province.*

carried them south as great dust clouds that were subsequently deposited over the landscape. In addition, winds crossing the vast deserts of Asia have lifted up and exported the dust southwards and southeastwards over the extensive grasslands.

Airborne dust is deposited either when the velocity of the wind is reduced, or when the particles are washed out of the air by falling rain. Accumulation is greatly assisted by a surface grass cover, which serves to hold and bind the loose material. Each season, new grasses grow on the slightly raised land surface and the older grass stems and roots wither and decay, forming a complex pattern of narrow tubes that are usually partly filled with calcium carbonate.

Close inspection of the many roadside cuttings or fields of loess reveals that the deposit is a light greyish yellow or light brown (buff) coloured material, which is very fine-grained, porous and friable. Upon exposure to the air the surface develops a thin cement-like covering. Individual loess grains are mostly silt-sized particles (0.002 to 0.06 millimetres in diameter), with some fine sand (0.06 to 0.2 millimetres in diameter). Over 50% of the grains are quartz (the material used to make window glass). The grains are characteristically irregular, with angular shapes, sharp edges, and fractured surfaces that reveal their dynamic origin, having being violently jostled around while carried for hundreds of kilometres by turbulent winds. Loess also contains carbonate, which generally occurs as rounded, silt-sized grains. This suggests that it originated as a primary sediment from the original source area. However, carbonate also occurs as calcareous coatings to the mineral grains, which were formed by groundwater precipitation or by biological activity. Fortunately, calcium carbonate increases the fertility of the loess soils.

The maximum grain size exhibits a decrease towards the southeast, in the direction of the prevailing winds. Thus, the coarser, more sandy particles were deposited in the north, nearer the source area. In general, the maximum particle size near the Yellow River exceeds 0.045 millimetres. This decreases to less than 0.015 millimetres in the region of Xi'an, almost 750 kilometres to the southeast. Travellers may notice that roadside cuttings through the loess in the south of the province are steeper and more stable than those in the north. This is because the finer grained loess in the south is more cohesive, the loess characteristically forming vertical walls that are very stable unless the exposures are disturbed. In contrast, the sandier loess in the north is less cohesive, Therefore, roadside slopes in the north are usually designed at a less-steep angle than in the south, although slope failures are still more common than in the south. Collapses are generally manifest as shallow scallops in the slopes, with cones of loose material on the hard shoulder at the base of the slope.

AGE OF THE LOESS DEPOSITS

Loess deposits are a valuable regional archive, preserving evidence of past geological conditions, climatic history, landscape development, and human evolution. Scientific keys to unlocking these stories include interpreting the pollen contained in the deposits, examination of the incorporated micro-fossils, analysis of buried soil horizons (ancient soils or palaeosols), dating of intercalated ash layers from major volcanic eruptions (tephra chronology), and determining the orientations of magnetic particles contained in the loess (palaeomagnetism).

Modern dating techniques have determined that, at its optimum development, the loess comprises four main units. An important scientific site is located at Luochuan, in Shaanxi province, about 200 kilometres north of Xi'an. There, the Hemgou Section at Potou Village (see photograph opposite) is 135 metres thick. The oldest unit at the base is termed the Wucheng (or Red) Loess (about 50 metres thick), which began accumulating about 2.4 million years ago in the Early Pleistocene Period. Overlying this is the Lishi Loess (about 75 metres thick) of Middle Pleistocene age, which began about 1.1 million years ago. More recently, the Late Pleistocene Malan Loess (about 6.5 metres thick) can be dated back to about 100,000 years ago. Finally, the uppermost Potou Loess (about 15 metres thick) is of Holocene age, less than 10,000 years old.

Unravelling the history of human evolution in the loess deposits has produced at least four generations of fossil hominids (human-like fossils), namely Lantian Man, Dali Man, Dingcun Man, and Hetao Man. Lantian Man remains were found near the village of Gongwan in Lantian County, about 60 kilometres east of Xi'an. Dated at 1.15 ma, the skull was of a 30 year old female preserved at the base of a loess deposit on a terrace of the Ba River. Teeth of Dingcun Man were found about 30 metres above the Fen River, at a site 26 kilometres south of Linfen. They were unearthed from 11 metres below the surface of a deposit of Malan Loess that had accumulated on a terrace developed adjacent to a former lake bed. East of Xi'an, the village of Banpo was unearthed from below a thin loess cover to reveal details of life in a matrilineal society that flourished by the Chan River about 6,000 years ago.

FEATURES OF THE LOESS

Loess does not exhibit any layering (stratification), but forms an homogeneous mass. Well-developed vertical cracks or fissures are the only apparent structure. Because loess is loose, porous, homogeneous, and contains organic matter and carbonate, it is both easy to cultivate and fertile. The major disadvantage is that the loess is subject to erosion by running water, or by wind, especially if the vegetation cover is removed. Also, loess is easily excavated, allowing early hominids to hollow caves out of the steep valley walls. Today, people still live in similar cave houses, sometimes two or three storeys high, with chimneys that emerge in the flat fields above the cliffs. Loess

(Top Left) *The Hemgou loess type-section in Luochuan county; a 135 metre thick exposure spanning 2.4 millon years of earth history.*

(Top Right) *Desertification is a major problem in northern Shaanxi province. Remedial tree planting traps and holds the encroaching sand dunes.*

(Bottom) *Saline flats in northern Shaanxi province; white salt encrustations on the surface, and a dust storm removing the soil.*

Village life—cave-style houses dug out of loess cliffs can still be seen in many areas of the Shaanxi countryside.

dwellings are warm and dry in the bitterly cold winters, and remain cool in the very hot summers. Most notably, between 1936 and 1947, Mao Zedong and his comrades lived worked and wrote in simple cave houses that were dug out of the loess at Yan'an (see pages 288–289). However, because the area is subject to earthquakes, tremors can cause the cliffs to collapse, endangering the lives of the cave occupants. Collapses bury facilities below and disrupt the fields above. For example, about 250,000 people died in 1920 as a result of a major earthquake in the province, either directly, or in the resulting famine.

Loess can be readily quarried and makes durable bricks, therefore, it has long been utilized as a building material. The most notable use was to build the existing city walls of Xi'an, erected in the Ming Dynasty between 1370 and 1380 (see Xi'an city walls on page 255). Interestingly, the foundations were formed of mixed lime, earth and glutinous rice. Above this, the emergent walls were constructed of layers of rammed loess faced with sun-dried bricks, which were probably also made from loess. The walls are about 9.7 kilometres west to east, and 8.6 kilometres north to south, 12 metres high and 15–18 metres wide at the base, tapering to 12–14 metres wide at the top. Thus, about 6.6 million cubic metres of loess had to be excavated to build the walls, and a further 5 million cubic metres was probably used to complete the many watch towers and gatehouses.

CLIMATE

The geological history of the region has determined the modern environment of Shaanxi province. Hence the climate, soils and vegetation of the province can be directly traced back to events in the geological record, as can the geological hazards that pose a danger to the infrastructure and population of Shaanxi.

In the case of Shaanxi province, the uplift of the Tibetan Plateau, which began about 2.5 million years ago, culminated in the establishment of the cold Siberian Anticyclone (a cold, high pressure air system) and the development of the Asian Monsoon climate. The strong monsoonal wind system was responsible for the removal of silt from the interior deserts of Asia southwards to the steppe zone, and ultimately for the formation of the Loess Plateau.

Today, the Asian Monsoon affects 10% of the world's land area, a region that supports more than 50% of the world's population. Northern China experiences a Continental Monsoon type climate, which is characterized by extremes. Conditions range from semi-arid in the northwest to subhumid in the southeast. There are marked seasonal contrasts, with a large daily and a large annual range of temperature, and moderate but highly concentrated rainfall. Winters are dry, very cold and windy, whereas summers are generally hot with light rainfall. The average annual temperature is 8° to 11° centigrade on the high Loess Plateau, but 11° to 15° centigrade on the lower North China Plain to the east.

During the winter, the area is covered by the Siberian Anticyclone, a cold high pressure air mass. Winters are long, with strong, bitterly cold northwest winds that sweep down over the hills, generating thick dust storms. The largest dust storms usually occur between March to May. The *Books of the Western Han Dynasty* by Ban Gu (32– 92 CE) reported strong winds from the northwest that carried red and yellow clouds of floating dust, and described *huangtu* (yellow dust) falling to the ground. Summer is the wet season when a low pressure system covers the area and warm, moisture laden winds blow in from the south. About 70% of the annual precipitation falls in the period from June to August, usually as scattered showers. However, precipitation is sparse and variable with the average annual rainfall ranging from a maximum of 1,400 millimetres in a year to as low as 100 millimetres in drier years. Average annual runoff depth increases from 25 millimetres in the drier west to 50 millimetres in the east. In wetter years the region is subject to destructive cloudbursts and hailstorms, during which several hundred millimetres can fall on one day. These rain stroms can cause severe soil erosion, mudflows and flooding, whereas in dry years the summer dust storms are usually more disruptive than winter ones.

The normally light rainfall, combined with the extremely dense drainage network, prevents the accumulation of large groundwater reserves. Thus dry years cause almost immediate drought, which is synonymous with famine in the region. Farmers around Lanzhou in neighbouring Gansu province suppress the intense evaporation by spreading sand and pebbles over the fields, creating the distinctive "sand farmland".

SOILS

Overall, it is estimated that only about 10% of the soils of China are residual, that is formed on bedrock in place. The majority, or about 90%, are formed on materials that have been transported by wind or by rivers. Over most of Shaanxi province, soils are developed on the wind blown loess deposits, and more locally on the alluvial deposits of the Yellow and Wei rivers.

Atmospheric and biological processes acting over the surface of the loess deposits have developed dark loessial soils, up to 2 to 3 metres thick. Under undisturbed conditions, loessial soils are a calcareous loam, which is a sandy silt containing calcium carbonate. They are characterised by a richly humic upper layer, up to 1 metre thick. However, most of the natural vegetation cover has been lost, largely as a result of ancient deforestation, but also because of poor land management practices, such as unwise cultivation, overgrazing, and the cutting and burning of grass and scrub. Depletion of organic matter causes a loss of structural stability of the soil. The natural crumb structure breaks down and porosity is reduced. Therefore, the treeless plains are extremely sensitive to rainfall, and rainfall intensity and distribution are

a critical factor in the province. The infrequent heavy rains cause exceptional damage because, with little vegetation cover to trap the rainwater, runoff is rapid and highly erosive, removing the topsoil by sheet and gully erosion. Erosional undercutting of the vertical sidewalls of the steep ravines causes rapid widening of the ravines. New ravines are created, houses and fields are threatened, and roads diverted. In contrast, in dry years natural desiccation allows deflation (wind action) to blow away the fine-grained loess. Thus, as development pressures increase, the loess is becoming an increasingly unstable and relatively transient resource.

VEGETATION

The natural, zonal vegetation of the region is transitional from deciduous broad-leaved forest in the warmer, moister southeast, through forest-steppe in the centre, to steppe (grasslands) in the semi-arid northwest. However, because the region has probably been cultivated for more than 7,000 years, most of the original vegetation has been destroyed. Today, the loess plains are mantled with bunch steppe grass, with some forest remaining on the higher mountains. Herbaceous plants distinguish the wetter areas, and remnants of the original broadleaf and evergreen forests, comprising oak, maple, poplar, birch, elm and willow, with some conifers, survive in the southeast and in the Wei valley.

GEOLOGICAL HAZARDS

Geological conditions present several important natural hazards that threaten both the lives and the livelihoods of Shaanxi province residents. Recently, as China has become more economically developed, all the provinces have been assigned insurance ratings for natural hazard consequence assessment. Shaanxi, Gansu and Sichuan provinces are considered to be moderately developed, and have been assigned an intermediate risk category. The far west and northwest of China are categorized as poor, and the remaining provinces are well-developed.

The major natural hazard is erosion of the loess. Loess is highly erodible, even on slopes as low as 3° to 5°, and erosion gullies up to 100 metres deep are common. About 430,000 square kilometres of the Loess Plateau are affected by erosion, with 110,000 square kilometres classified as severely damaged. The Yellow River is the major agent of sediment removal, carrying a mean annual silt load of about 1,600 million tons that is about 38 kilograms of suspended sediment in each cubic metre of water that passes along the channel. However, in the middle reaches where the river crosses the Loess Plateau the sediment load increases to 2,200 million tons, 80% of which is loess.

(Preceding pages) *Rapeseed and wheat fields outside Xi'an. Farmers in the region plant two crops per year—maize from July to October and winter wheat from November to June.*

Landslides are another serious hazard. They bury villages, disrupt traffic, damage factories, threaten mines, block rivers and destroy farmland. During the wet season between June and August, landslides, mudflows, and rockfalls are common. Saturation slumping and collapse due to undercutting are the main processes. In addition, the thick loess cover overlies active fractures in the rocks that, when shaken by earthquakes, can cause large collapses. In the 22,000 square kilometres of central Shaanxi province, hazard surveys have identified 1,100 landslides, 80 mudflows, and 130 rockfalls. Some failures are particularly large, such as the loess landslide at Bailuyuan on 11 April 1990 that was 70 metres wide, over 100 metres long and descended 70 metres.

Earthquakes are a hazard throughout China. Tremors with a magnitude greater than or equal to 5 have occurred in every province in China. In 1556, the deadliest earthquake in world history killed 830,000 people in northern Shaanxi (source: Jake Hooker in *China Review, Winter 2004/5*). Between 1900 and 1980 there were 9 earthquakes of magnitude 8, and 66 of magnitude 7.0 to 7.9. On average in China, there is one earthquake a year of magnitude 7 or less.

Ground cracks, affecting the surface Quaternary deposits (alluvium and loess), were discovered within and around the city of Xi'an in 1959. A system of 11 major cracks, aligned in a north-north-easterly direction and dipping steeply to the southeast, are evenly spaced across a zone 150 kilometres wide. Individual cracks are up to 10 kilometres long, with numerous lateral branches that create a fracture zone between 8 to 10 metres wide. The cracks are the surface expression of ground subsidence resulting from excessive groundwater pumping. Monitoring has demonstrated that the cracks are active, extending longitudinally at a rate of 10 to 50 metres a year prior to 1984, but increasing to between 130 and 160 metres a year after 1984. Tensional opening of between 4 to 6 millimetres a year, and subsidence of 12 to 14 millimetres a year, was also recorded. Ground cracking has caused the dislocation of buildings, deformation of roads, severing of underground pipes, and displacement of the Longhai Railway, resulting in massive costs for remedial measures. Future developments are required to take preventative action to avoid building across the cracks, and to stop surface water penetrating the fissures.

In the drier western areas, deforestation and soil erosion have led to an encroachment of the desert sands, a process known as desertification. Currently in China there are 1.16 million square kilometres of desert and gobi (stone desert), 0.176 million square kilometres of desertified land, and 0.158 million square kilometres of potentially desertified land in 11 provinces. Studies using historical aerial photographs have shown that in the 25 years between the 1950s and the late 1970s, desertified land in China expanded by 39,000 square kilometres. This is equivalent to an increase of about 1,560 square kilometres a year, resulting in losses of about 450 million yuan a year in agriculture and animal husbandry. Today, 60% of the poor counties of China are located in windblown sand areas. Desertification is a major problem in Northern Shaanxi province, and several remedial projects are being carried out (see photograph on page 63). Prolonged misuse of agricultural land, water supplies, grasslands, forests and other natural resources, has resulted in an already weak and fragile environment being destroyed. The loose and silty surface has been exposed to the rigours of the dry and windy climate, transforming large tracts of the landscape to sheets of wind blown sand and undulating dunes. Remedial measures include the planting of trees along river banks, reforesting of hillsides, terracing of slopes, and close-planting of crops.

Three important groundwater-related problems affect the region. Firstly, the discharge of the rivers that cross the Loess Plateau is low, therefore, with an increasing water demand from an expanding population, agriculture and industry, underground water has been severely exploited. Because seasonal rainfall is low, groundwater recharge is slow. Therefore, the groundwater table is being lowered to critical levels in several areas. Secondly, of major concern is the high sediment load of the rivers that cross the highly erodible loess. Their low water discharge combined with the large sediment load makes the water unsuitable for irrigation, drinking and other purposes without treatment. Thirdly, in a climate where the rate of surface water evaporation exceeds the amount of annual rainfall, salinisation is a serious geological hazard in many low-lying areas. Consequently, over large parts of the Yellow River floodplain, ground water containing dissolved salts is drawn towards the surface by capillary rise (see photograph on page 63). Intense evaporation results in the accumulation of crystallized salts in the upper parts of the soil profile. These salts decrease the soil fertility, leading to a lowering of crop yields and a reduction of local incomes. The problem is most commonly tackled by drilling numerous wells to regulate the water table.

Raynor Shaw studied geography and geology at London and Edinburgh universities, specializing in geomorphology. He lectured in geomorphology at McMaster University in Canada, and has worked in West Africa and Venezuela prospecting for alluvial diamonds and gold. Since 1983 he has been living in Hong Kong, making geological maps and publishing reports about the geomorphology, weathering and Quaternary sediments.

CHRONOLOGY OF PERIODS IN CHINESE HISTORY

NEOLITHIC	7000–1600 BCE
SHANG	1600–1027 BCE
WESTERN ZHOU	1027–771 BCE
EASTERN ZHOU	770–256 BCE
SPRING AND AUTUMN	770–476 BCE
WARRING STATES	475–221 BCE
QIN	221–206 BCE
WESTERN (FORMER) HAN	206 BCE–8 CE
XIN	9–24
EASTERN (LATER) HAN	25–220
THREE KINGDOMS	220–265
WESTERN JIN	265–316
EASTERN JIN	317–420
NORTHERN AND SOUTHERN DYNASTIES	386–589
SIXTEEN KINGDOMS	317–439
FORMER ZHAO	304–329
FORMER QIN	351–383
LATER QIN	384–417
NORTHERN WEI	386–534
WESTERN WEI	535–556
NORTHERN ZHOU	557–581
SUI	581–618
TANG	618–907
FIVE DYNASTIES	907–960
LIAO (KHITAN)	916–1125
NORTHERN SONG	960–1127
SOUTHERN SONG	1127–1279
JIN (JURCHEN)	1115–1234
YUAN (MONGOL)	1279–1368
MING	1368–1644
QING (MANCHU)	1644–1911
REPUBLIC OF CHINA	1911–1949
PEOPLE'S REPUBLIC OF CHINA	1949–

A Brief Guide to the Chinese Language

Mandarin (*Putonghua* or common speech), designated as the official Chinese language by the Guomindang government in 1912, is historically a dialect of the Beijing area. The Beijing dialect is one of five major dialect groups—another one being Wu that is spoken in the Shanghai region. The differences between the Shanghai and Beijing dialects can be compared to the differences between the English and French languages. Regardless of the differences in the spoken language it is consoling to find that the written script is uniform throughout China. The only quandary presented is that over 50,000 characters are entered in the largest dictionary. In practice, however, educated people ordinarily use just 4,000 to 5,000 characters. The mammoth 900,000 character *Selected Works of Chairman Mao* is based on a glossary of just over 3,000 different characters.

Each character is a syllable, many of which can stand alone as words. In fact words with one or two syllables account for over nine out of 10 of those found in the Chinese language. Characters based on pictures formed the basis for the development of the Chinese script. For instance the character for a person (人) is based on a side view of a human being, the character for big or large (大) resembles a man standing legs apart and arms widespread. Whilst there only a few hundred such pictographic characters there are many more which build upon them, though an association or indication to form other words. For example, one person behind another person (从) means to come from or follow and one person above two others (众) means a crowd.

The Chinese government introduced the pinyin system in 1958 allowing an approach to the spoken language through the 26 characters of the Roman alphabet and its associated numerals. Around the same time, the written script was 'simplified' with many characters being rewritten in a less complicated arrangement so as to make them easier to learn. The pinyin system enables foreigners to achieve a reasonable level of spoken Chinese without any knowledge of the characters. This approach is also used in primary education as an aid to basic character recognition.

You will encounter pinyin on road signs, some maps and store fronts and in the Western media. You will initially meet with some difficulty in pronouncing Romanised Chinese words, despite the fact that most sounds correspond to usual pronunciation of the letters in English. The exceptions are:

INITIALS

c   is like the *ts* in 'i*ts*'

q   is like the *ch* in '*cheese*'

x   has no English equivalent, and can best be described as a hissing consonant that lies somewhere between *sh* and *s*. The sound was rendered as *hs* under an earlier transcription system.

z   is like the *ds* in 'fa*ds*'

zh   is unaspirated, and sounds like the *j* in 'jug'.

FINALS

a   sounds like '*ah*'

e   is pronounced as in 'her'

i   is pronounced as in 'ski' (written as *yi* when not preceded by an initial consonant). However, in *ci, chi, ri, shi, zi* and *zhi*, the sound represented by the final is quite different and is similar to the *ir* in 'sir' but without much stressing of the *r* sound

o   sounds like the *aw* in 'law'

u   sounds like the *oo* in '*ooze*'

ü   is pronounced as the German *ü* (written as *yu* when not preceded by an initial consonant). The last two finals are usually written simply as *e* and *u*.

FINALS IN COMBINATION

When two or more finals are combined, such as in *hao, jiao* and *liu*, each letter retains its sound value as indicated in the list above, but note the following:

ai   is like the *ie* in 'tie'

ei   is like the *ay* in 'bay'

ian is like the *ien* in 'Vi*enna*'

ie   similar to '*ear*'

ou   is like the *o* in '*code*'

uai sounds like '*why*'

uan is like the *uan* in 'ig*uana*' (except when proceeded by *j, q, x* and *y*; in these cases a *u* following any of these four consonants is in fact *ü* and *uan* is similar to *uen*.)

ue   is like the *ue* in '*duet*'

ui   sounds like '*way*'

TONES

A Chinese syllable consists of not only an initial and a final or finals, but also a tone or pitch of the voice when the words are spoken. In *pinyin* the four basic tones are marked , ,   and . These marks are almost never shown in printed form except in pinyin text.

ARCHAEOLOGY IN SHAANXI PROVINCE

—Gerald Hatherly

Shaanxi province, with its remarkable place in the history of China and noted educational facilities, is one of the country's most important centres for archaeological research and training. Throughout the province there are ongoing excavations and research projects that continue to rewrite and refine the history of China.

Xi'an is the centre of archaeological research in Shaanxi—nationally it is ranked in the top five of all centres in China for archeological study and education. Northwest University is the leading university for archaeological research, and over the past 50 years it has graduated several leading archaeologists who have worked on the most important excavations within China, including the famed Terracotta Warriors and Horses Dig in Lingtong county.

First discovered by accident in 1974 by local farmers digging a well, the ongoing excavation that continued through the late 1990s (work has now been halted until further notice) has yielded a treasure trove of artefacts and information that have served as the basis for authenticating the legends and records concerning the Qin period. What has emerged from an extensive field of research is that the pits excavated at the Terracotta site—the three working pits—have provided historians of the Qin period a remarkable still of military life in 2nd century BCE. Each pit offers scholars a glimpse of military organization—the size of a battalion (Pit Number 1), the structure of a military encampment (Pit Number 2), and the planning command centre (Pit Number 3). In addition to this, the excavation has provided visual clues to period weaponry, armour and the equipment and tackle used with horses.

More recent excavations conducted within the greater area of the tomb site have yielded new finds, including pits containing stone suits of armour, another with terracotta acrobats, and yet another with terracotta images of civil officials.

Another important excavation is the 14-year dig at Yang Ling, the funerary site of the Han Emperor Jingdi who died in 141 BCE. While long known as a Han period burial site, it was only in 1990, when an access road to the then new airport was being constructed, that archaeologists were called into examine the site. Since that day, more than 90 satellite tombs have been fully excavated and over 100,000 artefacts catalogued. Today a fine site museum (under the directorship of lead archaeologist Wang Baoping) beautifully displays the remarkable cache of artefacts excavated over the past decade. Here the artistic achievements of the Han dynasty are a testament to the remarkable transition that occurred between the militaristic Qin empire and the nascent development of an era of aesthetically pleasing art. From the blocky and overpowering figures of the Qin excavation—the soldiers, horses and chariots—we are ushered into dazzling images of daily life—houses, farms, animals, implements, court attendants, musical instruments and much, much more. Figures in terracotta, wood and bronze, richly coloured lacquer boxes and delicately patterned silks all suggest the evolution of a new artistic culture during the Han period.

More recently, in 2003 and 2004, the archaeological community in Xi'an and the rest of China were excited to learn about the discovery of not one, but two Tang period excavations—the tombs of Persian officials who had lived and worked in Chang'an, the ancient capital of Tang China. These two stunning finds, rich in funerary objects that show the direct cultural and commercial links between China and Persia, further the ongoing research in Silk Road scholarship.

Archaeology in Xi'an and Shaanxi, as in other regions of China, is just beginning to unlock the wondrous record of China's amazing past.

Archaeologists unearthing the terracotta warriors/soldiers
work with infinite patience at their painstaking task.

Places of Interest in the Xi'an Area

Period One: Pre-Qin

BACKGROUND

Xi'an lies a few miles south of the Wei River, a western tributary of the Yellow River. Near the modern city is the ancient site of Chang'an (Everlasting Peace), which served as the capital of several ruling dynasties spanning a period of over 1,000 years. But the Wei valley had been settled much earlier. In fact, both the Wei valley and Shaanxi province are traditionally known as one of the 'cradles' of Chinese civilization. The Yellow Emperor—the mythical ancestor and first sovereign of the Han race who is said to have lived in the third millennium BCE—has his legendary burial place at Huangling, a town halfway between Xi'an and Yan'an in northern Shaanxi.

PALAEOLITHIC

Before the present landscape of the Wei valley was created from deposits of sand blown from the Mongolian Plateau, humanity's early ancestors lived in the area. Between 1963 and 1966 a skull (now in Beijing), jaw and various other bones of Lantian Man, a form of Homo erectus dating from around 800,000 BCE, were discovered 38 kilometres (24 miles) southwest of Xi'an.

In the spring of 1978 another startling discovery was made in Dali County, to the east of Xi'an near the provincial border with Shanxi: an almost complete skull of what is now known as Dali Man. He is thought to belong to an early subspecies of Homo sapiens, living in perhaps 300,000 or 200,000 BCE.

NEOLITHIC

The development of agriculture found an ideal setting in the Wei and middle Yellow River valleys, with their deep loess deposits containing all the necessary minerals for successful cultivation. From approximately 5000 BCE onwards settlements were formed, larger and more permanent than similar ones elsewhere in the world. The early Neolithic stage in China is called Yangshao Culture. The name 'Painted Pottery Culture' is sometimes preferred, which contrasts with the 'Black Pottery', or 'Longshan Culture', that followed it. Yangshao Culture lasted until 3000 BCE. A typical Yangshao or Painted Pottery Culture settlement has been excavated at Banpo, on the outskirts of Xi'an.

Banpo pottery decoration.

Sights

BANPO MUSEUM

In 1953 when workers were laying the foundations for a factory at Banpo, less than seven kilometres (four miles) east of Xi'an, they came upon the remains of an ancient settlement. The discovery of this New Stone Age village has been described as the 'greatest single contribution to prehistoric archaeology in East Asia' (John Hay, *Ancient China*, Bodley Head, 1973). Between 1954 and 1957,  archaeologists working at the site obtained the first detailed data on the layout of a Neolithhic village. Dating from approximately 5000 to 4000 BCE, it is the most complete example of an agricultural Neolithic settlement anywhere in the world. Its remarkably well-preserved condition makes it a major attraction for visitors to Xi'an.

An area of 4,000 square metres (one acre) has been fully excavated, enclosed and put on view to the public. Foundations of 45 houses have been uncovered, some round, some square. The largest dwelling may have been a communal meeting place, or alternatively the house of the chief. Among the other impressive finds are: 200 storage pots, a collection of pottery and tools, a pottery-making centre and a graveyard with more than 250 graves.

The museum is simply but sensibly laid out. The main hall, in the rear, was built over the excavation site. Two smaller exhibition halls by the entrance display unearthed items, drawings and explanatory notes in both Chinese and English.

From the implements and utensils discovered, archaeologists have learned a great deal about the daily life of Banpo. It was a typical Yangshao Culture community.

Two to three hundred people lived there, practising slash-and-burn agriculture. They depended on millet and pork for their existence. In addition to millet, they planted vegetables such as cabbage and mustard, and hemp which was used to make clothing. They kept pigs, dogs and perhaps chickens and other animals. They also hunted and fished. They fired and painted extraordinarily beautiful clay pots with both abstract and non-abstract designs. The earlier decorations on these vessels portrayed fish with mouths open, fishing-nets and deer on the run—subjects reflecting the main preoccupations of Banpo's inhabitants. Gradually, as the displayed pots show quite clearly, the designs became abstract: the fish motif, for instance, was later replaced by a geometric pattern.

Chinese archaeologists believe that a primitive communist matriarchal clan lived at Banpo.

(Above) *Banpo pottery designs.*

An earthenware pot excavated from the Neolithic site at Banpo displaying a typical fish design.
Just one of a wide variety of pots on display at the National Museum of Shaanxi History
and the Banpo Museum with the characteristic bold designs and abstract patterns
of the Yangshao Culture from about 6,000 years ago.

In the communal burial ground found to the north of the site, men and women were buried separately, usually by themselves, but sometimes in multiple single-sex graves. Examples of these graves are on display. Women were generally interred with a greater number of funeral objects than men. However, it has been pointed out by foreign archaeologists that in most early matriarchal settlements excavated elsewhere, whole families related through the female line have been found buried together. At Banpo, as in other Yangshao cultures, children buried in jars have been found near some houses, although the cemetery was placed outside the village.

The Banpo Museum is located at the eastern end of the city, a convenient stop on the way to or from the Terracotta Warriors. It can be reached by bus number 11 or 42 from the Railway Station. It is open every day 9:00 am–5:30 pm. The Banpo Museum was under renovation in late 2004, and so the excavation site was not open to the public. Officials said it would reopen sometime toward the end of 2005.

Remains of the Capitals of the Western Zhou

Bronze metallurgy was practised from about the middle of the second millennium BC, contemporary with the emergence of the Shang dynasty. During this period (1600–1027 BCE), the Wei and Jing valleys were dominated by a relatively backward people called the Zhou. Under their leader, King Wu, they attacked and captured Anyang, the capital of the Shang in 1027 BCE. The Zhou dynasty lasted formally until 29 BCE, but the kings only enjoyed real power until 771 BCE. This period is called the Western Zhou. Archaeologists have discovered the remains of two Zhou palaces

Bronze you with loop handle (Shang dynasty),
unearthed in 1971 at Jingyang county, Shaanxi province.

west of Xi'an, at Fengchu village, Qishan County, and at Zhaochen village, Fufeng County.

A Western Zhou chariot burial pit was unearthed at Zhangjiapo, Chang'an County, in 1955. The war chariot was the pre-eminent symbol of power during the Bronze Age. One of the pits excavated at Zhangjiapo contained two chariots and the remains of six horses and one slave, interred as part of the funeral of a lord. These are on display in a small museum west of the city, near Doumen village.

It is recorded that the Zhou established five different capitals in the Wei and Jing valleys at different times. Two of these have been identified. Fengjing on the eastern bank of the Feng River was an early capital. Haojing on the opposite bank was the capital from 1027 to 771 BCE. The sites have been excavated and the remains of

A bronze vessel of the Western Zhou dynasty.

houses, workshops, burials and some hoards of bronze articles have been found and removed to the Xianyang and Shaanxi History Museums. Nothing of the old capitals can now be seen at the original sites.

BAOJI BRONZE CULTURE MUSEUM

Baoji, located in the western part of the Guanzhong Plain, was the place where the Zhou and Qin dynasties originated. Chinese archaeologists have unearthed large quantities of inscribed bronzeware of the Western Zhou dynasty in the area, and many of these pieces are on display in the Baoji Bronze Culture Museum. The first floor houses the museum's collection of bronzeware. On the second floor, there is an exhibition on ancient Chinese characters and on the use of knotting in record-keeping in the selling and buying of land.

The museum is just 40 minutes southwest of the Famen Temple, and can be combined with a visit to the temple.

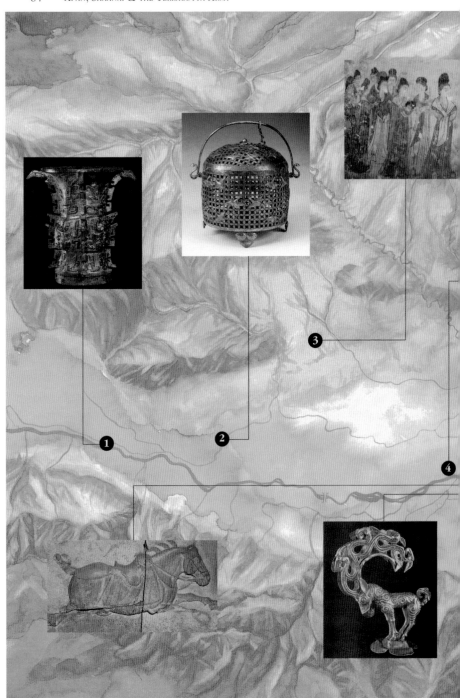

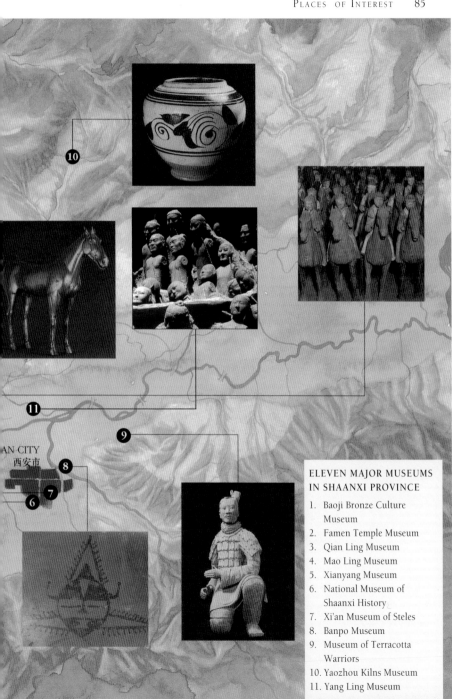

AN CITY
西安市

ELEVEN MAJOR MUSEUMS
IN SHAANXI PROVINCE

1. Baoji Bronze Culture
   Museum
2. Famen Temple Museum
3. Qian Ling Museum
4. Mao Ling Museum
5. Xianyang Museum
6. National Museum of
   Shaanxi History
7. Xi'an Museum of Steles
8. Banpo Museum
9. Museum of Terracotta
   Warriors
10. Yaozhou Kilns Museum
11. Yang Ling Museum

Characters of an *(peace), and* ma *(horse), used by the Six Warring States
(annexed by the Kingdom of Qin)*

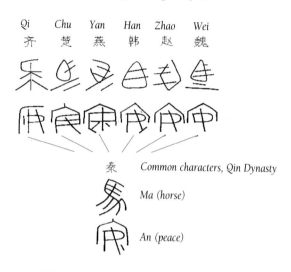

Qi   Chu   Yan   Han   Zhao   Wei
齐   楚   燕   韩   赵   魏

秦   *Common characters, Qin Dynasty*

Ma (horse)

An (peace)

Coins of the Six Warring States (annexed by the Kingdom of Qin)

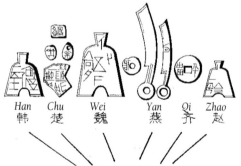

Han   Chu   Wei   Yan   Qi   Zhao
韩   楚   魏   燕   齐   赵

*After minting, the coins were
slotted onto a wooden pole and
the edges filed. Being square-
holed they did not rotate.*

*Common currency,
Qin Dynasty*

秦

*Characters for ban liang (half
liang). The liang was a unit of
weight; 16 liang equal 1 jin.
Each of these coins was
1/32nd of a jin.*

*Drawn by Wang Fan (not to
scale)*

*(Preceding pages) Just some of the 6,000 terracotta warriors thought to be buried in
Pit Number One of the Museum of Terracotta Warriors and Horses of Emperor
Qin Shihuangdi, over a third of which have been so far excavated.*

Period Two: The Qin Empire

BACKGROUND

THE RISE OF QIN

More than 2,400 years ago, the political map of China resembled a jigsaw. At least 12 kingdoms existed, spread across northern, central and eastern China as we know it today. At this time, the Eastern Zhou re-established the capital near Luoyang, Henan province, in 770 BCE. This dynasty is divided into two periods, the Spring and Autumn Annals (770–476 BCE) and the Warring States (475–221 BCE), both taken from the names of books. During the Warring States era the kingdoms were in a constant state of war; the Zhou kings were only nominal leaders and the Chinese world was divided into more than 100 petty principalities. This period is recognised as the beginning of the Iron Age in China, a time of tremendous technological progress in the arts of both war and peace. In due course Qin—based near modern Xi'an—became the most powerful of the contending states, and flourished as a result of a single-minded emphasis on military prowess, public works and food production. The Qin held sway over the middle reaches of the Yellow River, specifically much of present-day Shaanxi, southeast Gansu, northern Sichuan and the Ningxia Hui Autonomous Region.

THE FIRST EMPEROR

Qin Shihuangdi, who has been called both tyrant and reformer, ruled over a vast territory. Having gained predominance over various ruling states, he became the sole source of power and final authority for a centralized government in Xianyang.

Qin Shihuangdi (who was named Ying Zheng) came to the

The resolute expression of a kneeling archer freshly unearthed after having lain buried for over 2,000 years. Water is used to soften the surrounding earth during excavation which accounts for the statue appearing darker than normal.

Qin throne in 246 BCE—a mere boy of 13. His parentage is something of an enigma. His father Zichu, a son of the King of Qin, was sent as hostage to the Zhao State during a dispute between the neighbouring kingdoms. The young hostage, apparently allowed to live relatively freely in Zhao, became acquainted with a prosperous and conniving merchant named Lü Buwei. Lü Buwei had a favourite concubine, a dancer. When the hostage became infatuated with her, Lü Buwei not only stepped aside, but even helped him and the concubine to escape to Qin, where Zichu eventually became king. Shortly after their arrival in Qin, Ying Zheng was born to the dancer, but whether his natural father was Zichu, or Lü Buwei, has kept historians perplexed ever since.

Ascending the throne when he was only 13 years old, Ying Zheng appointed Lü Buwei as his counsellor, and thus the cunning ex-merchant effectively controlled the kingdom of Qin for a decade until he was finally banished and replaced by another adviser, Li Si.

With the ministerial talents of Li Si, complemented by the military capabilities of the officer Meng Tian, Qin grew more prosperous and increased its offensives against the rival kingdoms. During his reign Qin superiority was finally established when the six other states—Han, Zhao, Wei, Chu, Yan and Qi—were annexed between 230 and 221 BCE, unifying China for the first time. Ancient legends told of three saintly sovereigns, *huang*, and five ideal emperors, *di*. To reflect his supreme achievements and the unprecedented extent of his rule, Ying Zheng adopted the title *huangdi* ; this was prefixed by Qin, the name of his 'native' state, and *shi*, meaning the first. His full title thus proclaimed the establishment of an empire and dynasty (The term *huangdi* had previously only been used for deities and mythological hero-rulers such as the Yellow Emperor. Qin itself is the origin of the English word 'China').

Ying Zheng had acted with as much swiftness and determination as a 'silkworm devouring a mulberry leaf', in the words of the historian Sima Qian. The entire territory of what was then China had been united under him, and the first centralized empire had been established. It stretched from the east China coast to Lintao in the west, and from the Lang Mountains to the Yalu River in the north. A tongue of territory even extended south into present-day Vietnam. His capital was at Xianyang (see page 142), (25 kilometres northwest of today's Xi'an), on the north bank of the Wei River.

An emperor of vast ambitions and achievements, Qin Shihuangdi had a profound influence on Chinese history and culture, both in his life and death. To consolidate his power, Qin Shihuangdi embarked on a vast reform programme encompassing military, political, social and administrative matters. Inter-kingdom defensive walls, which stood in the way of centralization, were destroyed, but those of the former Zhao and Yan kingdoms in the north were utilized by General Meng Tian in building

(Left) *The watchful eyes of a terracotta soldier. No two faces look the same, leading to speculation that they were modelled on real people.*

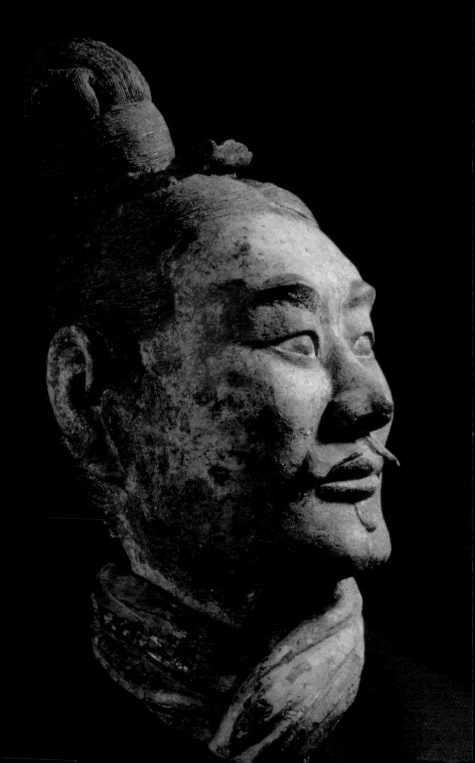

what was the first Great Wall—rebuilt and extended to safeguard the northern frontier—which stretched approximately 2,500 kilometres from Lintao, south of Lanzhou in the west, to the Yalu River in the northeast. This wall shielded the Qin empire from attacks by nomads of the north. Armies were sent as far south as today's Vietnam. Roads, irrigation schemes, palaces and above all his mausoleum all required hordes of reluctant labourers. Out of a total population of 20 million, one and a half million people are thought to have been called to some form of service to the State. Tens of thousands of the empire's richest and most powerful families were brought by force to live in the capital where they could be kept under observation.

The First Emperor's government was severe. He administered a strict legal code, whereby a whole family would be executed for the crimes of one of its members; he taxed people and conscripted millions of labourers for both military and civil projects.

Not all changes were on such a gargantuan scale. One peculiar reform standardized the axle lengths on carts to two metres to ease their passage along the wheel ruts of the ever-increasing number of roads which radiated from to all parts of the empire. These arteries guaranteed the swift deployment of the army to put down rebellions. To the same end, metal weapons were confiscated and taken to Xianyang where they were melted down. Legend has it that they were recast into 12 giant statues which lined the approach to the imperial palace.

Weights, measures and coinage were also standardized to strengthen commerce. In the Warring States period, the contending kingdoms had their own coinage, but now only the Qin form—a round coin with a hole in the middle—was circulated. Qin Shihuangdi also personally supervised the organization of a uniform Chinese written language—unified by the banning of old character forms and the compulsory adoption of the *xiaozhuan* and *lishu* scripts. He also prescribed 100 officially approved surnames for all his subjects. (See Special Topic on page 140)

The emperor's attempts to maintain a grasp on order went further. He divided his empire into 36 new administrative districts and posted garrisons at the most strategic locations. During the five inspection tours of his domain that he made during his rule, political propaganda was used to remind his subjects of the benefits he had brought them, for he had accounts of his achievements carved on steles and rocks on the summits of mountains.

As his rule wore on, Qin Shihuangdi resorted to more extreme policies. When scholars dared to criticize him by invoking the model rulers of antiquity, Qin Shihuangdi, on the advice of Li Si, launched a sort of 'cultural revolution'. He ordered all works of literature and philosophy, including *The Book of History*, *The Book of Morals* and *The Book of Songs*, to be burnt. Even discussion of the contents of such classics became a crime. At the same time, independent thought was suppressed:

(Left) *Green-faced terracotta warrior discovered in Pit Number Two. After firing, the figures were painted in a variety of colours, including green, red, purplish-red, flesh, purple, blue and white.*

books whose contents were considered subversive were burned, and eventually some 460 Confucian scholars were buried alive for their 'law-breaking'. These oppressive policies caused suffering on a huge scale, and on Qin Shihuangdi's death revolts swiftly followed.

Such draconian measures made many enemies for the emperor. Three attempts were made on his life, but in 210 BCE he died naturally of illness while on an inspection tour. Li Si realized the importance of keeping the death a secret, returning to Xianyang and naming the new emperor before opponents could seize the opportunity to wrest power. The minister had the corpse concealed in the imperial chariot, and to disguise the putrid stench, he cleverly loaded a cart with salted fish to accompany the chariot back to the capital.

Qin Shihuangdi's dream that the House of Qin might rule the empire for countless generations proved a folly, for within just five years rebels stormed Xianyang and soon after, one of the rebel leaders, Liu Bang, established the Han Dynasty (206 BCE – 220 CE). Nevertheless, the First Emperor's corpse did make it back to the capital, to be entombed one year later (209 BCE) in the magnificent mausoleum under the guard of the terracotta army. And in this way Qin Shihuangdi did achieve the immortality and recognition he expected for what turned out to be a short-lived dynasty.

The colossal scale and careful detail of his army of terracotta warriors shows beyond any doubt the advanced state of artistic and technological development of ancient Chinese culture during that period. The great clay army is certainly also a fitting memorial to the man who first really united what were until then disparate states.

All manner of treasures were piled inside for the emperor's opulent afterlife. Priceless treasures, live rare birds and animals were sealed inside while the emperor's body itself was enrobed in a funerary suit of gold and jade adorned with pearls. Crossbows were set up and positioned to shoot automatically if the interior was disturbed. After it was sealed the tomb was grassed over to appear as a natural hill. It is still like that today, although a stairway has now been built to the top, from which there is a good view of the surrounding area. Several ancillary graves have been found around that of the emperor. Some contained skeletons of horses while the occupants of others are almost certainly of royal lineage. Qin Shihuangdi fathered some 28 children and, after his death, they jostled bitterly for the succession. The direct heir, crown prince Fu Su, was killed by his younger brother Hu Hai, the second-in-line to the throne, who is also believed to have murdered many of his other brothers and sisters to secure his position. Some occupants were probably victims of the Second Emperor in the power struggle following the death of Qin Shihuangdi. In addition, some large graves, suspected to be those of Qin Shihuangdi's parents, have also been discovered in the area, as well as the graves of a general and of some 70 Qin labourers

(Left) *A standing archer excavated from Pit Number Two. This archer has no armour, only a simple robe, to allow freer movement and accurate marksmanship.*

together with large numbers of horse skeletons. Other pits have revealed terracotta birds and animals, symbolizing the emperor's love of hunting. So far more than 400 attendant burial pits and tombs have been discovered, covering an area of 56.25 square kilometres (nearly 22 square miles). The artefacts so far unearthed, combined with historical records, indicate

View of building spanning Pit Number Two where excavations have suggested that some 1,300 warriors, 450 horses and 89 chariots lie buried.

that Qin Shihuangdi's mausoleum was actually a miniature replica of the Qin Empire. None of the sites of these finds have so far been put on view to the public.

Sights

QIN LING

Qin Shihuangdi began supervising the construction of the Qin Ling, his burial tomb, as soon as he took the throne in 246 BCE. Work intensified after the conquest of the rival states, and continued for about 40 years, even after his death in 210 BCE. Only the fall of the dynasty itself in 206 BCE halted work on the elaborate funerary complex.

The site chosen was south of the Wei River beside the slopes of Black Horse Mountain in what is now Lintong County, 30 kilometres (18 miles) from Xi'an. The entire site measures approximately seven and a half kilometres square. Interior and exterior ramparts were built around its edge, probably out of the earth removed in the course of digging graves and chambers within the mausoleum. The exterior of the mausoleum is in the form of a low earth pyramid (see photograph page 4) with a wide base about 350 metres (382 yards) square. Originally it was 115 metres (377 feet) high, but more than 2,000 years of erosion have reduced this to 76 metres (249 feet). The emperor's grave itself, Qin Ling, which lies less than two kilometres west of the burial ground of the terracotta army, has not been excavated. Beneath it is thought to lie the underground palace in which the remains of Qin Shihuangdi were laid to rest over 22 centuries ago.

(Left) *A selection from the terracotta warriors; each one of the thousands of statues exhibits unique features.*

Army formation in Pit Number One showing the columns of warriors behind the vanguard.

Rebuilt wooden structure in Pit Number One.

Investigations have confirmed that there was an inner and outer enclosure and preliminary archaeological investigations have revealed what appears to be the underground palace's wall just four metres below the surface. What actually lies in the underground palace will remain a mystery for the moment, since the Chinese Ministry of Culture has no plans to excavate the site. The official line is that Chinese archaeologists are reluctant to open the tomb until they know a way to preserve what may be very delicate remains.

The mausoleum is thought to have been plundered at least once, by a rebel general called Xiang Yu in 206 BCE, but no excavations have yet been done. It is known, however, that not only was the body of Qin Shihuangdi interred in the tomb (in 209 BCE, a year after his death), but also those of his childless wives—who were buried alive—together with artisans who had knowledge of the inner structure of the mausoleum.

Information about the construction of the mausoleum comes almost entirely from Sima Qian, the chronicler of *The Historical Records*—China's first large-scale work of history which was written about a century after the fall of Qin. He recorded that a labour force of 700,000 was used to construct the mausoleum. The underground palace was said to comprise various chambers, the most important being the burial chamber. It featured bronze walls with heaven and the known world— the Qin empire—being reproduced on the ceiling and floor respectively. The sun, moon and stars—the last represented by pearls—were depicted, while features on the floor included the 100 rivers of the empire flowing mechanically into a sea on which floated golden boats. Tests on the mausoleum have shown minute traces of mercury over an estimated area of 12,000 square metres (14,352 square yards), adding substance to this claim. In all, some 17 skeletons, probably of princes and princesses, and perhaps of Qin Shihuangdi's parents, have been unearthed.

Museum of Terracotta Warriors and Horses of Qin Shihuangdi

The buried army of Qin Shihuangdi is one of the largest and most stunning archaeological finds of the 20th century. Discovered in 1974 at Lintong, 35 kilometres east of Xi'an, the warriors and horses have deservedly become known as a Wonder of the World. Now exhibited in situ, the life-size terracotta figures so far excavated testify to the power of the man for whom they were moulded to protect in afterlife.

This site is an archaeological find on a monumental scale. Literally an army of sculptured warriors, it is a stunning display that every visitor to China should see.

The discovery of the terracotta soldiers was like a legend come true for the villagers living in the area. For centuries they had been telling stories about the ghosts who lived underground and who were unearthed whenever they dug. Then in the

drought-stricken spring of March 1974, peasants were digging a well to tap the groundwater beneath woods east of Qin Ling, the first emperor's tomb. As the farmers dug, they came upon (in the words of *Newsweek*), 'the clay clones of an 8,000-man army'. When the first figures were unearthed, it was not appreciated how many there were, but gradually the significance of the discovery was realized: the emperor had decided to take an army with him to the nether world. The larger than life-size terracotta figures were found in a vault five metres (16 feet) below the surface, one and a half kilometres (less than a mile) east of the emperor's tomb itself. The positions of the pits, designated Pits One to Three according to their order of discovery, correspond to the prescribed military formation of a battle-ready army during Warring States and Qin times. In fact, the practice of burying statues with the dead began around the time of the Eastern Zhou dynasty (770–256 BCE) and continued until the Song dynasty (960–1279).

The museum, about 35 kilometres (22 miles) east of Xi'an, opened in 1979. The area was declared a World Heritage Site by UNESCO in 1987. The original museum, a large hangar-like building, is constructed over Pit Number One, the site of the original discovery in 1974. There are two other pits, only one of which (Pit Number Three) has been fully excavated. A fourth pit was discovered, but found to be empty and archaeologists have still to agree on its purpose.

THE EXCAVATIONS OF TERRACOTTA TROOPS

The terracotta soldiers are remarkably realistic pieces of sculpture. Each soldier's face has individual features, prompting speculation that they were modelled from life. They have square faces with broad foreheads and large, thick-lipped mouths, and they wear neat moustaches, and a number have beards. Some of them have their hair in a topknot. Expressions are generally austere, eyes focused far ahead. It is sobering to study the rows of soldiers and to compare not just their facial features, but also their varying heights, hairstyles, even the differences in the folds of their scarves, and to consider the amount of work that went into making them. The figures stand between 1.72 and 2 metres (nearly 5 feet 8 inches and 6 feet 7 inches) tall. The body, arms and legs are hollow and were formed by looping coils of clay into a kind of tube and then beating them together whilst placing a hand inside for support. This technique has been substantiated by the discovery of fingerprints and paddle marks on broken statues. The head and hands are solid and were moulded separately and fitted to the body after firing. A thin layer of clay was applied to each head and the individual features hand-sculpted. Details of the armour were also added to the body by hand.

The statues were originally painted using pigments made from minerals mixed with a binder such as animal blood or egg white. But the colour has been almost

(Left) A kneeling archer, typical of many excavated from Pit Number Two of the Museum of Terracotta Warriors.

(Above) *Archaeologists at work in Pit Number One. All warriors found thus far were smashed by tomb looters or crushed when the tunnel structure they were housed in collapsed 22 centuries ago. Every warrior now standing upright is the result of painstaking reconstruction and renovation by a dedicated team of archaeologists.*

(Below) *Archaeologists painstakingly unearth some of the terracotta warriors in Pit Number Two. Statues excavated from this pit in particular have retained a fair degree of their original paint, especially the red and pink pigments.*

entirely lost save for a few traces of red on tassels decorating armour and flakes of pigment on some of the faces.

Tests show that the pottery figures were fired at temperatures of between 950°C and 1,050°C with a level of skill that experts today have been unable to replicate with any degree of consistency.

The soldiers are divided into infantry armed with swords and spears, archers, crossbow archers, cavalry, chariot drivers, officers and generals. The wooden chariots no longer exist, having decayed over the centuries, but imprints of parts of them, especially wheels, remain visible in the compacted soil and their metal fittings have been excavated. Each chariot was drawn by four pottery horses, on average 1.5 metres (4 feet 11 inches) tall by 2 metres (6 feet 7 inches) long. The terracotta troops bear real arms, made of bronze. A huge number have been unearthed: swords, daggers, billhooks, spears, halberds, axes, crossbow triggers and arrowheads. The copper-tin alloy used was combined with 11 other elements such as nickel, magnesium, cobalt and chrome, and many weapons have emerged sharp, shiny and untarnished. The arrowheads contain a poisonous percentage of lead.

Head of a general denoted by double-tailed headgear, only worn by the highest ranking army personnel.

The vault housing the warriors was originally a five-metre (16 feet) deep pit with foundations of rammed earth. Three-metre (ten feet) high walls formed chambers which were paved with bricks. Pillars lining the pits supported pine-log beams and these in turn were overlaid with thick wooden planks, covered with reed mats and finally loess clay. The terracotta soldiers, horses and chariots were arranged inside. Rut marks are still visible on some of the original slopes down which the army was wheeled. The enclosure was then permanently sealed, or at least that was the intention. It appears, however, that the troops of General Xiang Yu, who had already plundered the nearby imperial tomb, Qin Ling, opened the vault in 206 BCE and set fire to the roof, which collapsed, smashing the figurines in site and preserving them in mud and ash.

INFANTRY AND CHARIOTEERS OF PIT NUMBER ONE

This pit, the first of three that were discovered over the period from May 1974 to June 1976, forms the main exhibition hall at the Qin Terracotta Army Museum complex. It is a rectangular pit measuring 230 metres in length from east to west and 62 metres

(Above) A seated horse groom, 68 cm in height, excavated from a horse grave within Qin Ling.

in width from north to south. Extensive excavation in the eastern half of this pit has so far revealed 1,087 warriors, 32 horses and the traces of eight chariots.

The display consists of infantry and charioteers arranged in battle formation. It consists of 11 parallel corridors running east to west, each corridor being 210 metres (230 yards) in length. The vault covers a total area of 14,260 square metres (17,055 square yards). So far, over 1,000 soldiers have been restored to standing position, in columns four abreast, standing on the original brick floor. At the head, facing east, is the vanguard, consisting of three rows of 70 archers each. They are followed by 38 columns of more heavily armoured infantry interspersed with some 40 war chariots, of which only the pottery horses remain. The south and north flanks are defended by single column of spearmen facing outwards, some clothed in battle dress, others in armour and holding weapons, while more warriors on the west flank form the rearguard. In the centre of the formation the warriors are lined up in nine columns, and among them are interspersed impressions of eight wooden chariots, now decayed. Each chariot is drawn by four horses and would have borne a driver and two warriors.

Visitors enter the vault through the east door and walk towards the south. At the foot of a staircase the very spot of the original discovery back in the drought-stricken spring of 1974 is marked. Proceeding down the southern flank of the vault you cross the excavations on an elevated walkway which affords views of both the completely excavated area looking back east and the partially excavated area to the western end

(Above) *Terracotta warriors standing as if at attention. The wooden weapons they once grasped are long disintegrated.* (Right) *A seated charioteer, made of solid bronze, concentrates on the road ahead, his hands stretched out to grasp the reins.*

of the vault. The grooves across the tops of the walls separating the corridors are the marks left by the decayed wooden beams. These are even more apparent in the unexcavated areas of Pit Number Two, where the imprints of entire beams can be seen as they sagged dramatically over the centuries.

Continuing down the northern flank of the vault you see corridors sometimes covered in protective plastic, and you may occasionally catch a glimpse of a half-excavated terracotta warrior, looking as if he was drowned in a sea of brown mud. At the unexcavated western end of the pit stand many half-reconstructed soldiers. Here it is often possible to observe archaeologists as they attempt to piece together the thousands of fragments of this enormous jigsaw. As it is unearthed, each piece is coded, marking where it was found and to which statue it might belong. Visitors exit the vault through a small door in the northwest corner. Archaeologists have estimated that if completely excavated the pit would yield more than 6,000 warriors, 160 horses and 40 chariots.

CAVALRY OF PIT NUMBER TWO

Twenty metres (22 yards) northeast of Pit Number One, this L-shaped pit was discovered in 1976 after extensive test drilling, but the official excavation did not begin until March 1994. Whereas Pit Number One contains mainly infantry, Pit Number Two has a greater number of archers, chariots and cavalrymen leading their horses—housing around 900 soldiers, including kneeling and standing archers, infantrymen and charioteers, together with some 350 chariot horses, 116 cavalry horses and the remains of 89 wooden chariots.

The pit covers an area of about 6,000 square metres (7,176 square yards) and is only partially excavated. It is contained in a modern building constructed over the excavation itself that allows visitors to walk around the pit and observe the ongoing excavations. The artificial lighting is subdued to help preserve the findings. These include a higher incidence of warriors with vestiges of their original colouring. This pit has 11 sloping entrances down which the terracotta warriors are believed to have been carted.

Trial digging at several places unearthed 70 archers, some kneeling, others standing. They show more brilliant colour than those in the other pits. Some 52 horses were

(Above) *A kneeling archer excavated from Pit Number Two.*
(Left) *A commander in armour, 1.90 metres in height, excavated from Pit Number One. He once held weapons in both hands: a spear in his right hand, but the strange twisted position of his left hand remains a mystery and the weapon he once held in it is unknown.*

also discovered. There is evidence—including two shafts and a well between 50 and 100 years old—to suggest that locals may have stumbled across the terracotta warriors decades before the announced discovery. On the north side of the building examples of some of the warriors unearthed in this pit are on display in glass cases. A stairway leads to a second floor exhibition hall where more exhibits are to be found, including just some of the more than 30,000 examples of Qin weaponry discovered in the three pits.

On 10 September 1999, workers painstakingly scraping and brushing away the compacted earth in this pit made a very unusual discovery—a kneeling archer with traces of green paint on its face. Archaeologists are still uncertain as to its significance. The theory that this could have been a mistake by a painter seems unlikely given the meticulous care that obviously went into the preparation of each of these figures.

Face of a general exhibiting racial characteristics common to the whole army: a squarish face, thick lips and facial hair in the form of a beard.

Archaeologists say the military formation of Pit Number Two is far more complex than that in Pit Number One. The more numerous array of archers, chariots and cavalry suggests that in the battles of the day those troops in Pit Number Two would have been engaged in launching offensives and breaking up the enemy ranks. Once the enemy troops were on the run the cavalry would have given chase.

Excavations are only at a very early stage. Archaeologists think that the pit might hold a total of 1,300 figures, more than 450 horses and the traces of 89 battle chariots.

THE COMMAND FORCE OF PIT NUMBER THREE

Discovered just one month after Pit Number Two, Pit Number Three lies 25 metres (27 yards) to the northwest of Pit Number One. It is U-shaped and only 28.8 metres (31.5 yards) in length from east to west, 24.6 metres (27 yards) in width from north to south and covering an area of less than 500 square metres (598 square yards),

Though the smallest of the three pits, Pit Number Three is strategically the most important since the command of the entire terracotta army was stationed here. Excavation of this battle headquarters has revealed the traces of a chariot, four horses and 68 warriors. The four horses pulling the chariot and the four warriors behind it are in good condition, but many of the pit's other figures are headless or smashed

(Left) An archer, 1.87 metres in height, standing at ease. Excavated from Pit Number One, this warrior once held a bow in his right hand. Most weapons were looted by tomb robbers when Xiang Yu's peasant army ransacked Qin Ling.

(Top) *Goose-shaped belt hook and* (Above) *Belt hook showing a man charging with a spear.*

completely. Numerous bronze weapons, and fragments of deer horn and animal bone have also been found. Animal sacrifice was probably part of the rites performed by commanders of a real army, who would have prayed to the gods for victory before a battle.

There is, however, one interesting omission. In Qin times, army commanders were normally issued a special token of identification, a palm-sized tally that came in two equal halves. As the token was usually carved in the form of a tiger, it was called a 'tiger tally' one half was held by the emperor, the other by the commander or general. To move troops, the general would have had to ask the emperor for permission. The emperor signified his agreement by giving his half of the tiger tally to the general. If the two halves fitted exactly, then all involved could be assured that the imperial order was genuine. No trace of a tiger tally, however, was found in Pit Number Three. This suggests that the commander of the terracotta army—which was above all an imperial guard—was probably in close attendance on the emperor himself.

Pit Number Three is housed within a modern building. The excavations are well labelled and atmospherically illuminated by spotlights rather than by natural light as in Pit Number One. Bilingual interpretive panels are positioned on the surrounding handrails, and colour photographs give the visitor a useful retrospective of the

excavation process, at the same time conveying something of the excitement at unearthing such a treasure trove. The excavations lie between 5.2 and 5.4 metres (17 and 17.7 feet) below ground. Terracotta warriors, mainly headless, and the four draught horses of a chariot, stand upon a fine Qin brick floor. Within the pit, rammed earth walls form chambers housing small detachments. Timber once completed this subterranean vault structure, but these collapsed and damaged the warriors beneath. Although many of the figures are decapitated, they compensate for their damage by exhibiting fine pigmentation.

(Above) *Head of a cavalryman showing simple headgear affixed by a chin strap.*
(Right) *A charioteer with outstretched arms that once held the reins of his steeds.*

Every figure is different and carefully and realistically modelled. Such individuality has prompted speculation that they were modelled on real personalities in Qin Shihuangdi's army. One can discern from their facial features and apparel differences of age, function and rank. Sometimes it is even possible to speculate about their character and temperament. However, collectively the figures do exhibit some general racial characteristics: they have squarish faces, wide foreheads, thick lips, moustaches and beards. The majority have alert expressions and a steely gaze.

The figures are all quite tall, with generals and commanders being the tallest and most portly. Apart from their larger size, generals can be clearly identified by their double-tailed headgear, longer tunics falling to below the knee, and minimal fish-scale pattern armour on the midriff, which hangs in an inverted V-shape a little below the waist. On the chest and neck they have bow-like decorations, while their feet are shod in boots with upturned toes. The sleeves of generals' tunics are usually long enough partly to cover the hands, since generals directed their troops and rarely engaged in direct combat themselves.

Officers have simpler headgear and usually wear a little more armour, sometimes on the shoulders, but not on the chest. Boots are flat-toed and box-shaped. Sleeves

(Above) *Three terracotta horses that once pulled a battle chariot; the wooden parts have since decayed.*
(Right) *Charioteer, 1.90 metres in height, excavated from Pit Number One.*

This bronze bell, inlaid with gold and silver, has a rhythmic interplay of curves and lines.

Bronze and stone equestrian implements.

leave the hands clear and free, for the officer both directs his troops and may need to lead them by example into combat.

Cavalrymen are found dismounted in front of their terracotta horses. They can be recognized by their sleeveless jackets of armour, which appear thick, and are composed of quite large, squarish plates that seem to be riveted together. Headgear is extremely simple and close-fitting and is secured with a chin strap to prevent it blowing off while riding. Shoes are the lightest and smallest of all those worn by the army.

Archers are portrayed in active, vigilant and carrying postures. The active ones usually wear simple battle robes with no armour, and their arms are in the process of drawing back their bows. Kneeling archers are more plentiful. They are crouched down on one knee in readiness for combat and they wear quite heavy armour on both their torsos and shoulders. Viewed from the rear their boots can be seen to have a distinct tread. But the bulk of the army's archers, in Pit Number One, are standing at ease.

The infantry wear either battle robes or bulkier armour. Their hair is usually tied into topknots and their hands are poised to carry spears. The charioteers are in more active poses. They have both arms stretched out slightly so as to hold the reins to drive their vehicles. Their horses, approximately 1.72 metres in height and slightly over 2 metres in length, look sturdy with big, bright, alert eyes, wide-open nostrils and impressive muscularity.

MOULDING AND PAINTING OF THE FIGURES

The warriors are composed of baked clay that was made by mixing loess with quartz sand. Anatomical parts the heads, ears, torsos, arms, hands, legs and feet were moulded separately. Individual adornments, such as hats, hair, tunics, armour and gaiters, were then moulded onto completed bodies from sheets of clay. At this stage the art of the craftsmen came into play as individual characteristics were produced, or perhaps copied. Some of the

Hollow bronze cudgel ends for mounting on poles. Triangular in shape at their apex, these weapons were used in close combat in either thrusting or beating fashion.

more delightful fine personal touches include the furrows on a general's forehead and the smile of a young warrior.

After the warriors had dried naturally in the shade they were placed in furnaces at temperatures of 950°C–1050°C . Once fired, they were painted in a variety of colours, including green, red, purplish-red, flesh, purple, blue and white. Craftsmen in the workshops were obliged to etch their names on the figures. In this way those producing substandard work could be identified. To date, 87 different family names have been found etched on the warriors, usually on the back of their belts.

BRONZE CHARIOTS AND HORSES

Two magnificent bronze chariots are housed in a relatively new exhibition hall, which stands to the right or north as you first enter the museum complex. In August 1978, archaeologists unearthed a small gold ornament the size of a walnut, some 20 metres (22 yards) to the west of the emperor's tomb, Qin Ling. Two years later in December 1980, two chariots, each with two-spoked wheels and drawn by four horses, were unearthed—totally smashed, apart from the solid bronze steeds and charioteers. Horsepower to weight ratio suggests that both these vehicles could have covered ground fairly swiftly.

These wonders of metalworking are about half the actual size of chariots used by Emperor Qin Shihuangdi on his inspection tours of the empire. Qin dynasty chariot construction won great admiration even from two of the state's greatest adversaries, Xiang Yu and Liu Bang, who also envied the grandeur and prowess of Qin charioteers.

(Top) *Bronze spearhead engraved with two characters* 'si gong'.
(Above) *The larger of the two bronze chariots on display at the Museum of Terracotta Warriors. Approximately half life size, this one was designed to carry the spirit of Qin Shihuangdi in the afterlife.*

The intricate detail of the battle chariot, known as the liche, clearly showing the superb craftsmanship involved in its creation.

The two bronze chariots were certainly crafted specifically for Qin Shihuangdi's afterlife. Since excavation they have been successfully pieced together. The chariots were originally placed one behind the other facing west in a wooden coffin about 7 metres (23 feet) long and 2.3 metres (7.5 feet) wide. The larger of the two chariots, the *anche*, weighs 1,241 kilograms (2,736 pounds), and at 2.86 metres (9.38 feet) in length, and 1.07 metres (3.51 feet) in height, it is thought to be half the size of an actual chariot. It is made of bronze, gold and silver components— about 3,462 separate metallic parts in all. It has a closed carriage with small, sliding, rhombus-shaped lattice windows on three sides for ventilation, and a door at the back. The domed roof, symbolizing the round sky, is of very thin bronze sheeting laid over a frame of 36 bow-shaped spokes (corresponding to the number of districts in the Qin Empire) which are about 6 millimetres in diameter. It covers the passenger carriage and the seated charioteer, which is also made of solid bronze. Stylized clouds are painted on the interior ceiling and include dragon and phoenix patterns and, based on silk fragments discovered inside, it is thought some accessories—maybe cushions or quilts—had once made the royal passenger comfortable. This predates the more widespread use and export of silk by several centuries. The chariot therefore seems likely to have been crafted specifically for Qin Shihuangdi's afterlife, although it is thought he used such a vehicle for his inspection tours. Called *wenliangche*, the chariot was the limousine of its day.

The second chariot, the *gaoche*, which was found in front of the other, may have been a vanguard vehicle with no covered compartment. It is also called *liche*, a battle chariot, and like the

(Top) *A commander found standing behind a chariot, excavated from Pit Number One.* (Middle) *Hand of a general with long, ruffled sleeves. The bronze sword he once held was probably looted.* (Bottom) *Armour on the shoulder of a warrior.*

(Left) *Head of a standing archer excavated from Pit Number Two.*

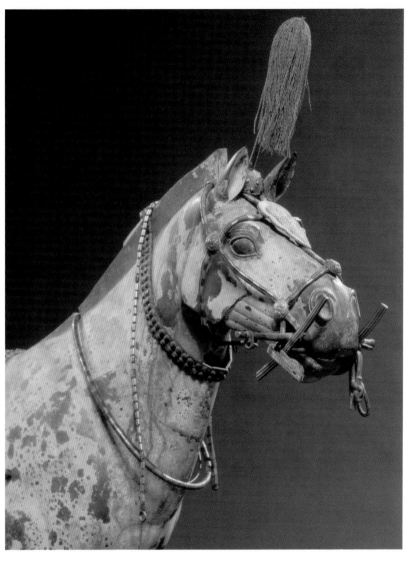

Bronze chariot horse—one-third life size.

second, is drawn by four horses. At 2.25 metres in length and weighing 1,061 kilograms, it is smaller and lighter than the *anche*, but it has the same number of horses. With its greater power to weight ratio this was a swifter vehicle and would have run ahead of the anche as an escort. There is no compartment in the vanguard chariot; to accommodate the standing driver the canopy is correspondingly much higher than that of the *wenliangche*—1.68 metres (5.5 feet) high—and displays superb gold decorative work on the post of the umbrella, which is locked in place by a special key. The chariot carries a pair of bronze shields, a crossbow and arrow, and a box containing 66 bronze arrowheads. The total weight of the first chariot is 1,061 kilograms (2,339 pounds) and consists of 3,064 components.

Both chariots highlight the superb metallurgical and metal-shaping technology of the Qin period as well as its highest artistic standards. Most chariot fittings are of solid bronze, often painted, although their pigments have faded. The harness and reins are inlaid with gold and silver, and each horse wears a halter made of some 84 one-centimetre (0.4-inch)-long tubes, fitted

Rear view of a middle-ranking warrior's head.

one onto another and thus endowed with a flexibility close to rope or leather. A tassel hangs down from each horse's neck. The canopies are incredibly thin bronze sheets but their casting is even and smooth. They are laid over a frame of 36 bow-shaped spokes about six millimetres (0.24 inches) in diameter. All these dimensions suggest to the archaeologists that both the temperature control and the casting methods were by this time highly advanced. Many parts of the chariots are overlaid with chains fashioned from extremely fine copper wire, with some of the strands just 0.5 millimetres (0.02 inches) in diameter. Microscopic examination shows that these strands were not forged but were drawn out to this size before being welded into rings and chains. The chariot drivers and horses are also of solid bronze, yet despite their material they appear lifelike. Artisans probably used files on the figures to reproduce the appearance of hair. The horses, painted white to mimic hide and given realistically flared nostrils, convey the impression that they are ready to stride forth at the crack of the charioteer's whip.

The other artefacts exhibited in this hall include more recently unearthed treasures such as the ten terracotta wrestlers and entertainers, 80 pieces of stone armour and a 212 kilogram (467 pound) bronze tripod vessel (*ding*). The life-size terracotta figures are carefully and realistically modelled. One of them, a headless stocky figure whose upper body is naked and who has muscular arms, holds what might be a pole used for acrobatics in his hands, which are placed in front of his protruding belly. When looked at in detail, the skirt is embellished with geometric designs. Another one of these figures, who might have also been part of

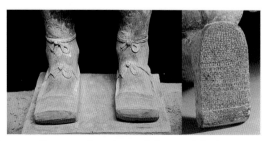

Footwear of warriors including treaded sole (right) of a kneeling archer.

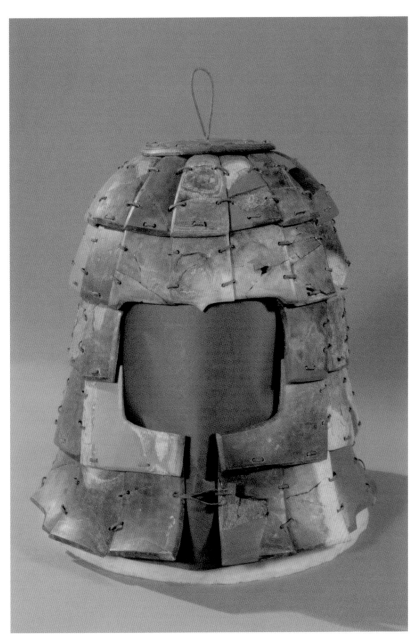

Reconstructed helmet composed of polished rectangular stone pieces held together with wire.

a troop of acrobats, wrestlers or entertainers, stands with his right arm raised above his head. It is thought that he might have been holding a weight. These are the earliest evidence found to date of the careful observation of the human body and the ability to recreate it in clay. In 1998, during a test excavation 150 metres to the southeast of the emperor's tomb mound, archaeologists came across thousands of pieces of stone. Not actually unearthed until August 1999, they included 80 pieces of stone armour. Found scattered in a pit, thousands of pieces of grey limestone plates, each bevelled and drilled with holes, were painstakingly reassembled to their original shapes. They were strung together with copper wire in a fish-scale formation similar to that sculpted on the terracotta warriors and characteristic of later Han-dynasty iron armour. Archaeologists have also been able to piece together stone helmets in the same way. One set of this ceremonial armour and helmet together weighs 20 kilograms (45 lbs). Work at this and other digs is continuing and is likely to yield yet more discoveries.

WEAPONS

An arsenal of weaponry has been found in all pits: they are actual armaments used in warfare during the Qin dynasty. They fall into three categories: daggers and swords used in close combat; long-handled arms such as spears and axes; and bows and arrows, and crossbows.

Weapons were made of bronze and copper alloys according to the demands of the particular armament. Among them, the long bronze sword draws particular attention. As slender as a willow leaf, it measures 90 centimetres in length and still possesses a keen cutting edge. It is thinner and longer than swords made in the Warring States period, and gives the swordsman greater thrusting power. Such bronze swords underwent the first rust-proofing in history with the application of chromium oxide coatings. Today, the swords are still rust-free, and they exhibit a bluish-grey shining lustre.

PIT CONSTRUCTION AND DESTRUCTION

All of the pits were tunnel structures built with clay and wood. None of them is particularly deep. The top of Pit Number Three, for example, is a little more than five metres below the ground surface. Once dug, the pit floors were levelled and paved with bricks, which have been well preserved. The pits' walls were lined with wood and sizeable roof beams were laid down and held up with the aid of timber supports. Curved impressions made by these heavy beams can be seen on the divisions between the passageways in Pit Number One. The distance from the pit floor to the roof is 3.2 metres.

Next began the sealing-up process. To prevent the infiltration of water, the wooden roofs were covered in reed matting onto which impervious clay was tamped.

(Above) *A general, more than 2 metres in height, excavated from Pit Number Two. Generals are the tallest and heaviest members of the army. This one highlights the skill of the artisan who made him: he exhibits advanced age denoting military experience, and appears calm in command of his men.*

(Right) *Archers, denoted by their absence of armour to allow freedom of movement, form the vanguard in Pit Number One.*

At this stage workmen would have carted in and positioned the thousands of terracotta warriors which range in height from 1.80 to 2.02 metres (kneeling warriors are approximately 1.2 metres high) and weigh approximately 150 kilograms. With the 8,000-man army in battle-ready position, the wooden doors were emplaced and also sealed with clay. The closed, underground barracks was now in complete darkness.

But not for long. Despite the meticulous planning for Qin Shihuangdi's afterlife, his underground fortress remained undisturbed for a mere five years. As his sons struggled to succeed him, discontented peasants rebelled. A warlord from the former Kingdom of Chu, Xiang Yu, eventually stormed Xianyang, the Qin capital, and shortly after the terracotta army did indeed face the atrocities of war when Xiang Yu's peasant rebels entered the mausoleum.

They probably carted off all that was precious and moveable. As for the pits, they might have remained intact but for the fact that the roofs on some had probably already collapsed. This was certainly caused by rainwater draining inside and rotting the wooden beams. Looters were therefore able to enter the pits. The terracotta warriors themselves were thought not to be worth removing, and were in any case too big and cumbersome. Nevertheless, most were smashed. The ransackers carried away instead valuable bronze weapons. Beams blackened with charcoal indicate that fires were started in the pits, but the warriors were only damaged, not destroyed. The fire did, however, burn off nearly all their paint and caused the collapse of the tunnel structures, though ironically that buried the army safely for the next 22 centuries.

Over two millennia later, the pits do indeed resemble battlefields. After painstaking archaeological work, many warriors now stand upright, while others lied beheaded and dismembered on the ground.

These are just a sample of the countless, astonishing details revealed by treasures excavated from the vast mausoleum of Emperor Qin Shihuangdi. In the future more wonderful discoveries are sure to be made in the precincts of the afterlife realm of China's first emperor.

360-DEGREE CINEMA
Behind Pit Number One is a 360-degree cinema. Here visitors can stand in a circular theatre and watch a dramatisation of scenes from Qin Shihuangdi's conquering of the six independent states, the construction of his mausoleum, the making of the terracotta figures and their eventual destruction by soldiers of the rebel general Xiang Yu. It is very useful to see this before entering the museum itself as it gives a better understanding of what is on display.

(Right) A commander in a plain gown. The absence of armour suggests the commander's superior role, directing troops rather than engaging in combat. Nevertheless, this warrior's right hand is poised to hold a spear.

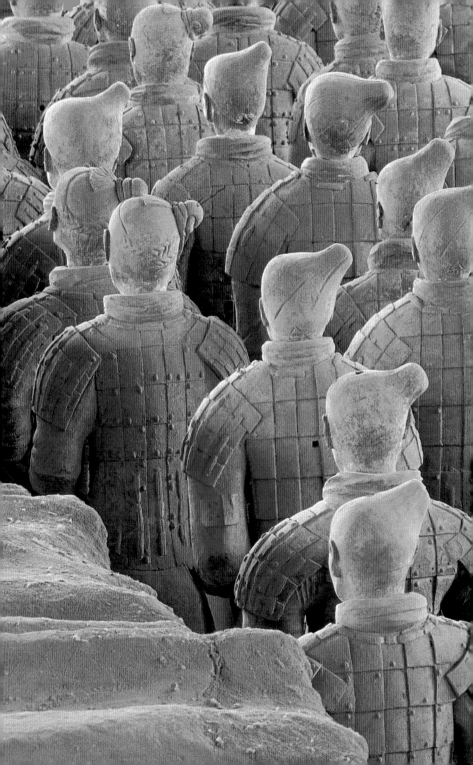

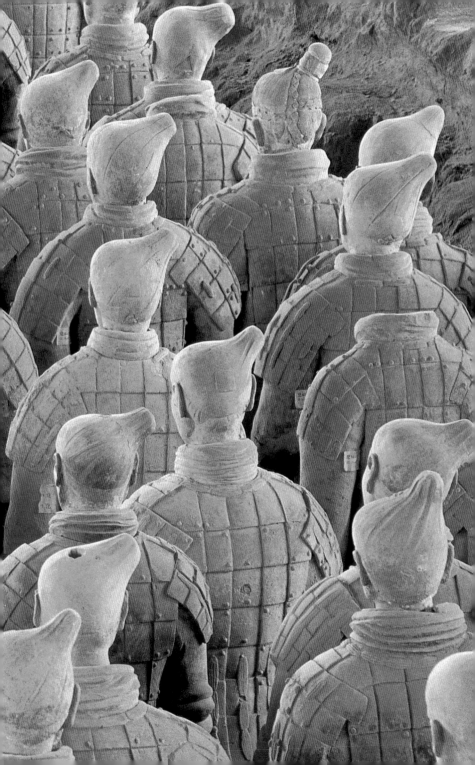

The Art of Grave Robbery —Ding Ye

In the dead of night on the outskirts of the ancient capital of Xi'an, shadows moved among the graves of ancient emperors, generals and ministers...the heads of terracotta figures at Qin Shihuangdi's mausoleum had disappeared. Nude figures of the Han dynasty unexpectedly appeared on the other side of the Pacific Ocean. Moreover, bronze wares of the Zhou dynasty, tri-colour glazed pottery of the Tang dynasty, pottery from the Yaozhou Kiln of the Song dynasty were all carried in a sea of trade out of the country under the cover of dark.

On the moonless, windy night of December 30, 1994, in the wake of a muffled sound breaking the still of the night, an earthen column shot into the sky at the southern side of Jing Ling mausoleum—the mausoleum of Li Huan, Emperor Xizong of the Tang Dynasty—in Qianxian County, Shaanxi province. This was another signal of robbery from an ancient imperial tomb. The thieves entered a 16-metre hole and broke into the grave. When police and personnel from the Cultural Relics Department arrived at the scene, the robbers had already made their getaway, leaving the mausoleum severely damaged. To save the other cultural relics in the grave, the Archaeological Research Institute of Shaanxi province undertook a salvage excavation of the mausoleum. This revealed that, in fact, the mausoleum had been robbed many times— seemingly in every dynasty.

Dying to Get Rich

Another crime began on the night of February 27, 1987, the first winter after the excavations of the legendary Qin Shihuangdi's terracotta warriors and horses. Wang Gengdi, a farmer from Lintong County, had been planning his escapade during the day. He jumped over the enclosure wall of the Hall of Qin Shihuangdi terracotta figures into the yard in which the Qin Shihuangdi Mausoleum archaeological team was stationed. He broke open the storage room and stole the head of a terracotta general that had just been repaired. Classified as a first rate, Grade A, national cultural relic, the head is one of 10 detailed terracotta figures of high-ranking officers unearthed from the mausoleum.

Wang Gengdi knew the crime was no ordinary burglary—he had mortgaged his life on this figurehead. Only 21 years old and anxious to get rich, frequently he stole and sold cultural relics. On June 17 that year, when the

(Preceding pages) *Rear view of column of infantrymen in Pit Number One.*
At bottom left the impressions left by roof beams of the original tunnel structure can be seen.

priceless treasure was about to change hands in Xi'an, for the price of 300,000 yuan, police officers, disguised as purchasers, arrested the dealers in a well-executed operation. Wang Gengdi became the first thief of cultural relics to be sentenced to death.

THE CRIME OF CENTURIES

In Chinese history, 13 dynasties set their capitals in Shaanxi and over 80 imperial mausoleums have been confirmed in the province. The number of royal treasures belonging to princes, ministers and generals is countless. The abundant buried gems and relics in the province are beyond imagination.The Zhou dynasty (1100–256 BCE) maintained a distinct social estate system that decided the arrangement of burial objects. The higher the official, the more the burial objects— luxurious burial accessories that would become valuable collector items for later generations and lucrative booty for grave robbers.

The earliest recorded grave robbery occurred when Xiang Yu (232–202 BCE), leader of a peasant revolt, burned down the Afanggong Palace, built during the Qin dynasty (within Shanglinguan Garden south of the Weihe River) while sending 30,000 men to dig up graves and loot all burial objects. Unfortunately, subsequent dynasties also carried on these traditions of the Zhou and today the abundant burial objects continue to lure the desperate. When Emperor Wudi died, the sacrificial objects were too many to place into Mao Ling. In the last years of the Western Han dynasty, an army of peasant revolutionaries dug up the Han imperial tombs and Mao Ling was one of the sites from where thousands of men took several weeks to carry away innumerable objects. Since the 1950s, archaeologists in Shaanxi have been exploring all the imperial tombs in the province. They have found signs of looting in every mausoleum. The mausoleums of the dynasties of Zhou, Han and Tang were the most seriously affected. They found traces of digging and burning in the tomb passage of the Qin Shihuangdi Mausoleum and this was confirmed in historical records. However, according to the latest archaeological findings, it is possible that the break-in did not severely damage the inner mausoleum.

Qian Ling is the joint burial place of Tang Emperor Gaozong and Empress Wu Zetian. In the second decade of last century, Liu Kan, a Kuomintang warlord, tried to dig up Qian Ling, but failed. It is said that large quantities of shifting sand hampered the digging. In recent years, a trial excavation of the mausoleum revealed a sloping tomb tunnel—63.1 metres long, 3.9 metres wide, and paved with thick stone slabs connected with iron bolting sheets. With melted iron poured into the crevices, the tunnel is very solid. There are no traces of digging in this tomb. It is the only well-preserved imperial tomb of the Tang dynasty.

Broken Horses

Thousands of cultural relics had been unearthed in Shaanxi over the years and grave robbery has been rampant. Until recently, there were no laws to forbid tomb excavation, theft, sale or export of cultural relics. Most of the unearthed relics passed through many hands privately and the situation worsened in the 19th Century with the theft of the famous stone carvings, 'Six Steeds' from Zhao Ling. In 636 CE (Tang dynasty), Li Shimin (Emperor Taizong) boasted of his own outstanding military exploits in the founding of the Tang Dynasty and was eager to display this prowess. He commanded master artisans to draw patterns of his six battle steeds that he had ridden into battle early in the dynasty and to make relief sculptures on large stones. He placed the carvings on display in the northern gate tower on Zhao Ling. Both in content and form, the carvings are unique in the history of Chinese sculpture. Drawing on the method of bas-relief from the art of Buddhist sculpture, the steeds differ in posture and disposition, and are unique in style—natural, powerful and lively. They are rare treasures of Tang dynasty stone carving. It is regrettable

that these valuable works were taken out of China early in the 20th century. The two best carvings—'Saluzi' and 'Quanmo'—are now in the Art Museum of the University of Pennsylvania, Philadelphia. The other four were sawn into pieces and packed, ready to ship abroad, but fortunately they were intercepted and captured, albeit not intact. Of the six carved steeds that are on display in the Museum of the Forest of Steles in Xi'an today, 'Saluzi' and 'Quanmo' are replicas and the others are pieced together from the fragments of the originals.

CASUALTIES OF WAR

From the early 1900s to 1949, when warlords battled constantly and the Chinese nation was in political turmoil, there was ample scope to plunder cultural relics. Much of the booty from Shaanxi was taken to Beijing and added to private collections, or sold and exported. The largest and most valuable bronze from Shaanxi is the *Guo Ji Zi Bai Pan* unearthed at Guochuansi, in Baoji. The bronze tray weighs 213.3 kilograms with 111 characters inscribed on it. Fortunately, this national treasure is now in the collection of the National Museum of China in Beijing. Epigraph experts praise the tripod, used as cooking vessel (*Maogong Ding*), as the greatest treasure— unearthed in Shaanxi during the Qing dynasty—with 499 characters inscribed in 32 lines. It has the most characters of any bronze discovered in China. In the early period of the 1910s, this bronze vessel was once left as a pledge at the Daosheng Bank run by Russians in Tianjin. Just prior to it being purchased by foreign interests and exported, the Palace Museum in Beijing redeemed it. However, the Nationalist Party took it to Taiwan just prior to 1949.

HISTORY FOR SALE

During the 1950s and 1960s, thanks to the comparatively stricter social controls and greater national awareness, the robbery of ancient tombs and the smuggling of cultural relics rarely occurred. In Shaanxi, those who earned their living by robbing ancient tombs disappeared. Nonetheless, after the implementation of many reforms including policies to open up China for foreign business, there is once again eager demand for China's cultural relics, with concomitant prospering of the black market. With so many imperial tombs of different dynasties scattered around the province, Shaanxi is the principle source of cultural relics and once more, grave robbery is thriving. The main targets are bronze wares and jades of the periods of the Shang (c. 16th–11th centuries BCE), Zhou, Spring and Autumn (770–476 BCE),

(Left) *Mao Ling has been robbed over 20 times.*

Warring States (475–221 BCE), the Han and Tang. Bronze wares, ceramics and pottery figures of Qin and Han dynasties are also popular, along with tri-colour potteries or objects; murals of the Tang dynasty as well as gold and silver vessels, bronze and stone figures of Buddha of the Sui (581–618CE) and Tang dynasties. Prices are determined by artistic value and the quality of the objects. Grave robbers concentrate on the tombs of the dynasties of Zhou, Qin, Han and Tang, but disdain those after the period of the Song dynasty (960–1279). The central government and local authorities have been enforcing strict retribution on offenders. However, since it is difficult to protect and administer ancient tombs in remote and rural areas that have no transport facilities, the crime in these areas is increasing.

A COMMUNITY OF THIEVES

In some places, village heads are taking the lead. The head of one village in Huayin County, Shaanxi, sent villagers on a special mission to Xi'an, Shanxi and Henan provinces to contact purchasers while simultaneously assuming personal command of the excavations. From 1996 to 1998, villagers dug up more than 40 ancient tombs, including one of the Western Zhou, 18 of the Eastern Zhou, three of the Warring States Period and more than 10 belonging to the Han. The northern highlands at Xianyang is thick with tomb groups belonging to the Warring States Period and the Han dynasty. At one time, almost every village carried out ancient tomb excavations. Every morning newly dug holes appeared around villages. In 2000, the discovery of Han dynasty tombs in Jingbian county, northern Shaanxi, became a magnet for group upon group of excavators. They worked openly and without conscience until a police officer fired a warning shot. Only then did they leave grudgingly.

STEALING FROM THE DEAD

One grave robber confessed the methods and techniques of his illicit profession: "Finding ancient tombs beneath crop fields, loess cliff sides or river shores and knowing where to start the excavation are not easy. It takes a lot of learning. First, it depends on the geographic conditions. Also the high officials and aristocrats of those times respected geomancy. They were particular about selection of tomb sites… after we have chosen a possible tomb site, we have to use a Luoyang spade (a kind of round iron spade, 50 cm in diameter, for taking samples of earth deep below the surface) to get soil vertically from the site. If the soil is in its natural state, we call it 'raw soil'. Otherwise, it is 'mellow soil'. If the soil at a depth of one to two metres remains raw, we move another place and test again. Mellow soil indicates that there may be tombs beneath the surface so we test soil again deeper. In this way, we can locate a tomb's protective layer, which comprises lime, charcoal, stones, cinnabar and wood dust. Then we test soil all around the area and so determine the position and depth of the tomb.... Generally, large tombs have a passage. If we dig out the passage, we can enter the tomb chamber that way. But small tombs have no passage. So then we have to dig a tunnel directly into the tomb. There are several ways to excavate tombs. The most common and practical way is to tunnel with the shaft slanting 45 degrees from the surface to the tomb. Then we can crawl in and out more easily. However, it takes extra time naturally, when the tunnel is long due to a steep slope. The second method, and less common these days, is to bore a hole vertically down to the edge of the tomb and enter from the side. Recently, we prefer to dig a small hole with Luoyang spades straight down to the bottom of the tomb and dynamite the tunnel to make it wide enough for a person to enter. This method is very fast." The ancient tomb builders often foresaw the possibility of theft and sometimes took measures to protect the tombs. For example, the builders paved the chambers with one-metre stone slabs and encased them in cobblestones or river sand—knowing that digging is extremely difficult in shifting sand. If groundwater were to seep into the tomb, the silt would have completely blocked any entrance. Of course, the robbers have ways to deal with problematic tombs. A typical example occurred in the eastern suburbs of Xi'an in January 2003. Robbers entered a tomb successfully at the imperial mausoleum of the Han dynasty using steel tubes (0.5 metres in length and 0. 7 metres in diameter) to control the shifting sand.

CONSTANT VIGILANCE

The most significant recent case of tomb robbery in Shaanxi was the one at Xianyang. This ancient tomb of the Western Zhou Dynasty on the northern shore of the Weihe River is the joint burial place of Emperor Yu Wenyong and his empress. As it has no grave mound on the surface, workers of the Cultural Relics and Archaeological Department of Shaanxi tried several times to locate the tomb, but failed. In June 1998, a group of robbers found the tomb in an eroded crop field. They stole scores of jade items and artefacts of gold and silver, which they sold to a trafficker for two million yuan. The police finally recovered the stolen relics overseas, including the solid gold 'Seal of Empress Dowager Tianyuan', 43 millimetres in diameter and nearly one kilogram in weight. On October 16, 2002, another group of robbers found the tomb chambers. After sawing through thick blocks of wood around the chambers, and falling dizzy with the foul air, they extracted the air and, wearing gas

masks, entered the chambers. They stole four pottery figurines blackened by burning for which they clinched a deal at 300 yuan per item on a "trial sale". Later, on three separate occasions, they snatched over 200 pieces and disposed of the booty very quickly. They received 4,600 yuan each. Two months later, grave robbers Huang Shimin and Zhang Xiaoyan stole 71 nude female figures. They sold them hastily at 700 yuan a piece. When the police noticed the suspicious-looking hole the robbers had made, they put the site under surveillance. Subsequently, they arrested the thieves and recovered 34 figurines. It is generally acknowledged that this is one of the most serious robbery cases in Xi'an in recent years in terms of both its scale and the quality of the tomb artefacts. According to historical records, the region around Jiangcun Village at Baqiao contained the subordinate tombs of Western Han imperial families. There are the tombs of Empress Dowager Bo, mother of Han Emperor Wendi, tomb of Empress Dou, those of her daughter Princess Guan Tao and her granddaughter Chen Ahjiao as well as the attendant tomb of Liu Xuan or Western Han Emperor Gengshi. Archaeologists who have studied the intercepted nude figurines believe they had clothes when they were buried, but the clothes decayed over time. The shape of the figurines is similar to the delicately shaped artefacts unearthed from Chang Ling, the mausoleum of Liu Bang or Emperor Gaodi and Yang Ling, the mausoleum of Emperor Jingdi. The genitals of both the male and female are lifelike. It is impossible to figure out how many ancient tombs have been robbed and how many stolen relics are sold every day from the loess land of Shaanxi.

BLACK MARKET DEALINGS IN XI'AN

The Antiques Exchange Market, built close to the city wall of Xiaodong Gate, east of Xi'an City, in the early 1890s, was moved to Baxian'an (Temple of the Eight Immortals) outside Xiaodong Gate in 1966. The Xi'an Antiques City was set up around the same time, occupying half of Zhongbei Flea Market at the crossing of Zhuque Road in the south of the city. In 2001, the 'Shaanxi Exchange Centre for Collections' was established in Dani'er Section inside Xiaodong Gate. Xi'an now has three antiques exchange markets, Xi'an Antiques City being the largest. These markets in Xi'an differ from their counterparts in Beijing, Shanghai and Tianjin. "Antiques" means things outside the range of "cultural relics" limited by China's Law of Cultural Relics. Goods available in the antiques markets in Beijing and other cities are jade, scrolls of calligraphy and paintings, porcelain vases, incense burners, mahogany furniture, secondhand timepieces and cameras. However, these

(Preceding pages) *Qian Ling, the mausoleum of Emporor Gaozu and Empress Wu Zetian, has not been plundered due to its solid construction.*

are not prominent in Xi'an's markets. They display some ordinary goods on the stands for the sake of appearance, but actually they deal in objects of all grades with many of them being from the predominant category of "cultural relics". For example, a Han dynasty pottery piece or an ordinary tile-end costs less than 100 yuan each. For seriously damaged pottery figurines of the Han and Tang dynasties and those with the coloured drawings peeled off, the bargain price could be less than 10 yuan each. Bronzes without inscriptions or patterns from the periods of the Warring States, Qin and Han such as cauldrons (*ding*), rectangular wine containers (*fang*), jars (*hu*) and swords can sell for a few thousand yuan each. The price of bronzes belonging to the periods of Shang and Zhou and choice items from the Spring and Autumn Period, the Warring States Period, and Han and Tang dynasties could sell for up to hundreds of thousands of yuan apiece. Judging by the quotations in the markets in recent years, the prices of cultural relics are rising. To evade investigation, no objects beyond the bounds of the law are displayed on the shop counters. Xi'an has about 120 antique shops in the three antique exchange markets. All are licensed to sell antiques. However, the bigger dealers probably have network links to relic distributors in Beijing, Shanghai, Guangdong, Hong Kong and Taiwan as well as to those acting as agents in rural areas. The proprietors of antique shops will never be involved in tomb excavation. Instead, the items generally pass from grave robbers to purchasing agents to proprietors in Xi'an to larger dealers outside Xi'an. In the late 1980s and the beginning of the 1990s, there was only one channel for the sale of cultural relics: export via the antique dealers in Hong Kong. However, Macau and Taiwan distributors also keep a close watch on the mainland's relics markets. It is apparent that they smuggle out large quantities of cultural relics every year that are intercepted by customs in all parts of the country. However, the seizures by customs are just a drop in the ocean. Since the late 1990s, China's economy has been developing rapidly, encouraging a domestic market for historical relics. Purchasers fall into three categories: gift givers, relics collectors, and those who buy artefacts as investments. Giving cultural relics as gifts has become fashionable. A gift of this kind can easily cost up to 10,000 yuan.

Translated by Anju K; Photography by Qiu Ziyu & Shi
Article supplied courtesy of China Tourism.

THE FIRST EMPEROR OF CHINA

Qin Shihuangdi, the first emperor of China, was both a reformer and a tyrant. Although his reign lasted little more than a decade, it was epoch-making in terms of its enduring influence on Chinese civilization.

While the emperor is best known by most people for his amazing tomb with its terracotta guards, perhaps his most valuable legacy is a uniform Chinese script which permits people speaking different regional dialects to have a means of communication. Qin Shihuangdi standardized more than the writing of characters, however. The demands of trade required a currency with recognized fixed value throughout his vast conquered territory, so he standardized the coinage, introducing a circular copper coin with a square hole in the centre. Equally important reforms were the standardization of weights and measures, and codification of the law. A very good exhibit on Qin Shihuangdi's reforms can be found in the National Museum of Shaanxi History.

To organize the empire Qin Shihuangdi abolished the prevailing feudal system and established prefectures and counties. These were put under the administration of officials appointed by the central government. Such extensive control required roads, which Qin Shihuangdi ordered to be built, the main ones radiating from his capital, Xianyang. To protect his northern border against hostile nomads, he strengthened the pre-existing fortifications, and the line of defence now known as the Great Wall is attributed to him. It is said that he joined up stretches of frontier walls that were constructed by his predecessors to make one long barrier.

Chinese tour guides and literature promote the Great Wall as a symbol of China's ancient civilization, but in the eyes of some modern Chinese it epitomizes their country's isolation and backwardness. Its construction was achieved at huge expense, particularly in terms of human lives. Labourers were conscripted to work on the wall, and convicts served out sentences there. Some convict labourers even had 'perpetual' sentences, which meant that when they died their places were inherited by family members.

There are many folk tales recounting the horrors of forced labour. The legend of Meng Jiangnu is the best known. Meng Jiangnu's husband had been conscripted to work for a season on the Great Wall. When, by the end of summer, he had still not returned to his Shaanxi home, she decided to take him warm clothes for the winter. After a difficult journey she found his work gang in Hebei, but his fellow conscripts told Meng that her husband had already died. At this tragic news, Meng began to cry hysterically, and her flood of tears broke open a part of the Great Wall, revealing her husband's remains. He had been buried where he fell and his body was used as part of the fill for the wall.

On hearing of the damage to his project, an enraged Qin Shihuangdi, coincidentally present on an inspection tour, ordered Meng to be brought before him. His fury soon subsided on seeing her beauty. Although he offered to take her as concubine, she decided that death was preferable and threw herself into the Yellow Sea.

The emperor did not live long and his death in 210 BC, while away from his capital on tour, led to the fall of his dynasty shortly after. There is a story of how his prime minister, fearful that news of the emperor's death would spark rebellion, tried to conceal it. The emperor's body was transported in haste back to Xianyang, the Qin capital near modern Xi'an. To mask the stench of the putrefying corpse,

Rubbing from a stele, exhibited in the National Museum of Shaanxi History, depicting an image of Qin Shihuangdi.

the minister filled his chariot with rotting fish. But the feared revolt was only postponed; four years later Qin Shihuangdi's heir was killed by rebels and the Han dynasty was established soon after.

Xianyang

Xianyang, a satellite city of Xi'an, was established on the north bank of the Wei River around 350 BCE, when Qin was one of several warring states vying for supremacy. The city was adopted as the Qin capital, and is said to have developed into a metropolis with 800,000 inhabitants before rebel general Xiang Yu set fire to it in 206 BCE.

In 1961 the exact location of the city was re-discovered in the Yaodian People's Commune northwest of Xi'an. Excavations in the 1960s and 1970s revealed the foundations of the Xianyang Palace, the first emperor's principal domicile, partly built on a terrace of pounded earth. The structure and function of different parts of the palace are now known. Important discoveries were made, including the remains of some murals. Building materials, decorated bricks and tiles were found in large quantities. These remains, other artifacts from the period, and a wooden model of the palace, can be seen in the Xianyang Museum.

Most visitors, however, go to the museum to view its collection of miniature terracotta soldiers dating from the Han dynasty. Apart from the Qin artefacts and Han figurines, the museum also has one exhibition hall dedicated to depictions of horses as well as a small display of steles and Buddhist statues and stonework. The latter is located to the back right of the museum and now functions as a Buddhist temple. The museum is on Zhongshan Jie, which is a continuation of Xining Jie. Xianyang is now Shaanxi's booming third city and site of the airport serving Xi'an, 28 kilometres (17 miles) away. It is accessible from Xi'an by road or rail. Mini buses depart frequently from the bus station near the southwest corner of the city wall. The ride takes about one hour.

XIANYANG MUSEUM

The Xianyang Museum was established in 1962 on the grounds of a former Confucian Temple, which dates back to 1371, when the Ming dynasty was under the reign of Emperor Hongwu. The small-scale museum, which is laid out in courtyard style, exudes considerable charm and peacefulness. It houses thousands of relics, numbering at least 15,000, of which 4,000 are on display. In addition to their famous painted terracotta army, the museum has significant numbers of jades, bronze wares and gold and silver vessels.

The Xianyang Museum houses a superb collection of miniature painted terracotta warriors, which were discovered in a group of Han tombs known as the Yangjiawan Tombs near the village of the same name, 20 kilometres (12 miles) to the east of Xianyang. That tomb is considered an 'attendant burial' to Chang Ling—the mausoleum of the Han Gaozu emperor, who as Liu Bang founded the Han dynasty in 206 BCE, and reigned until 195 BCE. The terracotta warriors were probably part of a tomb of a high-ranking military officials of the early Han period. Collectively known as the 3,000 warriors, they comprise 1,965 infantry, 583 cavalry and 410 shields. Of these, 1,500 are exhibited in a hall refurbished in 2003. They are well lit and stand against a panoramic background photograph of the area they were discovered in, with its many tomb hillocks. More photographs are displayed on the opposite wall. These show the original excavation pits, where many of the figures lay toppled on their backs and sides. The exhibition hall has large columns painted red and a beamed ceiling. The sense of drama is heightened with the infantry and cavalry displayed in a tightly packed formation, faithful to the original layout of the tomb which was discovered in 1962.

The terracotta infantrymen and cavalrymen were found in battle formation in two rows of five rectangular pits, to the east and west, with a pit containing war chariots in the centre. (The chariots were originally constructed of pottery and wood. The wood had decayed and the pottery remains were broken into so many pieces it was unfortunately impossible to reconstruct them.) Several subtle differences can be seen among the infantry: some hold halberds, some play musical instruments, some command, some hold flags, and some dance. Their facial features accurately depict their origins so that three distinct ethnic types can be distinguished amongst the statues: the soldiers from the Guanzhong plains in Shaanxi are approximately 49–51 centimetres tall, with square faces; the somewhat shorter 48 centimetres tall Cong people from Sichuan province have prominent cheekbones and are without protective head covering; and the soldiers from Longxi who stand about 44.5 centimetres tall, are the shortest. There is a considerable variety in the head ornaments, garments, trouser leggings, shoes and armour.

The eastern pits contained mostly infantrymen who once held wooden weapons and pottery shields. The figurines were originally painted and some show traces of colour, although the paint on a few is well-preserved. The cavalry were concentrated in the western pits and are of two distinct kinds: taller, heavy-uniformed cavalrymen, some in armour, riding larger and stronger horses making them about 68 centimetres tall, and relatively shorter men with light uniforms riding smaller horses, with an overall height of about 50 centimetres. The latter are archers and wear quivers on their backs.

Like a massive army poised for battle, the warriors are an impressive sight, making the ride from Xi'an well worthwhile on their own. The museum, however, is also noted for its carved jades, bronze vessels and some precious gold pieces (see photograph on page 149). From 1966 to 1976, some of the earliest jade wares of the Han dynasty were discovered in the vicinity. The craftsmen obviously gave considerable thought to the stone, its colour, texture and shape. Although most measure less than 10 centimetres long, the jades are conceived of as sculptures in the round, with images including bears, winged immortals astride jade horses, eagles of obvious power, figures with serious expressions, and mythical beasts of vigour and power,

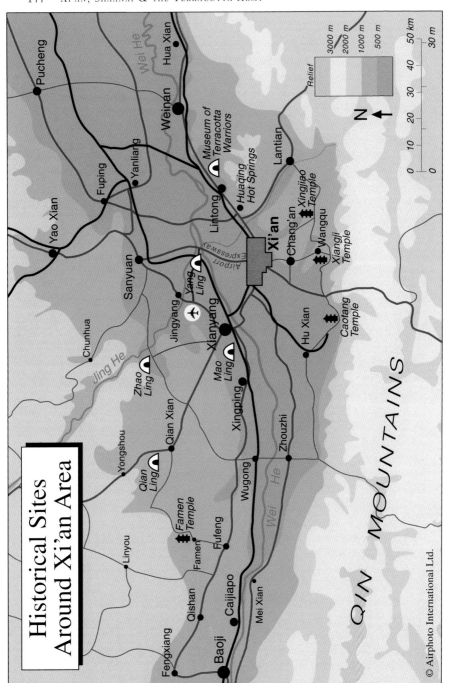

The small-scale Xianyang Museum is laid out in courtyard style. This view shows the building which features a special exhibition on the theme of horses.

called *bixie*, who ward off evil. When appropriate, the carvers have made excellent use of the various colours in the raw material, and all the jades have been beautifully polished. It is perhaps the carving of an immortal astride a galloping horse in white jade, only 7 centimetres long, which is most outstanding. It is carved from jade from Hotan, Xinjiang, famous for its smoothness and translucency.

The museum houses a number of bronzes, including vessels with gold inlay, inscribed bronze vessels, bronze musical instruments, and also bronze building elements like hinges, some of them gilt bronze, and connectors to hold wooden building columns together. They can be seen in the first exhibition hall and in the halls flanking the courtyard on the right and left as one proceeds inward.

In the second hall, directly in front of the first courtyard, there is a thematic display of 50 horses dating from the Warring States to the Tang dynasty. It is a superb exhibition, arranged chronologically and well thought out. The Chinese domesticated the horse from Neolithic times onwards and this exhibition demonstrates just how important the horse has been throughout the ages. Pottery examples are the most numerous, and these will surely appeal to lovers of Chinese ceramics who will quickly identify the differences between the monochrome and tri-colour examples as well as between the unglazed and glazed ones. The exhibits may also be enjoyed as sculptures—there are horses that pull carts and ones that dance for emperors. There are also ones that carry warriors into battle and ones that carry liberated ladies of the Tang dynasty playing polo. In addition to ceramic horses, there are reproduction frescoes and small bronzes. Though a small-scale exhibition, it is an extremely satisfying one. If time allows, and after a short rest in one of the quiet courtyards, the exhibition can be enjoyed more than once.

BETRAYAL

*Three nights were required to open a shaft. Most commonly the main
funeral passage lay directly below the earthen mound, and the crypt itself,
containing the sarcophagus, lay at some remove. Sometimes, to confuse
robbers, the main passage, the inner passage, and the crypt itself bore no
relation at all to the external mound. The several cuts would wind and twist,
and then the door to the crypt would be at the spot least expected. Sometimes
it was by no means easy even to find the crypt. Incomparably more difficult
was the task of getting the funeral treasures out. These were of course the
tombs of the rich and noble. They had been devised on the assumption that
there would be robbers.*

*For three nights the ten of them took turns at digging. Some forty feet
below the spot chosen by Ko they came upon a flat rock about a yard square
which might have been called the skylight. The stone was too large for two or
three men to move. Since they were confined to the narrow shaft they had
opened, they were two nights making their way into the passage below. When
finally they had succeeded, there was still a little time before daybreak. Some
in the band wanted to proceed immediately, but Ch'en said with some firmness
that they would wait until the next night. Against possible discovery, they had
yet to block the shaft and cover it with weeds. The secret of grave robbing was
to leave time for everything.*

*It was a cloudy night of fierce winds when they finally made their way
inside. The band seemed to gather from nowhere, work clothes beating in the
wind. The season was neither warm nor cold. The light of the lanterns was
now bright, now low.*

*Ch'en looked from one to another. They were not to have thoughts of
private booty, he said, they were to share alike. And he approached a young
woman, the only woman among them, and a tall young man.*

'You two will stand guard outside,' he said.

The woman was his third wife, the man his younger brother.

'Get inside, the rest of you.'

*As if in a sort of ceremonial capacity as leader, he took up a lantern and
bent over to enter the dark hold. Three men followed him and mattocks and*

shovels and hammers and the like were brought down, and the other four disappeared inside.

The darkness was more profound than on the surface. The only sound was the whistling of the wind. He had left as sentinels his wife and a brother with whom he shared the same blood, and in the choice had been considerations of a sort that Ch'en would make. Had he chosen anyone else, he could not have been sure when the stone would be toppled back into place. The others were his trusted comrades, but they were human, and he could not be sure when temptation would raise its head. If the stone were to fall, if only that were to happen, then the men inside would not see the light of day again. Ten days would pass and they would lie dead of starvation, and the treasure would be the property of him who had betrayed them. The men in the tomb were always conscious, therefore, of who it was that stood watch outside. Though it was the usual thing for a relative of someone inside the tomb to be drafted for the work, that was not always the safest procedure. There were wives who cursed husbands, sons who hated fathers. Ch'en's choice of his own wife and brother had much to recommend it to the others. Ch'en's young wife got along well with her husband, and she was a good-natured, amiable woman, pleasant to everyone. The brother had been reared like a son. He was of a wholesome nature such as to deny that he and Ch'en shared the same blood, and well thought of by everyone.

But it was not as wise a choice as the other thought it. The moment the two were alone the woman held out her hand to the man.

'Put the lid back on. Make up your mind to it. Go in and do it.'

She spoke in a low voice. The young man was startled. The same terrible thought had been with him from the moment he was appointed sentinel. He had been having an affair with the woman for a year and more. Though she was his brother's wife she did not seem like a sister-in-law. Ch'en had taken advantage of the fact that she was without resources, and had as good as kidnapped her, and had his way with her...

There was a rustling as the youth went off through the grass. The woman followed.

Yasushi Inoue, Princess Yung-t'ai's Necklace from Lou-lan and Other Stories, translated by James T Araki and Edward Seidensticker, New York, Kodansha International, 1981

FUNERARY FINERY

In a large grey building standing to one side of the Drum Tower, under a line of Chinese characters painted to read 'Municipal Theatre Costume Retail Department', there was a door with a curious sign on its lintel. It said: 'Funeral and Interment Clothes Sold Here'. The door was closed, but you could get into the shop by either one of two additional entrances; these had signs which said, 'Men's and Women's Fashions', and 'Theatrical Costumes, Props and Dance Costumes'.

I thought that this was worth more than a moment of my curiosity, and stepped into the darkness of the building. I made for the funeral clothes counter, which turned out to be in the far end of the shop. It was very dark there, but still it was not difficult to see the sign pinned up above the counter, which said, 'Burial suits, once sold, are without exception not returnable'. I asked to see one.

She took a minute to look through her stock—from where I stood I could see that she was plentifully supplied—and came up with something which I thought you nowadays only saw in the movies. It took my breath away, it was so sumptuous, a beautiful ensemble in silk, such as might have been worn by a court lady in the Qing dynasty. The robe was of purple silk, deep as the skin of an aubergine, and trimmed with a border of gold. The skirt, of a heavier silk, was midnight blue and splashed with a phoenix pattern embroidered in gold. (I supposed that the male version would be a dragon). Together the pieces cost 32 yuan, well over half of an average wage earner's monthly salary.

In such finery are the richer dead arrayed when they go to their graves in China. How incorrigible they are, those millions of Chinese in their baggy blue suits; if they don't dress very stylishly when they are alive they certainly make up for it when they die. And the thought came to me that all the chic, all the colour, all the money of China is expended on the children and the dead.

Lynn Pan, *China's Sorrow: Journeys around the Yellow River*,
Century Publishing, 1985

*Gold ewer and cover decorated with mandarin ducks and climbing plants,
height 21cm; diameter (at centre) 11cm. Excavated from Xianyang Northwest
Medical Apparatus and Instruments Factory site, 1969.*

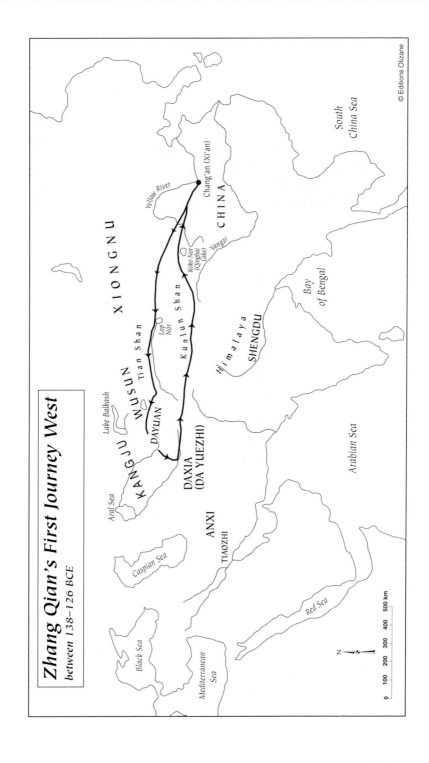

Zhang Qian's First Journey West

between 138–126 BCE

© Editions Olizane

Black Sea

Mediterranean Sea

Caspian Sea

Aral Sea

TIAOZHI

ANXI

Red Sea

Arabian Sea

KANGJU

Lake Balkash

WUSUN

DAYUAN

DAXIA
(DA YUEZHI)

Tian Shan

XIONGNU

Lop Nor

Kunlun Shan

Himalaya

SHENGDU

Bay
of Bengal

South
China Sea

Yellow River

Chang'an (Xi'an)

CHINA

Koko Nor
(Qinghai
Lake)

Yangzi

N

0 100 200 300 400 500 km

ZHANG QIAN AND THE CHINESE DISCOVERY OF THE WEST —Bijan Omrani

The greatest advances in the bounds of human knowledge often come not when man is satisfying his curiosity in times of peace, but rather when he is seeking new ways to defend himself in times of war. Such is the case with the Chinese discovery of the West.

Although, at the end of the third century BCE, the Chinese were able to attain a new unity under the dynasty of the Han emperors, they found themselves constantly menaced and harassed by a nomadic people to the north: the Xiongnu. Considered by many to be the ancestor of the Huns who later were to penetrate into Europe, the Xiongnu were, at that time, militarily superior to China: a force of archers and cavalrymen who would pillage and attack the sedentary populations unfortunate enough to live upon their borders. To defend against them, sections of the Great Wall had been built during and before the Qin dynasty (221–207 BCE); yet, this proved not enough of a defence, and throughout the second century BCE, the Chinese were incessantly harassed, losing their resources of manpower, horses, and money. In 138 BCE, the Emperor Wudi decided that a diplomatic solution should be attempted. In a distant and uncertain region of the west, he knew that another nomadic group known as 'the Yuezhi', had taken up residence after being displaced by the Xiongnu; indeed, their leader had been slain in battle, and his skull converted into a drinking vessel for the use of the Xiongnu chief. Thinking that if only they could be located and contacted, they would willingly accept an alliance with China against their enemies in order to regain their old homeland, he commanded the despatch of an ambassador charged with bringing this about.

The man he selected for this task was called Zhang Qian, an officer of the palace guard, originally from Chengu district in south-western Shaanxi. To accompany him, 99 junior officers and private soldiers were chosen, along with a renegade of the Xiongnu, a skilled archer named Ganfu. Having been invested by the Emperor with the ambassadorial insignia—a bamboo pole topped with three tufts of hair from the tail of a yak—he set out from the Imperial capital Chang'an (Xi'an), and made his way through southern Gansu province towards the Yellow River.

After the party had made its way beyond this obstacle, they discovered that the region into which they had crossed, known as the Hexi Corridor, was infested by the Xiongnu. Captured and led away by a detachment of cavalry, Zhang Qian was humiliated before the king, and given to a noble family to be employed as a slave. For eleven years, he lived as a herdsman, pasturing sheep and cows, even taking a Xiongnu wife and by her having a son. At length, with a number of the Chinese prisoners and his new family, he was able to escape. Fleeing westwards through the wilderness, relying on the skills of Ganfu and his companions to hunt down prey for their survival, they eventually came upon a vast salt lake, Lop Nor, in the ancient kingdom of Loulan. Enquiring from the local inhabitants a route to the Yuezhi, they continued on their course through a number of petty principalities in the region of Xinjiang. In time, they reached the kingdom of Dayuan, otherwise known as the region of Ferghana, in modern-day Uzbekistan. Here, not only were they received with courtesy and kindness—the King of Dayuan had heard of and respected China as a powerful and wealthy state—but also, they made a number of useful discoveries: grapes, carrots, garlic, and sesame. More importantly, they found that Dayuan produced a finer breed of horses than ever had been available in China as well as a variety of grass, called alfalfa or musu, which acted as excellent fodder.

Zhang Qian was, after a year, escorted to the realm of the Yuezhi; they had settled in Bactria, in the rich plains of northern Afghanistan. Although they listened to Zhang Qian's proposal of an alliance with sympathy, they decided not to enter into a military league with the Han emperor: China was too distant, they believed, to be a reliable partner, and the Xiongnu were still a close and ever-present threat. Nonetheless, Zhang Qian continued to collect useful information. He learnt of other, far off empires, the Persian and the Roman, and noted that native Chinese goods, such as cloth and bamboo, were available in the local markets, which led him to conjecture about trade routes as yet unknown to the Chinese court.

Zhang Qian and his remaining followers began their return to Chang'an by a different route towards the south, below the Kunlun Mountains by way of Qinghai. Again, he fell into the hands of a Tibetan tribe in league with the Xiongnu and was sentenced to hard labour. Nevertheless, in 126 BCE he again escaped, and managed to continue unmolested to the Chinese capital, where he presented to the Emperor Wudi the ambassadorial staff with which he had been entrusted thirteen years previously. Only he, along with his wife and Ganfu, remained of the original party of 100; they were hailed as pioneers, and showered by the emperor with honours.

Zhang Qian was able to report news of 36 kingdoms in the western regions. His description of the horses of Ferghana prompted the emperor to send further missions—the first led again by Zhang Qian—to the King of Dayuan, in order to secure them for use against the Xiongnu. Besides this, the Chinese court began to establish regular contacts with the kingdoms and principalities all the way to Kashgar, and later as far as Persia. It is thanks to Zhang Qian's perilous work and adventures that trade along the Silk Road with the West was able to come into being, and for this he is still remembered by the Chinese as a national hero under the title granted him by the emperor: The Great Traveller.

Period Three: The Han Dynasty

BACKGROUND

The Qin dynasty maintained its authority only until 209 BCE. The first emperor's death in 210 BCE was followed by outbreaks of rebellion and civil war, which led to the empire's dissolution. The final blow was dealt by General Xiang Yu, who conquered the Qin forces in 207 BCE. But then he himself was overthrown four years later by the founder of the Han dynasty.

The first Han emperor was a general of plebeian background called Liu Bang, known posthumously by his dynastic title of Han Gaozu, which literally means great-great-grandfather of Han. His capital, called Chang'an, was built in the strategic Wei valley. Accordingly, the first half of Han rule, lasting until 8 CE, is called the Western Han to distinguish it from the Eastern Han period, 25–220 CE, when the capital was at Luoyang to the east.

THE CAPITAL CITY OF CHANG'AN

In 202 BCE Liu Bang moved into a minor Qin palace on the southern side of the Wei River. Later the architect Xiao He added a large new complex of some 40 buildings to the west of it. This was the Weiyang Palace (see page 158), which was to remain the principal seat of the Western Han emperors. Together these two palaces formed the nucleus of Han-dynasty Chang'an.

The imperial establishment soon outgrew the two original palaces and more buildings were added during the time of the emperor Han Huidi (reigned 194–187 BCE). An irregular-shaped wall was built around the palaces, eventually forming a circumference of about 22 kilometres (nearly 14 miles). Within the wall there were eight main streets and 160 alleys. Outside the wall another city developed, a city of artisans, with markets, workshops and houses.

THE SILK ROAD

It was during the Han that the Chinese opened up routes to central and western Asia. This was to have a profound impact on Chang'an. From the capital, Han Wudi, the Martial Emperor (reigned 140–86 BCE), launched a series of campaigns against the Xiongnu, the warlike Turkish people of the steppes, who were a constant threat to the northern frontier of China. In 139 BCE Zhang Qian was sent officially to Central Asia to find allies against the Xiongnu (see Special Topic page 151). On his second journey in 119 BCE he went as far as the Ili Valley and from there dispatched envoys to India and the Iranian empire as well as kingdoms east of the Caspian Sea. One of the most influential finds that Zhang Qian made on this journey were the splendid horses in what is now Uzbekistan. Some of these were brought to China where they later became the inspiration of Chinese sculptors, painters and writers to an extent that was almost obsessional, especially during the Tang dynasty.

Merchant caravans followed the armies and established the routes of what Europeans later called the Silk Road. The eastern section opened by the Chinese linked with trade routes in western Asia to form links of trade and cultural exchange stretching from Chang'an to the ports of the eastern Mediterranean Sea. Official contact with the Roman Empire was attempted in 97 CE, but the envoy never got through. However, unofficial representatives of Rome, including a party of jugglers, reportedly arrived in Chang'an in 120 CE. There was a special street where foreigners were accommodated, and even a protocol department to arrange their reception.

Paper was one of many Chinese inventions that eventually reached Europe via the Silk Road. The world's earliest pieces of paper were discovered in 1957 at Ba Bridge, east of Xi'an. It was originally thought that paper was invented during the Eastern Han, but these pieces of hemp paper were made considerably earlier, during the reign of Han Wudi.

Sights

THE IMPERIAL TOMBS OF THE WESTERN HAN DYNASTY

There are nine tombs of the Western Han emperors on the north bank of the Wei River and two south of the present-day city of Xi'an. The construction of each one was started soon after the accession of the sovereign and, according to regulations, one third of all state revenues was devoted to the project. On the death of the emperor valuable objects were placed in the tomb and the body was interred in a suit of jade plates, sewn together with gold wire. A piece of jade was placed in the mouth of the emperor. Prominent members of the imperial family and important officials were buried in smaller ancillary or satellite tombs nearby.

None of the imperial mausoleums has been excavated, and they remain irregular flat-topped grassy pyramids, 33–46 metres (108–151 feet) high.

MAO LING

Mao Ling is the mausoleum the Western Han Emperor Wudi, the Martial Emperor, who reigned from 140-87 BCE. Like Qin Shihuangdi, he initiated a new period of dynamic expansion. Imperial rule was extended to the southeast coastal region of China, northern Vietnam and northern Korea. His tomb is 40 kilometres (25 miles) west of Xi'an. Although it has not been excavated, the commemorative area has been well laid out. The top of the small hill on which a monument has been built has a good view of many surrounding tombs, some of which have been excavated.

The Martial Emperor had tried to avoid his demise with attempts at making himself immortal. He put a bronze statue (the Brazen Immortal) in a high tower to catch the pure dew in a bowl, which he drank with powdered jade. However, the potion proved ineffective, and he died in his 70th year. Apparently there were so many treasures intended for his tomb that they could not all be fitted in. But many of his books are said to have been buried with him, as well as a number of live animals.

The mausoleum was desecrated, rather than robbed, by peasant rebels called the Red Eyebrows, just before the establishment of the Eastern Han. They removed articles from the tomb and threw them on a bonfire. Archaeologists believe that they have found the patch of burnt earth where this happened.

Mao Ling is situated northwest of Xi'an, a convenient stop on the way to or from Qian Ling, the Tang dynasty tombs (see page 191)

THE TOMB OF HUO QUBING

About one and a half kilometres (less than a mile) from Mao Ling lies the tomb of Emperor Han Wudi's eminent general. Nicknamed the 'Swift Cavalry General', Huo Qubing, later Grand Marshal, was born in 140 BCE. His uncle took him to fight the fierce northern nomads, the Xiongnu, when he was 18. He led a force of 800 cavalry which is reputed to have killed more than 2,000 of the enemy. In all, he defeated the Xiongnu in six battles and kept open the transportation route between Xi'an and the northwestern province of Gansu. He died at the age of only 24 from natural causes. According to the author Sima Qian, who was a contemporary, Han Wudi, the Martial Emperor, built a special tomb for the general in the shape of the Qilian Mountains (which marks the present-day border of Gansu and Qinghai provinces), where Huo had won a great victory.

The Mao Ling Museum, which stands at the base of Huo Qubing's tomb, showcases many important relics discovered among satellite tombs of Emperor Wudi's Mao Ling. In 1961, the State Council listed Mao Ling and the Tomb of Huo Qubing as important cultural relic sites to be protected, recognizing that the area is immensely rich in its cultural legacy. In its exhibition halls, the museum displays relics from a number of the satellite tombs, while its exterior corridor pavilions house sixteen large, remarkable stone sculptures. The stone sculptures were originally placed in front of Huo Qubing's tomb. In their selection of stone, and in its carving, chiseling and outlining, the Western Han sculptors have used the stone's natural shapes and contours with a high degree of skill to create vigorous, but simple, figures, both human and animal. Some of them have minimal carving and etching, but various poses such as crouching, leaping, reclining, resting and trampling are shown. There are two horses in front of Huo Qubing's tomb mound, one to the right and one to left, each in its own pavilion. Facing toward the tomb, there is a galloping horse on the right, measuring some 2.5 metres long, and a horse trampling a Xiongnu on the left. The other sculptures are displayed in two covered corridors, rich with luxuriant ivy, on either side of the mound. They house a prone horse, a crouching tiger ready to ambush, a toad, a frog and a fish, an elephant and an ox, both lying at

Han dynasty earthen tomb figure.

leisure, and a boar. There is also a beast preying on a sheep, and two human figures, one by itself, and the other wrestling with a bear. This last stone, about 2.77 metres (nine feet) high, may represent a Xiongnu idol, known as a 'Golden Man'.

The museum's two exhibition halls stand on either side of an attractively laid out garden with a large goldfish pond in the centre. The exhibits inside are almost all of the Western Han period and were discovered in the vicinity of Mao Ling. Four of them in particular,

Stone sculptures of a crouching tiger (2 metres long) in the foreground and a prone horse (2.6 metres long) behind; Mao Ling Museum.

designated national treasures, attest to the rich culture and techniques in bronze, gilded bronze, silver, gilded silver, gold, jade and stone. In 1963, while ploughing in his field, a farmer discovered a magnificent bronze wine container in the shape of a rhinoceros. The original can be seen in National Museum of China in Beijing. It is so

At 62 cm high and 76 cm long, this gilt-bronze horse is the largest known example of its type. Discovered near Mao Ling, it is from the Western Han period (206 BCE–8 CE).

naturalistic in its modeling, and so vividly shows the character of the animal, that it is almost lifelike. In fashioning its thick skin with many folds, the bronze has been inlaid with swirling gold and silver wires in the shape of clouds. In 1974 a jade door knocker with an animal face was excavated in the vicinity of Mao Ling. It is carved and the animals of the four directions—a green dragon, a white tiger, a scarlet bird and a black tortoise—are depicted in its four corners. At 34.2 centimetres high, 35.6 centimetres wide and 14.7 centimetres thick, it is the largest Western Han jade door knocker discovered so far. In 1981, a gilded bronze horse was excavated from a tomb at Mao Ling. It is the largest known gilded bronze horse yet discovered, and is approximately one-third life size, weighing 25 kilograms, standing 62 centimetres tall and 76 centimetres long. With a well proportioned body, the horse conveys great alertness, its ears pricked back and its full body taut. In the same year, an incense burner in bronze with gold and silver gilding and supported by a shaft shaped in the form of five bamboo sections, was discovered in a funerary pit in the Mao Ling area. The lid of the incense-burning compartment is shaped like a mountain and there is an inscription circling below. The mountain shape is significant because it symbolizes a belief in immortality and the afterlife. The entire piece stands 58 centimetres tall, and the diameter of the incense burning compartment is 9 centimetres and that of the bottom, 13.3 centimetres. The inscription tells us that it was made for one of the imperial palaces known as Weiyang Gong. It was found with other inscribed objects belonging to the Princess Yangxin, the elder sister of Emperor Wu. The base of the stand is shaped with dragon images, and below the inscription of the mountain censer are three dragons.

There are also a number of objects, perhaps less rare or masterful, which teach us about life in the Qin and Han eras. These include examples of the decorated building materials for which both the Qin and Han were famous, such as hollow bricks, carved with the creatures of four directions on the outside, and many bronze articles, including money and agricultural implements.

The Mao Ling museum is enchanting with its air of calm dignity. The buildings replicate Han architecture, with columns, beams and roof tiles, but given the rather insecure nature of these buildings, some of the rarest objects are reproductions, the originals being safely stored in the National Musuem of Shaanxi History in Xi'an or the National Museum of China in Beijing.

REMAINS OF THE HAN CITY OF CHANG'AN
HAN CITY WALLS
The site of the Han capital is on the northwestern edge of the present-day city of Xi'an. Today the walls are still there but inside the palaces have been replaced by fields of wheat and rape-seed (see map page 28).

REMAINS OF WEIYANG PALACE

The southern part of the Han city was excavated between 1957 and 1959 so the layout of the palaces is known. The raised area of the audience hall of Weiyang Palace, the principal seat of the Western Han emperors, can be reached by road. The platform is 101 metres (330 feet) long, much smaller than was thought for the original hall, but we know that Weiyang was rebuilt several times during the Tang period, so it is likely that the foundations have been altered.

HAN CITY ARMOURY

Built in 200 BCE, the armoury occupied 23 hectares (57 acres) near the present-day village of Daliuzhai, next to the site of Weiyang Palace. Excavations have revealed a large number of iron weapons, and some made of bronze. At the end of 1981 it was announced that a number of hefty suits of armour had been found weighing 35–40 kilograms (77–88 pounds).

YANG LING

The area of Yang Ling is the site of the tomb of Liu Qi, the fourth Han Emperor Jingdi, who reigned from 157 to 141 BCE. The archaeological site lies next to the road leading from Xi'an to the airport near Xianyang, just across the bridge spanning the Wei River. On the south side of the road lies the Yang Ling Museum, opened to the public at the end of September 1999, ten years after the site was first discovered. The principal exhibits in the museum are the thousands of unearthed pottery figures and animals. The emperor's tomb mound, which faces east, stands on the north side of the road opposite the museum, together with that of his wife, Empress Wang, who died some 15 years later. To date archaeologists have concentrated on excavating pits in the immediate surrounding area and, as with the mausoleum of Qin Shihuangdi, they have left the emperor's tomb untouched for the time being.

The significance of the site lies in the overall layout of the mausoleum, including the method of positioning and measuring the placement of the tombs and accompanying graves as well as the system of burial pits and structures. The existence of a large south gate and the vast number of pottery sculptures is also noteworthy.

The emperor's tomb mound was originally square-sided with a flat top in the shape of a truncated pyramid 31 metres (102 feet) high. It was contained within a square walled enclosure, each side of which was 410 metres (448 yards) long with a gate in the middle. Four brick culverts that acted as drains for the tomb have been unearthed, one at each of the four corners. A road led from each gate with a rammed-earth tower standing on either side. More than 90 pits have been discovered arranged in parallel rows running perpendicular to the four sides of the tomb. A further 28 pits have been found around the tomb of Empress Wang, who died in 126 BCE.

At some time between 153–141 BCE a large stone compass was placed about 450 metres southeast of the mausoleum. It was used during the building of the mausoleum to obtain measurements, and to determine level and height. It is in a square shape, one side measuring 1.8 metres and the other 1.83 metres. The diameter of the disc in the upper part of the compass is 1.4 metres and the cross in the middle of the disc points to the four directions of due north, due south, due east, and due west respectively. This large stone compass (known as the *luojing shi*), is the earliest known stone for measurement not only in China, but in the world, and has great value in the history of surveying and mapping.

The excavations of the mausoleum's south gate ruins took place between the summer of 1997 and the autumn of 1998. Since 2001, the remains of the gate have been housed inside an impressively large protective structure resembling the original Han dynasty building. Inside the structure, the rammed earth, tile fragments, and post holes of the original gate can be seen. Pebble stones around the perimeter make a walkway. The ruins are roped off and all along the inside walls of the structure are illustrations of gates throughout Chinese history. Although there are literary records of gates, their size and number of openings, the Yang Ling south gate is the earliest one found, the most grand and complete, and it provides vital information about Chinese architectural history. A pottery *weiqi* chessboard, the earliest of its kind, was also found in the south gate area. It is exhibited in the main museum.

Most visitors to Yang Ling will want to spend the majority of their time looking at the pottery figures. Their sheer number is staggering, approximately 50,000. When excavation work began on 24 pits to the south of the road containing the emperor's army, thousands of pottery warriors were revealed. Their bodies are approximately one-third life-size, without arms and naked. Their arms and hands were originally made of wood, with movable joints, but these, together with the leather armour they once wore, have long since decayed. There are, however, traces of red silk present on some of them. There are patches of bright vermillion around the heads of some, with traces of woven silk fabric, apparently the remains of a kind of headband worn during this period. Similar traces around the shins show that some wore red silk leggings. Among the warriors, there is realistic modeling suggestion motion such as moving and walking; in other words, the pieces are not in static poses. Some eunuch figures have also been found, providing the earliest known evidence of this practice.

All the figures were painted and many still retain at least their original basic ochre colouring representing the skin. Features such as hair, eyebrows, moustache, and pupils were painted in black. Archaeologists have concluded that the nude figures, which were originally clothed, were meant as burial objects for the royal family alone and are found in pits accompanying the emperor's tomb. It is thought that the practice of robing burial figures in textiles, which is characteristic of Chu tombs, shows the influence of that culture, whereas the figures with sculpted clothes are similar to the figures in Qin Shihuangdi's tomb.

For government ministers and members of the nobility, figures with clothes molded from clay were suitable. The figures include soldiers, male and female archers mounted on horseback, servants, both standing and kneeling, musicians and dancers. The latter, in particular, display a superb grace with lithe bodies and flowing, long sleeved dresses. Some servant figurines have been unearthed in almost perfect condition. These, like the dancers, wear molded clothes, in this case with white painted robes and yellow belts.

The excavated domesticated animals include horses, cows, pigs (some of which are clearly pregnant), sheep, goats, dogs and chickens. The horses have a slot along the back of the neck where a mane was once fixed and a hole for a tail, but these have

(Left and above) *Heads of the figurines excavated at Yang Ling exhibit facial characteristics of at least ten different ethnic variations. Many retain much of their original paintwork including the skin colour and black-painted hair, pupils and moustaches.*

decayed, perhaps because they were originally made from real horse's hair. It would appear that each pit represents a division or department of the emperor's palace. In fact, some of the pits have revealed rooms complete with servants and everyday utensils. The inclusion of domestic animals is of particular interest to archaeologists as this is the first time such a quantity and variety has been discovered. The sheer number of them and the high level of pottery modeling are unique to Yang Ling. Following the unification and standardisation of the Qin dynasty, the Chinese under the Han emperors experienced a relatively stable and prosperous period with the rapid development of agriculture.

It has been estimated that around 17, 000 workers, living in a city to the east of of Yang Ling, took 28 years to complete work on the main tombs and their associated pits.

This site is highly recommended. And with its convenient location beside the airport road, Yang Ling can easily be included on any itinerary. If time permits, try to see the three most important features of the site—the main museum building and its terracotta figures, the stone compass and the south gate. If time is tight, be sure to see the terracotta figures.

(Above) *Traces of silk fabric clearly visible on the head of this figurine from Yang Ling indicate it once wore some form of headdress. The vermillion patches are the remains of a kind of headband worn during this period.*

(Preceding pages) *The naked figures from Yang Ling, the mausoleum of Jingdi, the fourth emperor of the Han dynasty. The remains of iron swords lie beside some of them, but their once movable wooden arms and real clothes have long since decayed.*

(Right) *A Tang dynasty tri-colour, glazed pottery figurine displaying a 'wild bird' coiffure, with a central roll of hair hanging low over the brow. Height 43cm. Excavated in Xi'an, 1959.*

Period Four: The Tang Dynasty

Background
The collapse of the Han dynasty in 220 CE, after years of insoluble economic and political problems, was followed by centuries of power struggles, barbarian invasions and political fragmentation, with interludes of unity and order. In 581 CE a high ranking official, Yang Qian, seized the throne and founded the Sui dynasty.

The Sui and the Capital City of Daxingcheng
The old Han city of Chang'an was by then too derelict to serve as the symbol of power for the first Sui emperor, who reigned with the title of Wendi. He commissioned a brilliant engineer, Yuwen Kai, to build a new city—Daxingcheng, or the City of Great Revival—southeast of the old one.

Yang Qian and Yuwen Kai created perhaps one of the greatest planned cities. The huge rectangular area designated for the metropolis faced the four cardinal points and had an outer wall with a perimeter of over 36 kilometres (22 miles).

The Sui dynasty was, however, short lived. Wendi was succeeded by his even more ambitious son, the emperor Sui Yangdi. He, in turn, ordered the construction of a new capital at **Luoyang**, as well as a huge programme of canal building (the Grand Canal, the world's largest man-made waterway running from Luoyang to Hangzhou, was his most monumental legacy to China).

He also attempted a disastrous invasion of Korea. Rebellions followed and the emperor was assassinated in Yangzhou in 618 CE.

The Establishment of the Tang Dynasty
Power was next seized by the Li family. Li Yuan, hereditary Duke of Tang, marched on Daxingcheng in 617 CE and the following year made himself emperor with the title of Tang Gaozu. The capital was renamed Chang'an, a deliberate move to assume by implication the mantle of the Han. In turn, Tang Gaozu was ousted by his second son, Li Shimin, who took the throne himself with the title of Tang Taizong, and effectively consolidated the Tang.

The Tang dynasty (618–907 CE) is widely considered to be a Golden Age, the stage in history when Chinese civilization reached its most glorious and sophisticated era. Under one of its greatest emperors, Taizong (reigned 627–649 CE), military conquests extended Chinese domination as far as the Pamirs. A brilliant civilization that found expression in poetry, painting, dance, music and crafts flourished in a rich

(Right) As the eastern terminus of the Silk Road, Chang'an played host to thousands of foreign travellers. Foreign influence can be seen in some of the fashions shown on pottery figures such as the one opposite, who is dressed in Central Asian style. Excavated from tomb of Yang Jianchen in Bianfang Village, Xianyang, 1952.

and powerful empire. Contributing to this intellectual and artistic ferment were the ideas and customs of travellers from other lands, notably Persia, India and Central Asia, who flocked to work or trade or spread their faiths in the imperial capital Chang'an (on the site of the modern city of Xi'an)— again the centre and symbol of glory, the world's largest and most splendid city. Only the Baghdad of Harun al Rashid offered any comparison. During this period, the city wall of Chang'an stretched far beyond the one standing today, which was built during the later Ming period, and went as far as the Big Goose Pagoda. By the middle of the eighth century China had a population estimated at 53 million, of which nearly two million lived in the capital.

Chang'an's affluence and luxury, and the opportunities these created for leisure, were conducive to the development of a refined and sophisticated way of living. Women were not excluded from this civilized lifestyle—indeed they acquired in Tang society an equality and status unprecedented in the history of China up to that time. Those of the upper classes, in particular, and wives and daughters of wealthy merchants, were able to take an active part in social life, to walk freely in the streets and to flaunt their femininity. They also pursued such traditionally male activities as riding and playing polo. A fad developed during the middle years of the dynasty when

women, led by ladies of the court, took to wearing men's clothes. Princess Taiping, younger sister of the Emperor Gaozong, danced for her brother in a man's purple gown, belt and scarf.

EMPRESS WU

Taizong died in 649 CE and was succeeded by his ninth son, who reigned with the title of Gaozong until 683. However, the next effective ruler was a woman, not a man. Wu Zetian (see page 170) was born in 624 CE and became a concubine of Taizong. On his death she withdrew from court and became a Buddhist nun, only to be recalled by Gaozong, eventually becoming his empress in 655 CE.

(Above) *The 'just fallen off a horse look' hairstyle, popularized by the imperial concubine Yang Guifei, on a painted pottery model of a woman with a fashionably plump figure.*
(Right) *Another example of a figurine displaying a brightly-coloured dress with a high waistline.*

Empress Wu

The Golden Age of the Tang dynasty was ushered in not by an emperor but by an ex-concubine, who became the only woman sovereign in Chinese history. Wu Zhou's remarkable career began in 638 CE when she entered the palace, aged 13, as junior concubine to Emperor Taizong. On his death 11 years later she was relegated to a Buddhist nunnery, as custom dictated, but by then—so it is traditionally alleged—she had already become the mistress of his son, Gaozong. She returned to court as Gaozong's favourite concubine, set about arranging the murder of the empress and other female rivals, and within a few years gained the rank of imperial consort for herself. Her ascendancy was not achieved without the ruthless dispatch of many opponents—ministers who had enjoyed the emperor's trust, members of the imperial family, and all those courtiers who claimed that her friendship with Gaozong was incestuous.

For much of Gaozong's long reign (649–83 CE) real power was in the hands of Empress Wu. She fully exploited his weakness and her own skill for intrigue. Purges of rivals—who were murdered or exiled—kept her position secure, but historians agree that it could not have been sustained had she not possessed great intelligence and a genius for administration. Although she was whimsical, superstitious and highly susceptible to the flattery of any sorcerer and monk who could win her favour, she remained for most of her rule consistently adept at picking competent statesmen and military leaders to carry out her policies. The conquest of Korea and defeat of the Turks were accomplished during her time. The imperial examination system—by which government officials were chosen regardless of social standing—was promoted, so that in time political power was transferred from the aristocracy to a scholar-bureaucracy. She was, as one historian put it, 'not sparing in the bestowal of titles and ranks, because she wished to cage the bold and enterprising spirits of all regions... but those who proved unfit for their responsibilities were forthwith, in large numbers, cashiered or executed. Her broad aim was to select men of real talent and true virtue.' During her years in power the stability of the empire laid the foundation for the prosperity and cultural achievements that followed and culminated in the High Tang.

Empress Wu bore Gaozong four sons and one daughter. Their second son was named heir-apparent in 675 CE but Empress Wu, suspecting him of an attempted coup, banished the prince to Sichuan. It was there that he was subsequently made to take his own life, on his mother's orders. When the emperor died, another of Empress Wu's sons was enthroned. He proved to be as ineffectual as his father, and was speedily deposed and exiled as well. The reign of the next crown prince was equally short. In 690 CE, Empress Wu dispensed with puppet emperors altogether by proclaiming a new dynasty—Zhou—and usurping the throne.

While Wu Zetian continued to govern effectively, the last decade of her reign was overshadowed by several more savage murders. By now in her 70s, the old empress was becoming increasingly dependent on two corrupt courtiers, the Zhang brothers. Their malevolent presence was intensely loathed by the rest of the court, and it was insinuations against her favourites that impelled Wu Zetian to order the execution of her granddaughter, her step-grandson and another Wu relative on a charge of disloyalty. The Zhang brothers were finally killed in a palace coup in 705 CE, which forced the empress to abdicate in favour of her exiled son and restore the Tang. She died less than a year later.

White jade bracelets mounted with gold.
Unearthed from Hejia village, Xi'an, 1970.

A pottery figurine displaying a spectacular example of both dress and hairstyle.

After Gaozong's death Wu Zetian dethroned two of her sons and her official reign began in 690 CE. Although Empress Wu's rule was characterized by recurrent palace intrigues and ruthless political murders, China prospered greatly during this time. For economic as well as political reasons she preferred Luoyang to Chang'an and chose this as her capital from 683 to 701 CE. Just before her death in 705 CE, when she was in her 80s, she was finally removed from power, and the Tang re-established. Empress Wu Zetian was the only female sovereign in Chinese history.

EMPEROR TANG XUANZONG

The period of struggle over the Tang succession was ended by the emergence of the third great ruler of the dynasty, Emperor Xuanzong, Empress Wu's grand-son. Popularly known as Ming Huang, the Enlightened Emperor, his reign corresponds with what is called the High Tang, the apogee of the Tang dynasty, that most confident and cosmopolitan of all phases of Chinese civilization.

The emperor presided over a brilliant, extravagant court, patronizing the greatest concentration of literary and artistic genius in Chinese history. Xuanzong's contemporaries included the paramount poets of China, Du Fu (712–770 CE) and Li Bai (699–762 CE), and the great painter Wu Daozi (700–760 CE). After the death of his beloved

Imperial Concubine Yang Guifei (see page 196), Xuanzong died a broken man in 762 CE, having earlier abdicated in favour of his third son.

STYLES OF DRESS FOR TANG WOMEN

The more conventional style of dress for Tang women was based on a bodice or top and ankle-length skirt. Inevitably fashion dictated the refinements and details added to this basic style—the tops would either be tight-fitting or loose, hemlines rose and dropped, and the fabrics used were more or less luxurious, depending on the economic circumstances of the wearer. Nevertheless, three broad trends can be discerned over the period. First there was the style inherited from the previous Sui dynasty (581–618 CE), which consisted of short, close-fitting bodices and long skirts, generally in dark colours. Later, clothes modelled on foreign costumes were the rage, and by then more ornamentation, as well as bold and exotic colours, had become popular. In the third phase a more voluptuous, indeed plump, figure came into vogue, and brightly-coloured but loose-fitting garments with high waistlines and full sleeves were preferred. The favourite ornaments then were hairpins.

Women in Tang society enjoyed experimenting with ways to enhance their appearance and charms. As time went on the cut of their dresses also became less staid than those of the previous age. Tight, high-collared tops were abandoned in favour of garments with wider collars and even décolleté necklines, inspiring many an erotic reference to the barely covered snow-white breasts in the poems of the day. The trend towards greater exposure could also be observed in hats and veils, originally worn for modesty's sake, which gradually gave way to headgear that showed more and more of the wearer's face.

Descriptions in historical records of garments which belonged to a princess included silk brocade skirts embroidered with motifs of birds and flowers, shimmering with gold thread and coloured feathers. Another fine imperial outfit is a woollen skirt with gold embroidery, thought to have belonged to Empress Wu, which was discovered in the crypt of Famen Temple near Xi'an.

TANG HAIRSTYLES

It was customary to bury earthenware models of servants, horses, buildings and other objects in tombs, to accompany the deceased in their after-life. The most striking feature of the pottery figurines of women is undoubtedly their extraordinary hairstyles.

Examples of silver chai—*double-pronged hairpins decorated with bird and peony designs.*

The back of a gilt bronze mirror, inlaid with images of four phoenixes trailing ribbons, a design symbolising eternal love. Diameter 22.7cm.

People of ancient China believed that some part of the essence and life force of a human being was contained in the hair. Women traditionally grew their hair long and in the Tang dynasty they wore it in a multitude of different styles, most of them involving plaiting or coiling and piling up the tresses in towering edifices on top of the head. These elaborate coiffures were given delightful names, such as 'resembling clouds' (*yunji*), 'resembling a spiralling shell' (*luoji*), 'resembling the wings of a butterfly' (*hudie ji*), a high chignon, with thick bunches forward of the ears (*paojia ji*) and so on.

To hold up long coils of hair, pins could be a single pin with a decorative top (*zan*); a double-pronged pin with a decorative top (*chai*); or a double-pronged pin with a decorative top from which beads dangled (*buyao*). Like jewellery, hairpins made of precious metals and decorated with gems proclaimed the wealth of the wearer, like *The Salt Merchant's Wife* in the poem by Bai Juyi (772–846 CE):

> *Growing rich, many gold hair-pins adorn her glossy hair;*
> *Growing plump, the silver bracelet on her arm is tight.*

Tang women also tucked combs in their hair to hold it in place. Combs, too, were often made of gold and silver, as well as jade, horn and shell.

Hair as a beauty feature is celebrated in famous poems, such as *Song of Eternal Sorrow* also by Bai Juyi, which tells the story of Yang Guifei, an imperial concubine (see page 196). Reputed to be of outstanding beauty, Yang was one of several femmes fatales in Chinese history who were held responsible by later generations for the downfall of dynasties. It is said that the Tang emperor Xuanzong, smitten by Yang Guifei, put aside his duties of government to spend time with her.

He had his first sight of her as she emerged from her bath:

> *Her hair like a cloud,*
> *Her face like a flower,*
> *A gold hair-pin adorning her tresses.*
> *Behind the warm lotus-flower curtain,*
> *They took their pleasure in the spring night...*

(Right) *Painted pottery figure of a woman holding a mirror.*

Yang was allegedly the author of the coiffure known as the 'just fallen off a horse look'—a style she inadvertently created when, after taking a tumble when out riding, the high arrangement of her cloudy tresses came loose on one side. If anything, the delightfully dishevelled state of her hairdo made her look even more beautiful, so it was not surprising that the other palace ladies rushed to copy her.

A plum blossom in gold leaf, once used as a forehead decoration. It would have been stuck to the centre of the brow with glue.

Such interest in personal adornment was not admired by all, however. A high-ranking government official made so bold as to criticize these elaborate coiffures, describing them as too impractical for ordinary women, and urging the palace ladies to set a less frivolous example. Emperor Taizong angrily riposted: 'Are women in the palace expected to be like bald monks?'

COSMETICS AND MAKE-UP

From very early times women had used cosmetics to supply what nature did not endow. Besides dressing their hair in intricate coiffures and wearing hairpins and jewellery, women in the Tang dynasty had recourse to several types of make-up. They used face powder, of which there were two kinds—rice powder and white lead powder. The latter became more popular and eventually displaced rice powder as a cosmetic. White lead powder was used with rouge, which is thought to have originated from the Xiongnu tribal lands in the northwest. There, in the Yanzhi mountains, thrived a plant from which yellow and red pigments were extracted. The red was used as a dye to produce rouge; this was mixed with a little water before application.

There are many references in Chinese literature to beautiful women's 'moth eyebrows'. Clearly eyebrows were also considered a feature of beauty and much plucking and painting went on to enhance their attractiveness. Emperor Han Wudi

Cloud-shaped silver box embossed with a design of honeysuckle and parrots.

*Jade powder compact,
with carved mandarin ducks and lotus motif.*

(reigned 140–86 BCE) liked his concubines to have eyebrows rising to meet at the centre of the forehead, a fashion dubbed *ba-zimei*, after the Chinese character for eight (八). In the Three Kingdoms period (220–265 CE), when powerful regional warlords clashed to gain control of China, one of the contenders, Cao Cao, had a preference for long dark eyebrows on his women. Emperor Yangdi of the Sui, the short-lived dynasty that preceded the Tang, acquired large supplies of a substance from Persia that was used to draw eyebrows for his wife and concubines. The infatuated Xuanzong, during a period of exile from the capital while a rebellion raged in the north of the empire, had an artist draw for him a picture of ten eyebrow styles, no doubt to recall 'she with the moth-like eyebrows'—Yang Guifei, who had been killed by his mutinous troops on the journey into exile.

Cosmetics were applied to other parts of the face. Coloured foreheads were considered extremely chic at one time. Buddha statues were conventionally made with golden foreheads, and this inspired a fashion of decorating the skin above the eyebrows, either by painting it yellow or by sticking on a yellow patch cut out in the shape of a flower. A princess of the Southern dynasty is credited with originating this practice. It seems she was resting on a balcony in the Nanjing palace one day when a blossom from a nearby plum tree was blown onto her forehead. The outline of the petals remained there for three days, inspiring a host of imitators who resorted to other materials such as gold leaf, fish bones, mother-of-pearl and oyster shell, so that not only plum blossom patterns but outlines of birds and fish also began appearing over their brows.

Besides decorating their foreheads, Tang women also painted crescent-shaped red marks on their temples and, of course, applied colour to their lips. Indeed, lipsticks made a very early appearance in China, and the 'cherry mouth' was admired and celebrated in verse by Bai Juyi.

Silver box with flower and foliage design.

As in 18th-century Europe, imitation beauty spots were in vogue, but in China the appearance of the first one was said to have been the result of an accident. This happened during the Three Kingdoms period. A kinsman of the royal Wu clan, intoxicated after a heavy night of drinking, inadvertently struck his wife with a jade sceptre. A physician, summoned to treat her wound, concocted an ointment of otter bone marrow, ground jade and ground amber. This guaranteed that the wound would leave no scar, he assured the distraught husband. But the ointment contained a little too much amber, and this left the lady with a red spot where a dimple might be. Curiously, this made her more alluring, to the delight of the husband and the fury of his concubines.

By the Tang dynasty, much more deliberation was going into the preparation of beauty spots, which could be variously shaped (apricot-shaped and soya-bean-shaped ones were popular) and were chosen to match the clothes and hairstyles being worn. Generally the spots were made by dotting the cheek with rouge, but they could also be made of gold foil or kingfisher feather.

TANG WOMEN'S LOVE OF GOLD AND SILVER

All these methods of personal adornment led, inevitably, to a proliferation of paraphernalia for the dressing table, such as bronze mirrors, gold and silver receptacles for cosmetics, powder boxes and containers for potpourri.

Gold and silver have always had an allure for women, not just in the Tang. Objects made in these precious metals were generally the most prestigious and acceptable gifts from a father, husband or master. It was during the Tang, however, that metalworking skills attained the level of art. From the gold and silver relics of the period, it is clear that the artist-craftsmen were beginning to place as much emphasis on aesthetics as on function. Boxes for cosmetics, pieces of jewellery, and even everyday articles for the house were all made with the aim of creating shapes and styles that were not only useful but also attractive.

Decorative techniques included embossing, engraving, filigree and openwork. The designs reveal many influences; the bird and foliage motif, for example, was adopted by Chinese craftsmen from the Middle East. Auspicious feminine symbols, notably grapes and phoenixes (representing fertility and love respectively), embellished articles used by women such as mirrors. Mirrors made during the Tang show that the composition of bronze at the time was 70% copper, 25% tin and 5% lead. One side of the mirror was highly polished to provide a reflective surface; the reverse was usually decorated.

(Left) *Painted pottery figurine with plump figure showing one of the many elaborate hairstyles fashionable during the period.*

METALWORK TECHNIQUES

Xi'an in Shaanxi has a rich heritage of metal relics from the Tang dynasty, when it was the site of the imperial capital, Chang'an. Two of the three largest caches of Tang gold and silver treasures ever unearthed were found in the province: the first in 1970 at Hejia village, and the second beneath the Famen Temple in Fufeng County, which was discovered in 1987. (The third was excavated in 1982 at Dingmaoqiao, Dantu, in Jiangsu province.)

Sea beast and grapes motif on a bronze mirror.

The first gold articles in China were made during the Shang dynasty (16th–11th centuries BCE). By the Tang dynasty some 17 centuries later, metalworking had developed into a sophisticated craft. Both the prosperity of the age and the rise in gold production contributed to this development. The techniques used had their origins in the bronzeware manufacture of the Western and Eastern Han dynasties (206 BCE–8 CE and 25–220 CE). Later the popularity of bronze declined, although the material continued to be used in the manufacture of mirrors.

Gold and silver wares in the Tang were usually cast rather than turned and beaten, and their surfaces were chased or inlaid with mother of pearl or precious stones. Openwork was another technique, most appealingly employed in the manufacture of ball-shaped censers (*xiangnang*), two of which were discovered in the Famen Temple. Each censer consists of a hollow ball on a chain, with a bowl suspended on a circular axis inside. No matter how the censer was swung, the interior bowl would not spill its aromatic herbs or burning incense. To create one, the gold- or silversmith would have beaten his metal into a ball around 4.5 centimetres in diameter before hollowing it out. The material was then pierced to create the openwork decoration, which often depicted grapes or birds in flight.

Mirror back, with a motif known as 'palace of the moon'. The moon, phoenix and grapes, with their traditional feminine associations, were symbols of love and fertility.

Gilded silver incense burner (xiangnang) decorated with birds in flight and grapes. Diameter 4.5cm.

Not surprisingly, gold and silver articles were possessed only by the richest echelons of Tang society—the imperial family, the nobility, and well-patronised temples. A woman of refinement or one from a wealthy family could afford to be fastidious. She would order her ladies in waiting to carry censers, to scent a room or space she occupied. Censers were also hung on chariots and sedans and used at burials. Emperor Xuanzong, returning from exile in Sichuan, had the body of his beloved Yang Guifei exhumed so that she could be re-buried in a more appropriate grave. Her corpse and clothing had already begun to decay, but the heavy scent from numerous *xiangnang* masked the unpleasant smell. Princess Tongqiang, Yizong's daughter, hung censers burning imported incense from the four corners of her sedan chair. Some noblewomen put Buddhist sutras in their *xiangnang* to ward off evil.

The malleability of gold means that one gramme of pure gold can be stretched into filigree 0.00434 millimetres in diameter and 3,500 metres in length. A magnificent example of the goldsmith's elaborate workmanship is shown by the flowers-and-clouds decoration on the gold cup illustrated (see photograph below).

DESIGNS

Many of the gold and silver objects from the Tang show a foreign influence in their design, decoration and method of manufacture, an influence that was spread to China by merchants from west and Central Asia via the Silk Road.

The strongest design influence on early and mid-Tang gold and silverware came from Sute in Central Asia. The octagonal silver cup decorated with flowers and birds (see photograph on page 185) exhibits a Sute shape and ornamentation.

Gold cup decorated with flowers and clouds. Height 5.9cm, diameter 6.8cm. Excavated from Hejia village, Xi'an, 1970.

Gradually gold and silverware began to acquire Chinese characteristics. For a time hybrid wares were produced. The silver goblet with a hunting design has a shape that bears Byzantine traces, but its decoration is Chinese. An octagonal, petal-shaped silver cup depicting women and hunting combines foreign and Chinese features. Each petal depicts a scene, four showing men and four of women. The men are on horseback, poised to shoot their arrows. In contrast, the women look relaxed as they groom themselves, comb their hair and play with babies. The inside of the cup is also decorated with a pattern of fish and aquatic plants. When the cup is filled with water, it is supposed to resemble a pond.

A gold drinking vessel with *mojie* design (see photograph on page 184) is one example of a Chinese vessel with decoration showing Indian influence. In the centre of the inside base of the cup is the *mojie*, a mythical creature with a long nose, sharp

Silver goblet with a hunting design. Height 7cm, diameter 5.9cm.
Excavated from Hejia village, Xi'an, 1970.

teeth, and a fish's body and tail, which was respected as the spirit of rivers and the root of all life. It was featured in sutras brought to China during the Eastern Jin dynasty (317–420 CE). From then on, many *mojie* designs were used on gold and silver objects.

Octagonal, petal-shaped gilded silver cup depicting women and hunting. Height 5.1cm, diameter 9.1cm. Excavated from Hejia village, Xi'an, 1970.

The gold bowl patterned with lotus petals is an example of fretwork where two layers of the metal beaten into the shape of lotus petals form the main ornamental feature. The top layer of petals is adorned with animal motifs: rabbit, river deer, parrot and mandarin duck. The second layer is decorated with the outlines of honeysuckle, while the inside of the bowl is etched with thousands of little fish, which symbolize children and happiness. In another example featuring the lotus, the overlapping leaves on the gilded silver bowl look most realistic because of the thinness of the metal.

RELICS FROM THE TANG PALACE

Articles and ornaments were manufactured in gold and silver for everyday use in the imperial palace and as ritual vessels in temples. Gold was even taken internally as an elixir by those in search of a long life.

The gold basin illustrated below is the only surviving example of its kind from the Tang dynasty. Others were doubtless stolen from tombs, melted down and reworked. This basin was hammered into shape by hand, then polished, probably with the aid of some kind of rudimentary tool, to produce its fine surface sheen. The poet Wang Jian (c. 767–830), in *Palace*, gives a hint as to its use:

The emperor arrived and all the maids
Washed their faces and put on make-up.

Gold basins also had ceremonial uses. Whether it was the empress or an imperial concubine who gave birth, the arrival of a baby was a happy event. When the child was three days old, a ceremonial washing in a gold basin was held.

Gold basin. Height 6.5cm, diameter 28.6cm. Excavated from Hejia village, Xi'an, 1970.

Emperors often gave gifts in gold and silver to courtiers, ministers, local officials and concubines as tokens of favour. At the winter solstice, the emperor would grant silver cosmetic boxes to his maids. The exquisitely-made silver box (see photograph on page 185) was probably a gift from an emperor.

The Tang palace was normally home to over 3,000 beautiful women, but the emperor never noticed more than a lucky few. Vying for the emperor's favour, his concubines would throw gold coins to see whose turn it was to please him. Under the Emperor Xuanzong, gold coins known as *Kaiyuan* (the name denoting his reign) were used for this game. They bore the characters *kai yuan yong bao*, and were modelled on copper coins, the legal tender of the time.

Despite all the attention, however, Xuanzong's best-loved concubine remained Yang Guifei. After her arrival at the palace, the coin-tossing game stopped.

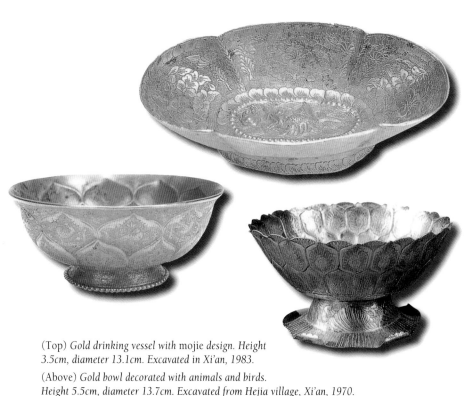

(Top) *Gold drinking vessel with* mojie *design. Height 3.5cm, diameter 13.1cm. Excavated in Xi'an, 1983.*

(Above) *Gold bowl decorated with animals and birds. Height 5.5cm, diameter 13.7cm. Excavated from Hejia village, Xi'an, 1970.*

(Above right) *Gilded silver bowl with overlapping lotus leaf pattern. Height 8cm, diameter 16cm. Excavated from the crypt of Famen Temple, Fufeng, 1987.*

Octagonal silver cup decorated with flowers and birds. Height 6.1cm, diameter 6.8cm. Excavated in Xi'an, 1982.

Gold and silver coins were also issued to celebrate the birth of babies to imperial concubines. One of the most bizarre of such coin issues was to mark the adoption of An Lushan by Yang Guifei. General An, only 15 years younger than Yang, was rumoured to be her lover rather than her adopted son.

Silver plates were made in several different shapes. The plate with a turtle design at its centre is in the shape of a peach (see photograph on page 186). The fruit is said to have originated in China. Peach stones dating back to the late Shang dynasty, at least 3,000 years old, have been excavated at Taixi in Gaocheng county, Hebei province.

There were several kinds of peach, the most popular being the peach of immortality which grew in the garden of Xiwangmu, the Queen Mother of the West. People believed that by eating the fruit they could shake off fatigue, while Taoists regarded the peach as a symbol of longevity. Another auspicious symbol of

Silver box decorated with interwoven flowers. Excavated from Hejia village, Xi'an, 1970.

Gold Kaiyuan coin.
Diameter 2.3cm. Excavated
from Hejia village, Xi'an, 1970.

longevity is the turtle. Legend has it that a Taoist presented a small gold turtle to Xuanzong and told him that by keeping the talisman he could enjoy a long life without encountering evil or disaster.

The silver plate with the gilded turtle is one of five such plates excavated in Hejia village. The other four are equally distinctive: there is one in the shape of two peaches decorated with a pair of foxes; another shows a flying ox (see photograph on page 187); the third is a round plate adorned with a pattern of rocks and flowers; and the fourth, a diamond-shaped plate, carries a design of phoenixes. All silver plates typify Chinese design and decoration.

Other favourite motifs included mandarin ducks and climbing plants, which stand out in the all-over decoration (*man di zhuang*) of the gold ewer and cover (see photograph on page 149).

The rarity, lustre and beauty of gold and silver were much prized by Tang rulers. The durability of these precious metals has meant that the wealth of ornaments they commissioned for their empresses and concubines as well as the articles for use in the palace still bear testimony to a glorious culture that continues to astonish and fascinate.

CHANG'AN IN THE EIGHTH CENTURY

Chang'an was a lively, crowded, and beautiful city in the eighth century. Appropriate, as the planned capital of a well-ordered society, it was also highly organized. In the centre was the Imperial City with the Imperial Secretariat, the Imperial Chancellery, the Censorate and the Department of State Affairs under which came the six Boards of Personnel, Revenue, Rites, War, Justice and Public Works. This organization of government lasted, in this form at least, for the next thousand years.

The central north-south avenue, with the delightful name of 'The Street of the Vermillion Bird', divided the Outer City into two districts: the area of the aristocrats to the east, and the rather

Gilded silver plate decorated with a turtle.
Diameter 12.3cm. Excavated from Hejia village, Xi'an, 1970.

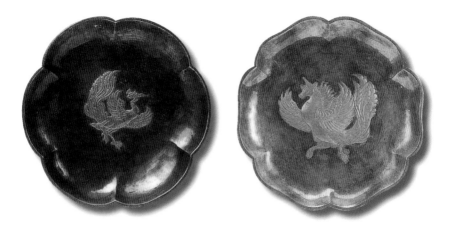

Gilded silver plates decorated with a phoenix (left) and flying ox (right). Diameter 15.3cm.
Both excavated from Hejia village, Xi'an, 1970.

more populated section of the merchants and lower classes to the west. The two
markets that served them were very large and extremely well run. We know that the
shops and workshops of the East Market were divided into 220 trades, each one with
its own exclusive area and bazaar.

Much of the colour in Chang'an was provided by the 'Westerners'—merchants
from Central Asia and Arabia, and particularly travellers from Persia. Central Asian
fashions dominated the capital. Women dressed in the Persian style and wore exotic
Western jewellery. Men played polo. The Buddhist temples and monasteries vied
with each other in offering unusual religious entertainment.

Foreigners congregated in the West Market, which was always full of excitement
and activity. Here were bazaars and artisans' workshops, merchants' houses and
hostelries, taverns and entertainment places, including wine shops where the songs
and dances of Central Asia were performed. There were Persian bazaars; shops of the
unpopular Uighur moneylenders; and markets selling precious jewels and pearls,
spices, medicinal herbs, silk, and a whole range of everyday items, including the
newly fashionable beverage, tea. This was where criminals were punished and where
courtesans could be found. Many of these ladies were from the lands bordering Persia
and some were reputedly even blonde and blue-eyed.

FOREIGN RELIGIONS IN CHANG'AN
For much of the Tang the authorities allowed the foreign communities freedom of
religion. Zoroastrianism, Manichaeism, Nestorianism and finally Islam all followed
Buddhism (see page 209) to Chang'an.

Top section of Xi'an's Nestorian Stele, dated 781 CE. The nine Chinese characters declare: 'Stele for the propagation of the Luminous Religion of Da Qin in the Middle Kingdom'. Above the text the Nestorian Cross of Resurrection is engraved standing between clouds and branches on a lotus flower. While the lotus symbolises purity of mind in Buddhism, and the clouds are associated with Taoism, the arrangement with the Cross in the centre implies that the fulfilment of Chinese religiosity is to be found in Nestorian Christianity.

If you are interested in tracing the development of these religions, Xi'an's Forest of Steles Museum (see page 237) provides some intriguing evidence. Here you can see a tomb stone, dated 874 CE, inscribed in Chinese and Persian Pahlavi script, originally marking the grave of Ma, wife of Suren, a Zoroastrian. Also at the museum is the celebrated Nestorian Stele.

Inscriptions on this stone, in Chinese and Syriac, recorded the establishment of Chang'an's second Nestorian Christian chapel in 781. Even the Manicheans, who believed in a combination of Gnostic Christianity and Zoroastrianism, had a place of worship in Chang'an in the eighth century.

THE INFLUENCE OF CHANG'AN

If Chang'an itself was cosmo-politan, it also had unparalleled influence throughout Central and Eastern Asia. The royal progeny of several Korean and Central Asian states as well as Tibet were educated in the schools and monasteries of the Tang capital. But by far the greatest transfer of Tang culture was to Japan. From the mid-seventh century to the end of the ninth century a whole series of official missions were sent by sea to China. The Japanese cities of Nara and Kyoto were built on the same plan as Chang'an, though naturally smaller. The grid layout of Kyoto still remains today, and the best examples of Tang wooden architecture also survive in Japan rather than in China.

THE DESTRUCTION OF CHANG'AN

In the ninth century the importance of Chang'an waned, with the Tang dynasty itself coming under pressure as factions jostled for power. Twice Chang'an was sacked by peasant rebels and troops of the imperial forces. In 904 CE the Tang court was moved to Luoyang. The main surviving buildings were dismantled and the beams were taken to the Wei River where they were lashed together to form rafts which were floated down to the new capital. From 904–906 CE the city walls were demolished and a new, more modest wall was built around the old Imperial City. In 907 CE the last Tang emperor was finally deposed and Chang'an was renamed Da'anfu.

HUAQING HOT SPRINGS

Huaqing Hot Springs has been a favourite spa since the Tang dynasty. For centuries emperors had come here to bathe and enjoy the scenic beauty. The more energetic visitors may climb some or all of Li Mountain, on which are situated several Taoist and Buddhist temples. A cable car has now been installed to make this possible for everyone. None of the buildings in the grounds are particularly important. Although many of them are named after Tang halls and pavilions, they were built either at the end of the last century or during this one.

Huaqing Hot Springs can be conveniently visited on returning from the Terracotta Army site. A principal pleasure spot for Chinese tourists, the place is often busy, especially on Sundays.

The resort dates back to the Western Zhou when construction began on a series of pleasure resort palaces at the hot springs site, which is 30 kilometres (18 miles) from Xi'an, at the foot of Black Horse Mountain. The First Emperor of Qin had a residence there, as did Han Wudi, the Martial Emperor. In more recent times even Chiang Kai-shek used some of the buildings. However, the strongest associations are with the Tang: Black Horse Mountain is still covered with the pine and cypress trees planted by Tang Xuanzong, and the present buildings have a Tang atmosphere.

Taizong commissioned his architect Yan Lide to design a palace, the Tangquan, in 644 CE. It became the favourite resort of Xuanzong who spent every winter there from 745 to 755 CE in the company of Yang Guifei, the Imperial Concubine (see page 196). The resort was greatly enlarged in 747 CE and renamed Huaqing Palace. The complex was destroyed at the end of the Tang.

However, imperial bathing pools from this period (618–907 CE), lost

Huaqing Hot Springs Park.

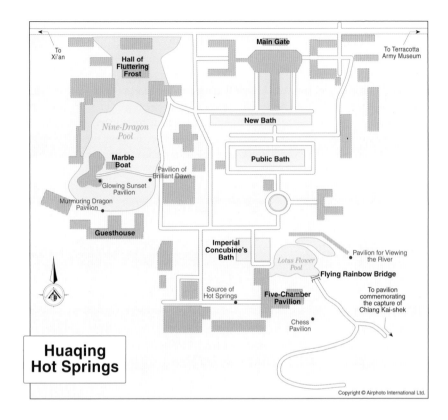

for almost a millennium, were discovered in 1982 by workmen renovating the Guifei Pavilion. They uncovered remains of palace architecture, including lotus-shaped roof tile-ends and four bathing pools—the Star, Long, Lotus and Guifei pools.

The Guifei or Hibiscus Pool, dating from 712–756 CE, has now been restored and is open to the public—but for viewing, not for bathing. It is a terraced structure with a central, empty, pool in the shape of a Chinese crab-apple blossom. The fountainhead, designed to represent the stamens of a flower, is a reproduction of the original.

THE BATHS

The best way to appreciate the Huaqing Hot Springs is, of course, to take a bath. The water maintains a constant temperature of 43°C (109°F) and contains various minerals, including lime and manganese carbonate.

The baths are exotically named. The Lotus, the Crab Apple and the Emperor's Nine Dragon Bath, for example, can be hired by the hour. Communal baths are a bargain if one does not mind mingling with 49 other bathers of the same sex. There are hot spring baths available at the Huaqing Guesthouse (see page 316) but they are reserved for guests.

THE SITE OF THE XI'AN INCIDENT

The Five Chamber Building, just behind the Imperial Concubine's Bath, contains the bedroom used by Chiang Kai-shek on the eve of the Xi'an Incident of 1936—also known as the Double Twelfth Incident as it happened on 12th December (see page 192). As the rebellious troops of Zhang Xueliang showered the pavilion with gunfire, Chiang escaped through a window and over the back wall. The broken panes of the windows can still be seen. Chiang was captured hours later on Li Mountain. His hiding place is now marked by an iron chain. The pavilion commemorating his capture was originally erected by the Nationalists to celebrate their leader's escape.

QIAN LING—THE IMPERIAL TOMBS OF THE TANG DYNASTY

From the tomb of the Emperor Xuanzong in the east to the tomb of Gaozong and Empress Wu in the west, the 18 Tang tombs are spread out in a line 120 kilometres (75 miles) long. Most of them are set into natural hills and mountains, rather than underneath artificial mounds. Each tomb was originally surrounded by a square wall and had a series of buildings for ceremonial purposes and for the use of guards. Each had its own 'Spirit Way', an avenue lined with stone sculptures. The Tang conception was much grander than that of the Ming, as all 13 of the well-known Ming Tombs in Beijing share one 'Spirit Way'.

The underground palaces of the Tang emperors remain untouched. Only the important subsidiary tombs of Zhao Ling and Qian Ling have been excavated. Of all the imperial tomb complexes near Xi'an, Qian Ling is probably the best preserved and the most complete. It is the mausoleum of Emperor Gaozong and Empress Wu Zetian (see page 170) and is situated 85 kilometres (53 miles) west of Xi'an. It has never been robbed or excavated but there are interesting relics in its vicinity.

If you stand at the southern approach to the mausoleum you can appreciate the original Tang layout and design. This main southern approach is between two prominent small hills, surmounted by reconstructed towers. From a distance the hills are said to resemble a pair of woman's breasts, and the story goes that Emperor Tang Gaozong had them constructed to honour the natural beauty of his wife.

This grand and imposing avenue of animal and human statues leading all the way to the tombs is perhaps Qian Ling's most impressive feature, creating a memorable and awe-inspiring effect. Nowadays, visitors usually arrive via the car park part way along the route. It is well worth taking the time to stroll to the southern end of the Spirit Way to fully appreciate the grandiose nature of the project. Standing at the top of the flight of steps that disappears out of view below, one has a tremendous view over the countryside to the south—if the weather is clear.

The Xi'an Incident

Xi'an has always been known to the Chinese as a city rich with history, but it only gained recognition in much of the Western world in 1936 when Generalissimo Chiang Kai-shek was kidnapped there by some of his own generals.

The Xi'an Incident, as it became known, held the leadership of China hanging in the balance for a couple of tension-wracked weeks. An intriguing sequence of events brought on the kidnapping and its solution.

In 1936, while Hitler marched in Europe, the Japanese army was steadily tightening its grip on China. Chiang Kai-shek was not so much in control as simply being at the top of a fragile coalition of Chinese warlords and armies spread over China. The Communists had escaped Chiang's pursuit on the Long March and established themselves securely at Yan'an, in the mountains north of Xi'an.

Chiang knew that a head-on conflict with the Japanese army would, if not demolish him, at least weaken his position, and make him vulnerable to the communists. He decided to appease the Japanese instead, and send many of his troops to fight the Communists.

But for Zhang Xueliang, one of Chiang's allied generals, this policy of foot-dragging against the Japanese was unacceptable. A bright and courageous young general, Zhang was head of a Manchurian army and was incensed at the way his home in northeast China had been overrun by the Japanese since 1931. Zhang saw the situation deteriorating further in 1936, when the Japanese made a dramatic attack into Suiyan, a key area north of Beijing. On 4 December, a Nationalist attack on the Communists failed, resulting in a widespread refusal amongst Chiang's troops to continue fighting. Chiang flew to Xi'an to direct the campaign himself.

Zhang saw this as an ideal moment to make a move. He discreetly made contact with the Communists and at dawn on 12 December, his troops surrounded the palace at Huaqing Hot Springs, where Chiang was quartered. Hearing gunfire, Chiang escaped barefoot in his nightshirt—leaving his dentures behind—scaled a wall, injuring his back, and scurried up an old path on Black Horse Mountain. Thirty of his men were killed defending him.

Zhang's officers combed the area, and one of them found their Generalissimo later that afternoon, shivering and in pain, crouched in a crevice between the rocks. As the officer moved to bind Chiang's hands, the Generalissimo reminded his captor that he was the Commander-in-Chief. The officer is said to have bowed politely to Chiang and replied, 'You are also our prisoner.'

Two weeks of tough negotiations followed. Chiang and his formidable wife, Soong May-ling, were on one side, with Zhang and Zhou Enlai, later Communist China's premier, on the other, while the rest of China waited impatiently. Many of the Communist leaders wanted to execute Chiang, or at least keep him imprisoned. But a cable arrived from Moscow with an order from Stalin to release Chiang and get on with the task of fighting the Japanese.

The Chinese Communists bristled at being told by 'Uncle Joe' how to handle what they saw as their own affair. But they also knew they could win some useful concessions out of Chiang if they released him.

In the end, a compromise was reached. Chiang was allowed to fly back to Nanjing a free man, but had to give up the pretence of being the sole leader of China. Ostensibly he joined with the Communists in a 'National Front' against the Japanese. Zhang Xueliang, also went back to Nanjing as a prisoner of Chiang's and was branded a traitor.

The visitor to Huaqing Hot Springs can still see the site of this famous incident. The rooms where Chiang stayed and worked are marked, as is the spot up the hill where the Generalissimo was actually caught. The hiding place is marked by a chain and nearby, commemorating the capture, is a pavilion of dignified Grecian structure.

At the head of the avenue are two obelisk-like Cloud Pillars followed by a series of pairs of stone statues lining the 'Spirit Way' to the mausoleum. First there are two winged horses, then two ostrich-like vermillion birds. Five pairs of saddled horses come next, originally each had a groom but now two are missing. These are followed by ten pairs of tall, almost hieratic, guardians. They have very large heads, wear long sleeved robes, and hold the hilts of long swords that rest on the ground between their feet.

Beyond the guardians are two stone memorials; the one on the left (west) commemorates the reign of Emperor Gaozong and is balanced on the east side by the so called 'Blank Tablet' in honour of Empress Wu. The original implication was apparently that the old empress was beyond praise, but memorials were in fact inscribed on it during the Song and Jin dynasties (960–1234).

North of two small earthen remains—the ruins of two watch-towers—is a remarkable collection of 61 stone figures, now headless (see photograph page 198). From the inscriptions on the backs of these figures it appears that they represent actual foreigners who came to the Chinese court in the seventh century; some were envoys of Central Asian countries, others were barbarian chiefs. Behind them are two powerful sculptures of stone lions, guarding the southern entrance to the original inner enclosure, now no longer extant. There are similar pairs of animals at the north, east and west entrances. Just inside the old southern entrance is an 18th-century stele.

The Marble Boat and Nine Dragon Pool at Huaqing Hot Springs.

THE QIAN LING SATELLITE TOMBS

To the southeast of the principal mausoleum are 17 satellite tombs beneath man-made mounds. The names of the occupants are all known. Five of the tombs were excavated between 1960 and 1972. They had previously been robbed, but evidently of only gold, silver and precious gems. Archaeologists found a large number of pieces of pottery. But by far the most exciting discoveries at the sites were the mural paintings in the interiors. These provide valuable information about Tang court life, and are exquisite examples of the quality of the period's art. Unfortunately the paintings started to deteriorate soon after the tombs had been opened. All the principal ones have now been taken to the National Museum of Shaanxi History (see page 239), where they are kept in a special climate-controlled environment and only accessible by special arrangement. They have been replaced with reproductions and, as with many copies, they do not capture the vitality of the original.

THE TOMB OF PRINCESS YONGTAI

This was the first tomb to be excavated and remains the most impressive of all the tombs that can be seen. Princess Yongtai was a granddaughter of Emperor Gaozong and Empress Wu. She died in 701 CE at the age of 17.

The circumstances surrounding her death were mysterious. According to the records, she was executed by her ruthless grandmother on suspicion of having

YANG GUIFEI

Yang Guifei was a concubine whose love affair with Emperor Xuanzong of the Tang dynasty eventually brought about his downfall and the collapse of Xi'an's Golden Era. Her renowned beauty, and her power, have become legendary in China.

When Emperor Xuanzong had established a strong empire with a cosmopolitan capital at Chang'an (present-day Xi'an), he ordered a search throughout the land to find China's greatest beauty. Thousands of young women—one from as far away as Japan—are said to have been brought before him, only to be discarded or relegated to a secondary status in the back rooms of his palace.

One day, at Huaqing Hot Springs, Yang, the 18-year-old daughter of a high official and concubine of one of the emperor's many sons, caught Xuanzong's eye. Amidst protestations from his son, Xuanzong took Yang to be his own concubine, and she grew to wield enormous influence over the emperor, who began neglecting matters of state to spend time with her. He renamed her Yang Guifei—Yang the Imperial Concubine.

Tang-dynasty paintings indicate that—like other beauties of the time—Yang Guifei was as plump as a harem queen. Taking great pains to please her, the emperor had the palace at Huaqing Hot Springs enlarged, and she spent many languorous hours bathing there to keep her skin fresh. As the eminent Chinese poet Bai Juyi recounted:

> One cold spring day she was ordered
> To bathe in the Huaqing Palace baths,
> The warm water slipped down
> Her glistening jade-like body.
> When maids helped her rise
> She looked so frail and lovely,
> At once she won the emperor's favour…
> Behind the warm lotus-flower curtain,
> They took their pleasure in the spring nights,

Regretting only that the nights were too short,
Rising only when the sun was high,
He stopped attending court sessions…
Constantly she amused and feasted with him,
Accompanying him on spring outings,
Spending every night with him.
Though many beauties were in the palace,
More than three thousand of them,
All his favours were centred on her.

(Translated by Yang Xianyi and Gladys Yang)

As Yang Guifei's spell over the emperor grew, so did her demands. Fresh lychees, her favourite fruit, were brought by pony express from the southern coastal city of Guangzhou every week. Many of her relatives took positions at court, with her cousin becoming prime minister.

Yang Guifei also caught the eye of a Mongolian Turk, An Lushan, who had become military governor in north China. Visiting the Tang court often, he was rumoured to have become Yang's lover. Although 15 years her elder, he was—in a bizarre ceremony—adopted as her son. An Lushan became impatient for power, and soon attempted a forceful take-over of the capital.

As his troops neared Xi'an, the emperor fled with Yang Guifei to the west. Years of neglect had weakened the imperial army, and its remaining soldiers were determined to remove Yang Guifei, whom they blamed for the military decline. When stopping to change horses at Mawei, the soldiers mutinied, killing the prime minister, and demanding that the 'moth-like eyebrows' of Yang Guifei be surrendered as well.

A more valiant lover might have given his own life first, but Xuanzong stood helplessly by as Yang Guifei was strangled in the courtyard of a small Buddhist temple.

The An Lushan rebellion dragged on for several years, but was eventually crushed. The emperor, however, never recovered from his loss of Yang Guifei, and he died a broken man a few years later. The Tang dynasty survived nominally, but a steady decline had set in, and its former glory was never regained.

Stone figures, now headless, of foreigners who came to the Chinese court.

criticized some court favourites. Five years after her death, her remains were exhumed and her tomb built in the Qian Ling complex. The memorial tablet inside the tomb states she died in childbirth, perhaps because the manner of her actual death was considered shameful.

When the tomb was excavated, between 1960 and 1962, archaeologists came across an unexpected and gruesome discovery: the skeleton of a tomb robber, evidently murdered by his accomplices. The modern Japanese writer Yasushi Inoue has written a short story, *Princess Yung-tai's Necklace*, based on the incident (see page 146). Although the tomb had been plundered, archaeologists still found over 1,300 artefacts, including many fine examples of tri-colour pottery.

The passage leading down to the tomb is very steep—take care, as there are no steps. The walls on either side are decorated by reproductions of the original murals. They represent court attendants, almost all of them women, wearing the elegant fashions of the day. Set into the walls are deep alcoves containing reproductions of the tri-colour figurines, some standing, others on horseback, and everyday utensils that were originally buried with the princess.

Towards the bottom of the passage are two large, square tombstones, the first of which is inscribed with large, ancient seal script characters; the two representing Yongtai are at the top of the centre column. Nearby is the hole in the roof of the passage used by the tomb robbers.

Ducking through the heavy stone doorway, one enters the crypt with its huge sarcophagus made of black jade-stone. Called *mo yu shi* in Chinese, this stone is the same used to make the door and tombstones, and was quarried in Fuping County about 60 kilometres (37 miles) northeast of Xi'an. The sarcophagus is beautifully engraved with maidservants, phoenixes, mandarin ducks, vines and flowers and has a top carved in the form of a tiled roof. It originally contained the bodies of both the princess and her husband, Wu Yanji, who was the son of a nephew of Empress Wu and is said to have been also killed in the same year. Their remains are preserved for research in the Xi'an Medical College.

The small museum next to the tomb entrance displays a reproduction of the stone sarcophagus with part of one side removed to show the carvings both inside and out. There are also some of the original tomb figurines, reproduction frescoes and rubbings from this and other Qian Ling tombs.

THE TOMB OF PRINCE YIDE

The tomb of Princess Yongtai's half-brother, who died at the age of 19, apparently executed for the same reason and at the same time as his half-sister, is dated the same year as hers, 706 CE. Although the prince was unmarried when he died, his parents arranged a posthumous marriage for him and his 'wife' was buried with him at a later date. The tomb was excavated in 1970 and revealed some 1,600 figures.

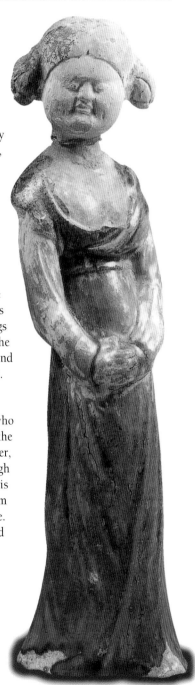

A maidservant similiar to many pottery figures from Princess Yongtai's tomb—wearing her hair in two coils on either side of the ears—in a dress with a décolleté neckline. Unearthed in Xi'an City, 1989.

The layout of the tomb is much the same as that of Princess Yongtai, but in this case the walls are decorated with frescoes showing court ladies and eunuchs, palace guards and hunting attendants. There is also a long mural at the entrance with a 196-man procession of guards massed below the high watch-towers of Chang'an. The stone sarcophagus is slightly smaller, but similarly engraved.

Examples of pottery figures found in the tomb, including some fine tri-colour glazed figures on horseback and a superb, large tri-colour glazed horse, may be seen in adjacent buildings.

THE TOMB OF THE HEIR-APPARENT PRINCE ZHANGHUAI

Prince Zhanghuai was one of Empress Wu's sons and he too fell foul of this formidable lady. He was heir-apparent from 675 to 680 CE, but was then disgraced by his mother and banished to Sichuan province, where he was forced to commit suicide in 684 CE, at the age of 31. His younger brother later had the body exhumed and reburied here. The tomb was built in about 706 CE. The two main paintings in the tomb are of a polo match on one side, and a hunting cavalcade on the other. There are also representations of foreign emissaries with court officials. The two other tombs that have been opened are those of Prime Minister Xue Yuanzhao and General Li Jinxing, and are of lesser importance.

Zhao Ling

Zhao Ling is the tomb of Emperor Taizong, who founded the Tang dynasty. It is located in the main peak of Mount Jiuzong, approximately 60 kilometres (40 miles) northwest of Xi'an. Although 14 of the satellite tombs have been excavated, the emperor's mausoleum itself has not. The whole necropolis covers an area of some 200 square kilometres (77 square miles). Visitors are normally taken to see Zhao Ling Museum, but not the site on Mount Jiuzong itself. 'Spirit Way'. Zhao Ling can be reached by private car but the condition of the roads should be checked before starting out.

Taizong was a great military commander who loved horses. Six bas-reliefs of his favourite mounts including his most famous horse, 'Quanmo', were originally placed at the northern entrance to the tomb. Considered masterpieces of Tang sculpture, they are unfortunately no longer in site. The 'Quanmo stone', together with the 'Saluzi stone', was taken to the United States in 1914 (see Special Topic, page 130). The other four stones are in the Stone Sculpture Gallery of the Forest of Steles Museum, along with plaster reproductions of the two in America, and are well worth a visit. The originals were sadly broken in several places in 1918, apparently in an attempt to facilitate their transport abroad.

The museum at Zhao Ling displays all the artefacts removed from the excavated satellite tombs. There is a splendid selection of Tang funerary pottery, both glazed and unglazed, including figurines of Chinese and Central Asians, horses and camels. There are some fragments of wall paintings, a ceremonial crown from a satellite tomb and a massive pottery roof finial from the Hall of Offerings, the main building of the original enclosure in front of the emperor's mausoleum.

There is also a selection of frescoes found in the satellite tombs. Although they are reproductions and poorly captioned, they are nonetheless splendid examples of Tang art and the costumes and fashions of the period. Those depicting dancers and musicians are especially delightful.

The museum also features a Forest of Steles (not to be confused with the famous one at Forest of Steles Museum in Xi'an). This is a collection of 42 vertical memorial tablets which originally stood outside the tomb mounds, together with ten black jade-stone tombstones from the interiors.

Unfortunately, the majority of the thousands of laboriously etched characters on these steles are illegible. They were damaged by vandals in the contemporary Tang and succeeding Song dynasties who, having made rubbings of the inscriptions, sought to inflate the value of their paper copies by defacing the source tablets.

XINGQING PARK

This is the largest park in Xi'an. Located east of the city wall's southeast corner opposite Xi'an Jiaotong University, it is quiet and full of trees. On weekdays it is an excellent place to get away from the crowds.

The park was originally the site of a Tang palace, where the sons of Emperor Tang Ruizong (reigned 684–690 CE and 710–712 CE) lived at the beginning of the eighth century. It became known as the Xingqing Palace in 714 CE after Emperor Xuanzong succeeded his father.

Famous for its peonies, Xingqing was a favourite palace of Emperor Xuanzong and Imperial Concubine Yang. After the Tang, the land on which the palace had been built eventually reverted to agricultural use.

The transformation of the site into a park came about in 1958 during the Great Leap Forward. Thousands of citizens were involved in laying out the park, taking only 120 days to complete the 50-hectare (123-acre) project.

It has an ornamental lake and a number of Tang-style buildings bearing the names of famous halls and pavilions in the palace of Xuanzong. There is also a white marble memorial, erected in 1979, to Abe no Nakamaro (701–770 CE), a famous secular Japanese visitor to Chang'an during the Tang, who rose to become Collator of Texts in the Imperial Library.

REMAINS OF DAMING PALACE

Daming Palace, or the Palace of Great Luminosity, was begun by Taizong in 634 CE for the use of his father, although Gaozu died before it was completed. In 663 CE it was enlarged for Emperor Gaozong and from then on became the principal palace of the Tang emperors.

The site of Daming Palace is to the northeast of the walled city, on the fringe of the modern urban area. The terraces on which once stood Hanyuan Hall (where important ceremonies were held) and Linde Hall (another large, but informal complex) may still be seen, together with a depression which was the ornamental Penglai Pool in Tang times. The whole area was excavated between 1957 and 1959, and the foundations of some 20 buildings were discovered. The Linde Hall, in particular, was completely excavated, although the site has now been filled in again.

THE TANG DYNASTY ARTS MUSEUM

Situated just around the corner from the Big Goose Pagoda, the Tang Dynasty Arts Museum is an offshoot of the Sino-Japanese joint venture hotel, the Xi'an Garden, or *Tanghua Fandian*. It consists of four exhibition rooms.

Rooms one and two display a selection of reproduction frescoes and cultural relics recovered from various Tang dynasty tombs. Room three is devoted to the theme of 'Chang'an—capital of the Tang dynasty', with models of Daming Palace and the Little Goose Pagoda (see page 214). A map of the city compares its layout with those of contemporary Rome, Alexandria in Egypt, and Nara in Japan, and shows how these cities were dwarfed by Chang'an at the time. There are also some artefacts, including some bronze mirrors, demonstrating the prevailing style of dress, with interesting information on women's hairdos, make-up and clothing. Room four is the art gallery with a variety of original works by professors of Xi'an Art College. Monies from the sale of these paintings go to assist with the maintenance of the museum. A good selection of original art by the peasant painters of Huxian is also available (see page 32).

There is also a small shadow puppet theatre, where performances by the Shaanxi Folk Art Shadow Play Company are arranged for tour groups. Many examples of these colourful puppets, whose origin dates back to the Western Han dynasty, are for sale. This is a place to enjoy relative peace and quiet amongst exhibition halls laid out between attractive gardens. Open to the public 9:00 am–5:00 pm.

YAOZHOU KILNS MUSEUM

A day visit to the Yaozhou Kilns Museum would ideally include seeing the museum, the excavated kilns of the Tang and Song dynasties and contemporary pottery workshops nestled in the surrounding hills. The Yaozhou kilns are located in the

(Preceding pages) *Polo players, from a mural at Prince Zhanghuai's tomb, Qian Ling.*

Huangpu township in Tongchuan city, about two hours drive north of Xi'an and accessible by good roads all the way. Yaozhou is best reached by hiring a private car in Xi'an.

In the Song dynasty (960–1279) the kilns were under the Tongguan county of Yaozhou prefecture, hence the name. The principal excavated kilns, housed in protective buildings constructed in 1987, lie to the east of the highway and give visitors the opportunity to see Tang and Song dynasty workrooms, a storage area for raw materials, areas to sun dry ceramics before firing, and glaze vats and kilns.

The museum opened in 1993 and its exhibition rooms follow a chronological sequence. A quick survey of the exhibited ceramics shows a steady acquisition of objects over five decades, beginning in the 1950s. Since 1959, specialists from the Archaeological Institute of the Chinese Academy of Sciences, the Shaanxi Provincial Archaeological Institute and the Tongchuan Municipal Museum, have investigated the area in Huangpu township and nearby villages. They have found 67 kilns and more than one million ceramics, which date from the Tang dynasty and the following 700 years. The museum also has fine storage facilities and areas where shards and other excavated materials are kept for study and research.

The museum exhibition rooms show Tang dynasty tri-colour glazed wares. One of the most important is a dragon head with bulging eyes and a wide-open jaw, unearthed in 1985, and designated a national treasure. Other tri-colour glazed wares discovered in 1987 include a cart, a standing male servant, a seated lady, a horse and camel. In 1987 a model of a house with courtyard, modelled in diminutive scale with a maximum height of 25 centimetres was excavated. The group of architectural models comprises a gate, main rooms, square pavilions, a well, a mill, an archery target, beds, human figures and horses. One of the most interesting figures among the group is a Central Asian man riding an elephant. As recently as 1999, a tri-colour glazed jug with applied decoration in the shape of a medallion was found. Most of the Tang dynasty tri-colour glazed wares were funerary in purpose. From the Tang dynasty, the exhibition hall also displays important black glazed wares and white glazed wares.

By the Song dynasty, Yaozhou wares really came into their own. Production reached its height at this time, with kilns active along a 5 kilometre length.

The genius of Yaozhou wares lies in the shaping of the clay and the development of glazes. Images, selected from a wide range of motifs, were carved into the clay with bamboo knives. Animal designs include deer, lions, rhinos and tigers as well as fish. Birds include cranes, ducks, geese and mandarin ducks. Plant designs include bamboo, chrysanthemum, honeysuckle, lotus, peony, pine and plum. After carving, which could be deeply incised to a depth as much 5 millimetres, the piece was then placed in a glaze vat and subsequently fired in the kiln at a temperature of 1250°C.

(Above) *Reproduction of a mural originally decorating the tomb of Prince Zhanghuai. Showing foreign emissaries with Chinese court officials, it illustrates the cosmopolitan nature of Chang'an, capital of the Tang dynasty.*

(Left) *A reproduction of one of the murals originally decorating the tomb of Princess Yongtai, showing court attendants wearing the elegant fashions and hairstyles typical of the time.*

Glaze would pool near the contours of the raised image and be lighter near the relief areas, to create contrasts. This insured that the pieces had a strong visual appeal as well as a marvellous tactile one. The tone of colours could range from teadust, to olive-green, grey-green, blue-green or ginger-green; many are described by the generic term celadon. The carved images produced the richest and most intense designs, but there were other decorative methods, including incising and impressing. In the latter, the soft, warm clay would be pressed against a mould with the design in reverse and while the contrast of the raised and depressed areas was not as great as that of carved ones, the designs could be very pleasing. The process was also much speedier than hand carving each detail.

The meticulous workmanship, fine carving and skillful glazing is epitomized in a vessel which has become virtually synonymous with the museum. Reproductions in a wide variety of sizes can be purchased at the museum shop. The original 19 centimetres tall vessel from the Song dynasty has a handle in the shape of a phoenix and a spout in the shape of a lioness suckling her cub. Having no lid, there is an ingenious method of filling the pot. Its mouth opening is on the bottom and the vessel must be held upside down to fill it with water. When turned upright, there are no annoying drips or leaks, only liquid that effortlessly streams out of the spout. It is a witty feat of ingenuity and technical mastery. The original, designated as a national treasure, is displayed in the National Museum of Shaanxi History. A copy of the vessel in absolutely huge dimensions is at the entrance of the Yaozhou Museum, where water streams from its spout into an artificial pond.

After the Song dynasty wares, the display halls show celadon wares of the Five dynasties, pale blue glazed porcelain of the Jin dynasty and white glazed porcelain of black flowers of the Yuan. The Mongols, who established the Yuan dynasty, originally did not have their own tradition of ceramic production, and under their rule taste changed. The once popular wares from the Yaozhou kilns in Shaanxi waned in the Yuan, while robust blue and purple ceramics were popular. During the Song dynasty, the Yaozhou kilns copied some of the Ding ware from Hebei while there were imitations in other parts of China of Yaozhou ware. In the Northern Song dynasty, the Yaozhou kilns ranked on par with five other prestigious and well-known kilns: Ruyao and Junyao in Henan province, Guanyao and Geyao in Zhejiang province and Dingyao in Hebei province.

Buddhism during and after the Tang

Simple but exquisite bowl with celadon glaze at the Yaozhou Kilns Museum.

During the Tang, Chang'an became the main centre for Buddhist learning in East Asia. The first contacts between adherents of Buddhism and the Chinese were probably made with the opening of the Silk Road during the reign of the Martial Emperor, Han Wudi (reigned 140–86 BCE). During the following centuries this Central Asian route, with Chang'an at its eastern terminus, remained the principal one by which Buddhism reached China.

Today a number of monuments bear witness to the importance of Buddhism in the city's history. Most famous are the two prominent landmarks with unforgettable names: the Big and the Little Goose Pagodas. Also in reasonable condition is Da Ci'en Temple (of which the Big Goose Pagoda is a part), and two interesting temples south of the city, the Xingjiao and the Xiangji Temples. Some other Buddhist temples have survived in various states of disrepair but may prove worth visiting, as much for the setting and the journey there as for the temple buildings themselves.

Several of the surviving temples and pagodas have particular associations with Buddhist monks, scholars and translators who made the journey from Chang'an to India in search of enlightenment, the Buddhist scriptures and, perhaps, adventure. Some 200 Chinese monks are recorded as travelling from Chang'an to India between the third and eighth centuries. A number of Central Asian and Indian monks also came to Chang'an, but they are less well documented than the Chinese travellers.

This ingenious Song dynasty Yaozhou vessel is filled from the bottom as it has no lid.

Of these monks the best known is Xuan Zang, who is today the most popular figure in the whole history of Chinese Buddhism. The Tang monk, as he is often simply called, is the hero of the long 16th-century Chinese novel *Pilgrimage to the West*, sometimes known as *Monkey*, which is loosely based on Xuan Zang's travels. A scholar and translator, Xuan Zang made a 17-year journey which took him to Nalanda (near Patna), then the greatest centre of Buddhist learning in India. Upon his return he became abbot of Da Ci'en Temple, where he spent the rest of his life working on translations of the Buddhist texts that he had brought with him from India. His remains were interred under a pagoda which is part of the Xingjiao Temple (see page 215).

By the early eighth century, Chang'an had a total of 64 monasteries and 27 nunneries and was the place where much of the scholarship resulted in the development of important Buddhist sects. These sects included the widely popular 'Pure Land', which emphasized an ideal Buddhist land, also known as the 'Western Paradise', and 'Esoteric' or Tantric Buddhism, which relied on initiation and consecration and made wide use of sacred sounds (*mantras*), sacred hand gestures (*mudras*) and cosmic diagrams (*mandalas*). At Famen Temple, some 118 kilometres (73 miles) west of Xi'an, more than 20,000 monks, followers of various Buddhist sects, lived in the monastery's 24 compounds which covered an area of over 4 square kilometres. The monasteries (and their monks and nuns) fulfilled a number of different roles, not only translating, studying and propagating religion, but also patronizing the arts, providing accommodation and even offering some banking facilities. They grew extremely rich, and Buddhism began to enjoy immense popularity at every level of society.

A succession of emperors either came to Famen Temple themselves or had its famous finger bone relic taken to Chang'an. It is recorded that the relic was taken to the capital city in 660, 790, 819 and 873 CE, and it was during this time that the temple gained nationwide fame. The relic was taken to the capital and the ensuing festival honouring the relics of the Buddha was an important occasion, rich in pageantry. It was also an opportunity for the common people to express their piety by offering grains such as rice or millet, foods, flowers or medicine. Equally, it was an opportunity for the imperial family to offer precious golden and silver vessels or sublime textiles. The Famen Temple underground vault included many artefacts for daily use offered by the royal families, including tableware, tea items, censers, clothes, coins and jewellery.

Although rulers such as Empress Wu Zetian (reigned 684–705), Emperor Yizong (reigned 859–873) and his son Xizong (reigned 873–888) were ardent Buddhists, other Tang emperors, however, were ambivalent in their support of the religion. They claimed that Laozi, the founder of China's indigenous religion Taoism, was their ancestor. Increasingly the success of the great temple-monasteries provoked resistance, and attempts were made to limit their power and wealth. Finally in 841 CE, a crackdown came when the Taoist Emperor Wuzong (reigned 840–846) ordered the dissolution of the monasteries and the return of monks and nuns to secular life. During the following four years, widespread persecution of Buddhism led to the destruction of almost all the Buddhist temple complexes. Many of them were re-established after 845 CE, and some of them survive to this day.

Sights

THE BIG GOOSE PAGODA AND DA CI'EN TEMPLE

The Big Goose Pagoda (*Dayan Ta*), perhaps the most beautiful building left in Xi'an today, is one of the city's most distinctive and outstanding landmarks. The adjacent Da Ci'en Temple is the city's best-preserved Buddhist temple complex.

Situated four kilometres (two-and-a-half miles) south of the walled city at the end of Yanta Lu, or Goose Pagoda Road, the temple and pagoda are on the sites of earlier Sui temple. Da Ci'en Temple was established in 647 CE by Li Zhi (who became Emperor Tang Gaozong in 649 CE) in memory of his mother Empress Wende.

Completed in 652 CE, the pagoda was built at the request of the Tang monk, Xuan Zang, whose pilgrimage to India is immortalized in the 16th-century Chinese novel *Pilgrimage to the West* or *Monkey*. Xuan Zang asked Emperor Gaozong to build a large stone stupa like those he had seen on his travels. The emperor offered a compromise brick structure of five storeys, about 53 metres (174 feet) high, which was completed in 652 CE. Originally called the Scripture Pagoda, it is said to be where Xuan Zang translated into Chinese the Buddhist scriptures he brought back from India. Its present name, Big Goose Pagoda, has never been satisfactorily explained.

Between 701 and 704 CE, at the end of the reign of Empress Wu, five more storeys were added to the pagoda, giving a sharper, more pointed form than it has today. Later damage, probably by fire, reduced it to the seven storeys it now has. It is a simple, powerful, harmonious structure, although ironically not how Xuan Zang wanted it to be.

The pagoda rises 64 metres (210 feet) to the north of the other temple buildings, and is the only remaining Tang building in the complex. On the pedestal, at the entrance to the first storey, are some rather faded photographs providing a useful and fascinating survey of other famous pagodas in China as well as a number of Tang inscriptions and engravings set in the base of the pagoda. There are some delightful tendril designs in bas-relief on the borders of the tablets and at the top of the tablets some exquisite coiling dragons and singing angels.

At the southern entrance of the pagoda are copies of the Emperors Taizong and Gaozong's prefaces to the translations of Xuan Zang. Over the lintel of the western entrance is an engraving of Sakyamuni and other Buddhist figures. Some tablets, inscribed during the Ming (1368–1644), recount the exploits of the Tang monk. On a fine day, climb up inside the internal wooden staircase to the top of the pagoda for a panoramic view.

During the Tang, Da Ci'en Temple was a considerable establishment. There were about 300 resident monks and no fewer than 1,897 rooms around 13 courtyards. It contained paintings by the leading artists of the day, and had the finest peony garden in the capital.

Although the temple was one of four to continue functioning after the great persecution of Buddhism in the middle of the ninth century, it was destroyed at the end of the Tang (907 CE). Since then it has been ruined and restored several times, but on a diminished scale. The last major restoration occurred in 1954, when the pagoda pedestal was widened.

The temple entrance is on the south side. Inside, to the right and left, are the Bell and Drum Towers, and a path leading to the Great Hall. This contains three statues of Buddhas, surrounded by 18 clay figures of Sakyamuni Buddha's disciples. Both the building and the statues inside are said to date from 1466. In front of the Scripture Library is a stone lamp from the Japanese city of Kyoto. To the east of the Great Hall are several small stone pagodas marking the remains of monks of the Qing period (1644–1911). Some new temple buildings are being constructed behind the pagoda. Built in Tang style around a courtyard, they will serve as a monument to Xuan Zang and house Buddhist scriptures and details of his life and achievements.

The temple is open from 8:30 am to 5:30 pm. Just around the corner is the Tang Dynasty Arts Museum (see page 204)

THE LITTLE GOOSE PAGODA AND DA JIANFU TEMPLE

The Little Goose Pagoda (Xiaoyan Ta) is one of Xi'an's major landmarks. Situated to the south of the walled city, the 13-storey, eighth-century pagoda is all that remains of the once flourishing Da Jianfu Temple. The temple, established in 684 CE in honour of Emperor Gaozong, was particularly associated with pilgrim Yijing, who settled there in the early eighth century to translate texts he had brought back from India. Although the temple continued to function after the persecutions of Buddhists, everything was destroyed save the Little Goose Pagoda, and an old locust tree said to have been planted during the Tang. Later, more modest temple buildings were erected next to the pagoda.

(Preceding pages) *The Big Goose Pagoda (Dayan Ta), first constructed in 652 at the request of the Tang monk Xuan Zang following his pilgrimage to India.*

The pagoda has not survived completely unscathed. When it was completed in 707 CE the brick structure had 15 storeys, but it was damaged during a series of earthquakes in the late 15th and 16th centuries. In 1487, the pagoda was split from top to bottom by the impact of an earthquake. Amazingly, it did not fall. In 1556 another quake had its epicentre some 75 kilometres (47 miles) east of Xi'an. This one had the effect of throwing the two sides of the pagoda together again, but it also dislodged the top two storeys.

The Little Goose Pagoda has remained to this day only 13 storeys, 43 metres (141 feet) high. There have been conflicting opinions about the original appearance of the building, which is partly why a complete restoration has never been attempted. (Drawings of the different designs are on display, alongside photographs of the restoration work, in a pavilion beside the pagoda. There are also dramatic photographs showing the temple rent in two following the earthquake.) Meanwhile, however, the slightly crumbling, open part of its apex gives it a distinct style. A new internal staircase was put up in 1965 so you can climb to the top. Unlike the Big Goose Pagoda, which has only narrow windows, here you can climb out to an open roof to enjoy an untrammelled view of the surroundings.

Among the noteworthy features of the pagoda are some Tang-period engravings of bodhisattvas on the stone lintels at its base. There is also a tablet commemorating the restoration of the pagoda in 1116 and another engraved during the Qing (1644–1911) with information about the earthquakes. A stone table dated 1692 gives an interesting idea of what the temple and pagoda would have looked like at that date, except that the pagoda is represented with 15 storeys.

Standing in one of the courtyards behind the pagoda is a small Bell Tower, housing a large bell measuring 3.55 metres (11.6 feet) high and weighing 8,000 kilograms (over 17,000 pounds). It was cast in 1192 in Wugong County, west of Xi'an, and moved to the temple about five centuries later. Beside it is a modern replica which can be struck by visitors for a small fee. Opposite the Bell Tower is the Drum Tower. Traditionally a Buddhist monk struck a bell before noon and a drum in the afternoon and evening. It is worth visiting the exhibition rooms of Shaanxi handicrafts at this pagoda. The Little Goose Pagoda is open from 8:30 am to 5:30 pm.

XINGJIAO TEMPLE

This temple is in a very pleasant setting, overlooking the Fanchuan River, 22 kilometres (14 miles) southeast of Xi'an, just beyond the village of Duqu. Xingjiao Temple, or the Temple of the Flourishing Teaching, was one of the Eight Great Temples of Fanchuan. It was built in 669 CE by Tang Gaozong as a memorial to the Tang monk Xuan Zang (see page 210), together with a tall brick pagoda covering his ashes. The temple was restored in 828 CE, though by 839 CE it again lay abandoned

according to the inscription on Xuan Zang's pagoda. However, it managed to survive until the 19th century when all the buildings were destroyed except the main pagoda and two smaller ones belonging to two of Xuan Zang's disciples. The temple was again rebuilt, partly in 1922, partly in 1939.

The three pagodas stand in a walled enclosure called Cien Pagoda Courtyard. The tall central pagoda is dedicated to Xuan Zang. It is a beautiful five-storey brick structure, with brackets in relief, in imitation of the old wooden-style pagodas. It probably dates from the ninth century. A small pavilion next to the pagoda has a modern copy of a stone engraving of Xuan Zang, carrying the scriptures in what might be described as a sutra-backpack.

On either side of the principal pagoda are those of Xuan Zang's two translation assistants. Each is of three storeys. On the east side is that of Kuiji (632–682 CE), nephew of General Yuchi Jingde (a general of Emperor Tang Taizong). It was erected during the Tang. On the other side stands the pagoda of Yuance, a Korean follower of Xuan Zang . This was built later, in 1115.

At the entrance to the complex are the Bell and Drum Towers. These are 20th century constructions but retain the original instruments from the 19th century or earlier. Facing the entrance is the Great Hall of the Buddha, built in 1939, which contains a bronze, Ming-period Buddha. The Preaching Hall behind was built in 1922 and contains a number of statues including a bronze, Ming-period Amitabha Buddha and a Sakyamuni Buddha of the same date as the hall.

In the eastern courtyard is the two-storey library, built in 1922 and restored in 1939. It contains a white jade Buddha from Burma. The library proper is on the upper floor and possesses some Tang dynasty sutras, written in Sanskrit, as well as 20th-century editions of the great Tang translations of Xuan Zang and others.

You can reach the temple by bus number 215 which leaves from Xi'an's South Gate. The trip takes about 40 minutes.

DAXINGSHAN TEMPLE

Daxingshan Temple was the greatest Buddhist establishment of the Sui and Tang, but since the tenth century it has been destroyed and rebuilt several times. The last reconstruction was in 1956. In 1999, the buildings around the front courtyard were either completely reconstructed or extensively renovated, and some of the main temple buildings have recently been repainted. A number of monks live and worship there. The temple complex stands in well-wooded, peaceful surroundings and is more extensive than it at first seems.

The temple is said to date back to the third century when it was known as the Zunshan Temple. It was refounded during the Sui when it was given its present name, and became the headquarters of an order with a network of 45 prefectural temples,

(Left) *Xingiao Temple.*

all established by Yang Qian, founder of the Sui dynasty. During the Tang it became a great centre of Buddhist art and learning and the Tang monk, Xuan Zang, hero of the famous Chinese novel *Monkey*, stayed there during the seventh century. Most of the buildings were destroyed during the Buddhist persecution of 841–845, and whatever survived disappeared at the end of the Tang. The temple was rebuilt under the Ming and again restored in 1785 by an expert on Tang dynasty Chang'an called Bi Yuan (1730–97). After its reconstruction in 1956 it was used by a community of Lamaist monks until the Cultural Revolution (1966–76). Today it houses the Xi'an Buddhist Association. The temple is located south of the Little Goose Pagoda on a small street called Xingshan Si Jie, near the open market of Xiaozhai.

XIANGJI TEMPLE
Xiangji Temple, which has an 11-storey pagoda built in 706 CE, lies due south of Xi'an some 20 kilometres (12 miles), close to the town of Wangqu. The square brick pagoda was built over the ashes of the Buddhist Shandao, one of the patriarchs of Pure Land Buddhism which preached salvation through faith rather than meditation. It was built by a disciple named Jingye, who is himself commemorated by a small five-storey brick pagoda nearby. Around the pagodas were originally the buildings of one of the great temple-monasteries of Tang Chang'an, although these have long since disappeared.

The pagoda of Shandao is similar in some respects to that of Xuan Zang at the Temple of Flourishing Teaching. It has brackets in relief and imitates a wooden structure. If you want to climb the pagoda, try persuading one of the monks for permission.

On 14 May 1980, which was, by Chinese reckoning, the 1,300th anniversary of Shandao's death in 681 CE, a major restoration of the temple was completed. The Great Hall of the Buddha was rebuilt, and a Japanese Buddhist delegation presented a figure of the monk Shandao. It is now on view inside the hall together with a figure of Amitabha Buddha which was brought from a Beijing museum.

It is difficult to reach the temple by bus and a taxi is the most realistic option. But the beautiful surrounding countryside and, of course, the pagodas themselves make the trip well worthwhile.

CAOTANG TEMPLE
Sometimes translated as the Straw Hut Temple, Caotang Temple was founded during the Tang dynasty. Surrounded by fields, it lies about 55 kilometres (34 miles) southwest of Xi'an.

The temple was built on the side of a palace where Kumarajiva, a fourth century translator of Buddhist scriptures, once worked and taught. Kumarajiva's translations, known for their elegant style rather than for their accuracy, have been used continuously down to modern times. The ashes of Kumarajiva are beneath a stone stupa, thought to be Tang, about two metres (6.5 feet) high, inside a small pavilion. In front there are some old cypress trees and a well. Other temple buildings include bell and tablet pavilions and a main hall The temple is on the road to Huxian and accessible by taxi or long-distance bus.

HUAYAN TEMPLE

Huayan Temple was founded by the first patriarch of the Huayan sect of Buddhism, the monk Dushan (557–640 CE), during the reign of Tang Taizong. In its heyday, the temple, situated in the Fanchuan area 20 kilometres (12 miles) south of Xi'an, was one of the Eight Great Temples of Fanchuan which flourished during the Tang.

Today, the only part of the temple to have survived are two brick pagodas on the side of the hill. One of them is 23 metres (75 feet) high and is square, like the Big Goose Pagoda, with seven storeys; the other is small with four storeys and is hexagonal in form. There is a good view of the surrounding area from the pagodas.

Located on the road that passes through Chang'an, southeast of Xi'an, the pagodas are accessible by bus number 215 that leaves from the South Gate (a trip of about 45 minutes) and can be visited conveniently on the way to Xingjiao Temple.

THE TEMPLE OF THE RECUMBENT DRAGON

The Temple of the Recumbent Dragon (*Wo Long Si*), believed to have been built during the Eastern Han in about 168 CE, was served by some 300 monks during the Ming dynasty (1368–1644). The name apparently comes from the fact that the Emperor Zhao Kuangyin (the dragon always symbolized the emperor), who founded the Song dynasty in 960, enjoyed coming to this temple to rest and play chess with the monks. It suffered particularly badly during the Cultural Revolution (1966–76), when virtually all the artwork was destroyed as everything but the strongest walls and foundations were razed.

For almost two decades the temple site was used to house a factory. Since 1982, three quarters of the floor area has been returned to the temple's jurisdiction in compliance with government policy promoting freedom of religious beliefs. Monks still stay at the temple, and three large halls and several peripheral structures have been built, one of which is a dining hall.

Access to the temple is down a lane between numbers 25 and 27 Baishulin Jie, a five-minute walk from the Forest of Steles Museum. Walk straight out of the museum gate to Baishulin Jie, turn left and take the second lane on the right.

Xuan Zang, 7th century CE Chinese Buddhist pilgrim, Big Goose Pagoda.

GUANGREN TEMPLE

The Guangren Temple is a Lama temple, located on Xibei Yi Lu within the north-westernmost corner of the city wall. It is one of only four such temples outside Tibet, the others being the Labrang Lamasery in southern Gansu, the Ta'er Lamasery in Qinghai, and the Lama Temple in Beijing. This temple, however, is by no means as grand as its cousins. Built in 1705 during the Qing dynasty, Guangren Temple functioned as a place of worship and lodging for monks and pilgrims travelling between Beijing and Tibet. According to the monks now serving at the temple, the Dalai Lama himself once stayed here briefly in 1952.

As with most religious sites during the Cultural Revolution, Guangren Temple suffered from officially sanctioned destruction

View of Tang dynasty style buildings in Famen Temple from the museum's 'Treasure Hall'.

by Red Guards. The old east section is still occupied by a factory, although there is talk about possibly one day restoring this, and the front courtyard is partly occupied by another building. All this makes the temple appear quite small and insignificant on entering the gate, particularly as it stands in the shadow of the imposing Ming city wall. However, appearances are deceptive and there are three main courtyards tucked away behind the first hall.

Calligraphy on a stele housed in a pavilion in the front courtyard was written by Kangxi, the second Qing emperor. The name plaque over the entrance to the main hall also bears his calligraphy, while inside the hall itself hang two lamps that were gifts to the temple from the Empress Dowager Cixi.

To get there by bus, take the number 10 running west along Lianhu Lu and alight at Yuxiang Men. Walk back east along Lianhu Lu, turn left into Xibei Yi Lu and the temple is right at the end of the street against the wall.

Famen Temple

Famen Temple is situated some 118 kilometres (73 miles) west of Xi'an, at a site on the Silk Road en route to Baoji, Tianshui and Lanzhou. It will thus appeal to travellers who are journeying west to retrace that ancient trade route, or indeed those visitors to Xi'an who can fit Famen Temple into a day's tour to the west, which also encompasses Qian Ling and the Baoji Bronze Culture Museum. Others may consider a famous temple housing sacred Buddhist relics worth a day trip in itself. When the Tang dynasty underground vault was excavated in 1987 and the diversity and quality of objects known, it quickly became clear that the Famen Temple finds were unprecedented. It is the largest underground religious vault or crypt ever found in China. Consisting of the Buddha's finger bone, gold and silver vessels, bronze, glass, porcelain, stone carvings, pearls, gems, jades, silks and other textiles, the finds provide rare insights into Buddhist practices and imperial sponsorship of a temple.

Although the origins of the Famen Temple can be traced back to the Eastern Han dynasty, between 147 and 189 CE, the temple underwent many changes during successive dynasties. The temple enshrined one of Sakyamuni Buddha's finger bones, believed to have been divided and distributed by the Indian King Asoka (died 232 CE). Relics such as these are known by their Sanskrit name *sarira*. During the Tang dynasty when the temple gained nationwide fame, the temple's pagoda was rebuilt and relics stored in a crypt beneath it. Later in 1609 of the Ming dynasty, a 45-metre 13-storey octagonal brick pagoda was built above the crypt. This pagoda was badly damaged by heavy rains in 1981, and in 1987, the three-chamber underground vault was discovered directly beneath it.

During the Tang dynasty the temple gained nationwide fame, but the popularity of Buddhism waxed and waned and when Buddhism was under wide attack, an imperial edict ordered that the finger bone of Sakyamuni be destroyed. Fortunately, the monks hid the relic. This would not be the first or last time the relics were safeguarded. When the Japanese army was about to invade Shaanxi in 1939, a Mr. Zhu Ziqiao, who knew about the underground palace, swore with other insiders to keep the secret and cast a bronze statue of the Buddha to guard the national treasures. Later, during the decade of turmoil of the Cultural Revolution (1966–1976) the Famen monk, Master Liangqing, burnt himself to death in front of Red Guards in order to protect the temple and its relics from destruction. Confronted by the burning monk, the Red Guards desisted.

On 24 August 1981, the Ming dynasty pagoda partially collapsed, leaving exactly half the structure standing and the other half a pile of rubble. By 1987 the damaged pagoda had been completely cleared away, leaving the stairway to the underground vault exposed. Similar in architecture to imperial tombs, there was a sloping passageway leading to a series of chambers. Four finger bone relics of Sakyamuni

Buddha were discovered: the front chamber containing one stored in a reliquary known as 'the Asoka Pagoda', the middle chamber housing one in a marble bier; the back chamber one in an eight-fold casket; and finally, in a secret shrine underneath the back chamber, one placed in a five-fold casket. As only one of the bones is a genuine *sarira*, the other three are known as 'shadow bones'. They are meant to protect the genuine one in case of persecution of Buddhism.

The temple complex, which has been faithfully reconstructed from original Tang drawings, houses a working monastery and resident monks. The rebuilt pagoda is set in pleasant garden surroundings tended by the monks. Today, visitors to the pagoda enter the renovated underground vault area by stairs leading inside and downwards. The entrance to the original crypt can be seen by crouching down in front of a window at floor level. Behind it is a gaudily decorated and brightly lit white marble chamber, today an important focus for devotees, both lay people and monks and nuns, who pray and chant in front of it. This acts as a reminder that the temple was once one of the four most sacred Buddhist sanctuaries in China and today, with the resurgence of religion, still has tremendous drawing power. To see the unearthed treasures, one must go to the Famen Museum, adjacent to the temple.

The museum consists of three buildings in Tang architectural style. Looking directly ahead from the entrance to the museum, you see the Treasure House. On your left is the exhibition hall documenting the history of Famen Temple, and to the right lies the exhibition hall housing gold and silver objects, textiles and other imperial offerings. The museum is of international standard with well-displayed objects, excellent lighting and informative explanation panels, in Chinese and English. Because of their enormous archaeological or religious importance, a number of the vault's treasures are often away on tour either in China or overseas, but with three exhibition halls, all so rich in content, there is more than enough to see.

The most precious treasures of the crypt are undoubtedly the finger bone relics and the reliquaries made to house them, which are displayed in the Treasure Hall. Measuring some 25 metres high and with over 2,500 square metres of exhibition space, this hall was the first to be opened to the public in 1988. You should be able to see at least some, if not all, of the set of eight caskets, originally nested one inside another, which contained the finger bone. The eight-layer casket, which was filled with fragrant herbs and spices and consecrated by Emperor Yizong (reigned 859–873), was placed in the centre of the back chamber with thousands of consecrated items and offerings systematically placed around it. The outermost casket was of carved sandalwood. Working from the outside and towards the centre, is a gilded silver casket with pictures of four guardian gods of the north, south, east and west and a cover of two dragons holding pearls. Inside this is a silver casket with a plain surface; next is a gilded silver casket showing preaching Buddhas. Next comes a pure

Gilded silver basket for storing or cooking tea, decorated with geese in flight. Height 17.8cm, diameter (at mouth) 16.1cm. Excavated from the crypt of Famen Temple, Fufeng, March 1987.

gold casket with Buddhas on the sides and a cover of flowers and birds with a double phoenix. This is followed by a pure gold casket with semi precious stones and pearls, followed by a stone casket similarly decorated. The innermost container is a pure gold pagoda with four doors and a pearl cover. Here, the genuine finger bone, with its whitish outer crust, and dark yellow inner crust dotted in black, was set standing on a silver rod.

When the underground crypt was opened in 1987, a stele dated 873 CE was found. It is an invaluable record listing the objects, their size and weight as well as the offerers' name. The treasures recorded on this tablet correspond to the actual objects: 121 gold and silver vessels, eight bronze vessels, 20 pieces of glassware, 19 porcelains, 11 stone carvings, 400-odd pearls and pieces of jade and hundreds of silk fabrics.

The exhibition hall to the right of the Treasure Hall displays many examples of Tang gold and silverware, demonstrating the advanced metalworking techniques and skills of the craftsmen of that period. About 100 of the gold and silver vessels, mainly imperial wares made in the royal workshop "Wensi Bureau", were offered by Emperor Yizong (reigned 859–873) and his son Emperor Xizong (reigned 873–888). Examples include a gilded silver bowl with an overlapping lotus petal design; the four gilded silver ewers (ritual vessels for the consecration of the image of Buddha; see photograph page 230–231), found in each corner of the crypt; an exquisite gilded silver basket with an open-work design decorated with geese in flight (see photograph opposite); eight small gilded silver plates with a peony design. In addition to wares from the imperial workshops, there are also objects of tribute from southern China, and a special section is dedicated to tea wares. These include a silver tea mortar decorated with a gold-gilt design of wild geese and a silver tea strainer with a design of an immortal on a flying crane, both dated 869.

Another group of rare objects are the *mise* or 'secret colour' celadon ceramics and more than 700 pieces of silk, including brocade, satin, embroidery, thin silk, gauze and many other types. A number of the textiles were donated by the imperial family or aristocracy. Other textiles were used to wrap objects. Some were imperially consecrated by Empress Wu Zetian (684–705) and later in the dynasty by Emperor Yizong and his son Xizong. Perhaps the most outstanding is a miniature garment embroidered in gold-wrapped thread and lined in red silk. The gold thread was only 0.06 millimetres thick, even finer than a strand of hair.

Those wishing to spend longer than a day at Famen can stay overnight at the Famen Temple Hotel, a short distance down the road from the temple (turn right out of the temple gate). See useful addresses page 323.

ON CLIMBING
THE BIG GOOSE PAGODA IN CHANG'AN —Du Fu

Written by Du Fu while on an excursion with some other poets to the Pagoda of Kindness
and Grace, better known now as the Dayan Ta or Big Goose Pagoda.

> At the top of the pagoda one feels
> To have truly entered the sky;
> Wind drums incessantly; I am
> Not one free of care and here my worry increases;
> And this structure,
> Representing the power of Buddha,
> Makes one wish to understand
> And penetrate the depths of his secrets;
> Looking through the dragon and snake
> Openings, one marvels at their intricacy
> Of construction; the seven
> Stars come into view and the Milky Way;
> One knows that the sun has been forced down,
> And that it is autumn already; clouds
> Obscure the mountain; the waters
> Of the clear Wei and the muddy Ching
> Seem to have come together; below us
> Is the mist, so can one hardly realize
> Down there lies our capital;
> There is a hardly-to-be-defined air
> Near the grave of the ancient Emperor Shun,
> And one cries for his awakening; but now
> By the Jade Lake, the Queen of the Western
> Heavens disports herself with wine, as
> The sun sets behind Mount Kunlun
> And yellow cranes fly aimlessly,
> While the wild geese stream into
> The sunset, searching for life.

Du Fu (712–770), the Sage of Poets, lived in a period of change when the prosperity of
the Tang began to decline. Having suffered obstacles in his official career, he began to
travel around the country and to write poetry. Living as a refugee during the Rebellion
of An and Shi gave him a personal empathy with the sufferings of the poor. His work
shows a great depth of feeling for the plight of the common people. In 759, Du Fu went
to live in Chengdu and it is here that his former residence, the Thatched Cottage, is open
for viewing by visitors. Recording as they do both the military and political situations
pertaining at this time, Du Fu's poems are referred to as 'the mirror of his time'.

(Right) *Big Goose Pagoda, Xi'an.*

SWISS EFFICIENCY

Sian is remarkable for its rickshaws. They have blue or white hood-covers, embroidered with big flowers, of an oddly Victorian design. We used the rickshaws a good deal, out of laziness, despite Dr Mooser's warning that their upholstery often contained typhus-lice. Typhus is one of the great scourges of Shen-si Province. One of Mooser's two colleagues, an engineer, went down with it soon after his arrival, but, thanks to an inoculation, the attack was comparatively slight.

Dr Mooser himself was a stocky figure, eagle-eyed with a bitter mouth and a smashed, rugged face. He wore a leather jerkin, riding-breeches, and big strapped boots. He rushed at life, at China, at his job, with his head down, stamping and roaring like a bull. The dishonesty and laziness of the average Chinese official was driving him nearly frantic. 'While I'm here,' he bellowed at his assistants, 'you are all Swiss. When I go away you can be Chinese again, if you like—or anything else you Goddam well please.'

Not that Mooser had much use for his countrymen either, or, indeed, for any Europeans at all. 'The Swiss are crooks, the Germans are crooks, the English are the damn lousiest crooks of the lot... It was you lousy bastards who wouldn't let ambulances be sent to China. I have all the facts. I shall not rest until they are published in the newspaper.' With his colleagues he spoke Swiss dialect, or English—boycotting High German, the language of the Nazis.

Dr Mooser had established several refugee camps in Sian, as well as a delousing station. The refugees were housed in empty buildings. As soon as could be arranged they were sent off into the country and distributed amongst the neighbouring villages. There were about eight thousand of them in the city, including one thousand Mohammedans, who had a special camp to themselves. These people belonged mostly to the middle class of China—nearly all of them had a little money. The really poor had no choice but to stay where they were, and await the coming of the Japanese. The really rich were already safe in Hong Kong.

There was no doubt of Mooser's efficiency. The camps were well run, the floors and bedding clean, the children's faces washed, and there was hardly any spitting. Mooser was a great favourite with the children. Whenever he visited them his pockets were full of sweets. 'I had to sack three camp commandants in the first week,' he told us. 'They call me The Chaser.'

Mooser didn't quite know what to make of us—especially after he had heard from me that Auden was a poet. He had no use for poetry because 'it changes the order of the words'. While he was working in Mexico he was summoned to the bedside of an Englishman named David H Lawrence, 'a queer-looking fellow with a red beard. I told him: "I thought you were Jesus Christ." And he laughed. There was a big German woman sitting beside him. She was his wife. I asked him what his profession was. He said he was a writer. "Are you a famous writer?" I asked him. "Oh no," he said. "Not so famous." His wife didn't like that. "Didn't you really know my husband was a writer?" she said to me. "No," I said. " Never heard of him." And Lawrence said: "Don't be silly, Frieda. How should he know I was a writer? I didn't know he was a doctor, either, till he told me."

Dr Mooser then examined Lawrence and told him that he was suffering from tuberculosis—not from malaria, as the Mexican doctor had assured him. Lawrence took it very quietly. He only asked how long Mooser thought he would live. 'Two years,' said Mooser. 'If you're careful.' This was in 1928.

Journey to a War,
W H Auden and Christopher Isherwood,
Random House, 1939

Dr Mooser and his two Swiss colleagues, of the League of Nations Commission, were advising the Chinese government on the prevention of infectious diseases.

Period Five: Medieval and Modern Xi'an

Background

With the destruction of Chang'an at the end of the Tang dynasty, the city lost its political splendour and power for good. Thereafter it remained a regional centre, usually out of the mainstream of political developments. The real economic centre of China had already moved away from Chang'an, further to the southwest, during the late Tang. After 907 CE the Xi'an area became progressively more impoverished and culturally backward. Much of the history in the following millennium is a dismally repetitious account of droughts and floods, famines and peasant insurrections.

However, Taoism continued to find adherents and remnants of Taoist temples (see page 258) can be seen in Xi'an today, despite the destruction caused during the Cultural Revolution. Islam, which had first been introduced into Chang'an by Arab merchants during the Tang, also flourished. Xi'an's beautiful Great Mosque is still functioning and welcomes foreign visitors (see page 256).

Between the fall of the Tang and the establishment of the Ming dynasty in 1368, the city changed its name many times. In 1368 the city was renamed Xi'an Fu, the Prefecture of Western Peace. It was to remain as Xi'an from then on, except for the last year of the Ming dynasty (1644), when the peasant leader Li Zicheng captured the city and renamed it Chang'an. (The name Chang'an survives today as the name of the county town immediately south of Xi'an).

The Ming Dynasty

In 1370 Zhu Yuanzhang, the first emperor of the Ming dynasty, put his second son, Zhu Shuang, in control of Xi'an. Zhu Shuang became Prince of Qin, using the old name for the area. A palace was constructed for him and the city substantially rebuilt on the site of the Imperial City section of the Tang capital, covering approximately one sixth of the original area. The prince did not take up residence until 1378, when the palace and the walls and gates of the city had already been completed. Although the palace, which was in the northeast part of the city, no longer exists, part of 14th-century Xi'an still survives, notably the Bell and Drum towers and the city wall and gates.

The Qing Dynasty

When the Manchus established the last imperial dynasty of China, the Qing, in 1644, Xi'an was garrisoned by Manchu troops. They occupied the northeast section of the city, which was walled off. In European accounts, these soldiers were referred to inaccurately, as 'Tartars'.

(Preceding pages) Two of the four gilded silver ewers from the Tang dynasty decorated with a variety of auspicious Buddhist symbols including vajras and lotus petals. Height 19.8 cm, width 13.2 cm. Unearthed in March 1987 from the crypt of Famen Temple, Fufeng.

During the 18th century the city, or at least its officials and merchants, enjoyed some prosperity, as indicated by the great development of Qingqiang opera at this time (see page 43). However, the 19th century was less happy with natural calamities following fast on the heels of a disastrous Muslim rebellion (1862–73).

In 1900 Xi'an again became a capital of sorts during the Boxer Rebellion when the Empress Dowager Cixi (1835–1908), with her captive nephew, the powerless Emperor Guangxu, fled in disguise from Beijing. They stayed for over a year in Xi'an, beyond the reach of the Western powers, while peace was negotiated.

In 1911 when a nationwide revolution overthrew the Qing regime, resistance by the garrison in Xi'an collapsed without much of a struggle. But a terrible massacre of the Manchus ensued. Between 10,000 and 20,000 were killed, including a few unlucky foreigners. Most of the buildings in the Manchu quarter were burned down. Such blood-letting and destruction did not occur in other cities. Much of the killing in Xi'an was evidently led by the Muslims, in revenge for the suppression of their rebellion 40 years earlier.

XI'AN IN THE REPUBLICAN ERA

During the Republican period of 1911 to 1949 Xi'an gradually became less isolated from the outer world. Before the revolution the city had already established its first telegraph office (in 1885) and international post office (in 1902). The railway did not reach Xi'an until 1934, but Westerners started to visit the city in increasing numbers from the turn of the century onwards, usually making contact with the China Inland Mission, the Scandinavian Alliance Mission or the English Baptists, all of whom were represented in the city. They returned, frequently to write books, informing (and often misinforming) the outside world about 'ancient Sian-fu':

> It will be long before the city of Western Peace becomes the resort of sightseers. Yet Sian and its neighbourhood provide more sights to see than most inland Chinese capitals, in case the blessed day of trains de luxe and steam-heated hotels should ever draw for it. The rolling plain, all round as far as you can see, is full of mounds and barrows; and two noble pagodas invite inspection. Or you can mount the wall and study the whole flat extent of the city; you can ascend the Drum Tower, and from the vast darkness of its loft look out towards the turquoise roofs of the Mahometan mosque, and beyond these, to the orange gables of the Imperial Palace, where the Grand Dowager pitched her flying tents in 1900.

> (From *On the Eaves of the World* by Reginald Farrar, 1917)

(Top right) *The Great Mosque: Door holder with a traditional flower design.*
(Top left) *Muslim men chatting inside the door of the Great Mosque before evening prayers.*
(Bottom) *Zhang Jianchang, carrying on the family tradition of paper making begun in the Qing dynasty, dips a bamboo frame into pool of mulberry pulp.*

Zhang Pengxue, fifth generation mulberry papermaker.

Li Fenglan, pioneer peasant painter, at work in her courtyard in the 1950s.

During the struggle for power in the 1920s and 1930s, Xi'an was of some strategic importance and once again in its history played a dramatic role: in 1926, it was occupied by a pro-Nationalist Shaanxi general, Yang Hucheng, and was promptly surrounded by an anti-Nationalist force. So began the six-month Siege of Xi'an. When it was finally lifted, some 50,000 were said to have died. Revolution Park marks the place where they were buried (see page 259).

In the struggle between communist and Nationalist forces, Xi'an came to the forefront in 1936, when Huaqing Hot Springs was the scene of the so-called Xi'an Incident (see page 192). Chiang Kai-shek, intent on getting rid of domestic communist opposition before putting up resistance to the invading Japanese, was arrested by two Nationalist generals, Yang Hucheng and the leader of the displaced Northeastern Army, Zhang Xueliang, and forced to agree to join the Communists against the common enemy, the Japanese. Xi'an became a vital link between the Communist headquarters in Yan'an and the outside world through the establishment of the Eighth Route Army Office (see page 259).

During the Sino-Japanese War, Xi'an was bombed, but never occupied by the Japanese. After the war, the city was controlled by Nationalist troops until it was taken by Communist forces on 20 May 1949. The People's Republic of China was inaugurated less than five months later.

Xi'an in the People's Republic

Xi'an has grown much larger in the past 40 years, both in size and population. Many new industries have also been established. The initial impetus for this growth came from the government whose policy was to give priority to the development of the cities in the interior. Recent years have also seen the rise of shiny tall, new modern buildings and shopping centres.

In 1949 Xi'an did not extend much farther than the walled city, covering only 13.2 square kilometres (5 square miles). Today the city has spread to 100 square kilometres (38.6 square miles), an extent even larger than the Tang capital of Chang'an, which occupied an area of 81 square kilometres (31.3 square miles) within the outer walls. The modern city is not so regular in its layout as its great predecessor, and it extends further to the east and west than the Tang city.

The population has increased rapidly since the 1930s when it was between 200,000 and 300,000. In 2003, the population in the metropolitan area, including people living both within the urban area and the outlying villages, was 7.16 million.

Sights

The Forest of Steles

The Forest of Steles Museum was formally established in 1952 and occupies the former Temple of Confucius along the inside of the southern section of the city wall, on Baishulin Jie. It was once the principal museum for Shaanxi and displayed antiquities from every part of the province. Today, those exhibits illustrating the history of Shaanxi are in the National Museum of Shaanxi History (see page 239) which opened in July 1991.

The famous collection of over 1,000 inscribed stones known as the Forest of Steles began in 1090 when a large Confucian collection of steles cut in 837 CE—the oldest existing texts of the Confucian classics—was moved for safekeeping to the back of the Temple of Confucius. The collection slowly grew until the 18th century when it was already called by its present name. It is the largest collection of its kind in China. The art of inscribing on stone began in China at least as early as the fourth century BCE. The earliest examples that have survived from this time are the ten Stone Drums of Qin. Recording a hunting party led by a Duke of Qin, they were discovered during the Tang dynasty at Fengxiang, about 145 kilometres (90 miles) west of Xi'an. The originals are now in Beijing but a reproduction of one of them is on display in the National Museum of Shaanxi History.

From the Han dynasty onwards flat stones were cut with either text or pictures, not only for commemorative purposes but also to make it possible to reproduce them on paper by taking rubbings. These rubbings, made into either scrolls or books, often serve as models for calligraphy practice.

As a rough guide, the contents of the Forest of Steles can be divided into four groups: works of literature and philosophy, historical records, calligraphy and pictorial stones. Of most immediate interest and appeal are the pictorial stones in Room Four, which are displayed with some stones engraved with historical records. They are almost all relatively late, from the Ming (1368–1644) or Qing (1644–1911). As well as landscapes and portraits—notably of Confucius and Bodhidarma, the founder of Zen Buddhism—there are some fascinating stones with allegorical pictures and some texts written to appear like pictures (it was a Qing fashion to create pictures composed of Chinese characters). Unlike the other halls which house steles dense with Chinese characters, the more pictorial stones can be appreciated without the ability to read Chinese.

Room Three houses a calligraphy collection which is of great importance. The first stone on the right was carved by Shi Mengying in 999 during the Northern Song dynasty. It shows characters in ancient seal script with, written very small below each of these, the corresponding character in regular script. This is of particular interest for those studying the origin and evolution of Chinese writing. There are also two reconstructed examples of the calligraphy of Wang Xizhi (321–379 CE) which have had immense influence on the art of the brush, together with pieces by many of the Tang dynasty masters. If you would like to see the famous Nestorian Stele (see page 188), cut in 781CE, it is in Room Two, immediately to the left of the entrance. It records the history of the Nestorian Christian community in Chang'an from its founding in the seventh century by a Syrian missionary. Note the tiny cross inscribed at the top and the decorative Arabic script at the bottom. Room One contains the nucleus of the collection, the set of 114 stones engraved in 837 CE with the definitive text of the Confucian classics. Inscribed on both sides of the stones, the text uses a staggering total of 650,252 characters. Regardless of whether one can read Chinese, the sheer number of characters makes it abundantly clear that the written word was highly venerated.

Room Five exhibits stone tablets of the Song, Yuan, Ming and Qing dynasties. They are mainly concerned with temple renovation and records of merit, although

some are also noted for their calligraphic artistic value. In Room Six most of the inscriptions are poetic, inscribed by the literati of the Yuan, Ming and Qing. Emperors, noted ministers and famous calligraphers of various dynasties have left many inscriptions, examples of which are displayed in Room Seven.

THE STONE SCULPTURE GALLERY

This gallery, which is beside the Forest of Steles, has a collection of about 70 sculptures and relief carvings of unrivalled quality. The exhibits are very well presented and stylishly lit, with good captions in English. The most famous exhibits are the six bas-reliefs from Zhao Ling (see page 200), the mausoleum of Emperor Tang Taizong, a great military commander who was particularly fond of horses. The six bas-reliefs of his favourite mounts, including his most famous horse, 'Quanmo', were originally placed at the northern entrance to the tomb. The 'Quanmo' stone, together with one other, was taken to the United States by an American archaeologist in 1914. They are now in the Art Museum of the University of Pennsylvania. The other four original stones are on display, along with plaster reproductions of the two in America. The originals were sadly broken in several places in 1918, apparently in an attempt to facilitate their transport abroad.

A number of large animals which once lined the approaches to imperial tombs of the Han and Tang are also exhibited, including lions, a tiger, a rhinoceros and an ostrich. There is also the inscribed black jade-stone sarcophagus and tomb door of Li Shou, the cousin of first Tang Emperor Gaozu, which was unearthed in 1973.

The exhibition also contains several Buddhist statues including a very beautiful torso of a bodhisattva, showing the strong Indian influence typical of the Tang dynasty, and an Avalokitesvara on an elaborate lotus throne, from the same period. Outside the sculpture gallery stands a collection of stone hitching posts, used during the Ming and Qing dynasties for tying up horses. The tops are usually decorated with carved lions. There are two rows of these, on either side of the path, just inside the entrance to the museum.

Just before exiting the museum, an exhibition hall on the right hand side displays recently unearthed Buddha statues. The sculptures are imposing in size. There is minimal captioning in Chinese, but none in English. The fact that they are recently excavated is a reminder of how very rich the Xi'an area is in historical artefacts.

THE NATIONAL MUSEUM OF SHAANXI HISTORY

The National Museum of Shaanxi History opened in 1991, eighteen years after Premier Zhou Enlai first suggested that such an establishment was needed to exhibit the province's archaeological treasures. Occupying a large site in Xi'an's southern

(Left) *A stone rubbing being made at the Forest of Steles Museum. A sheet of damp paper is first placed on the stone and allowed to dry and then pounded with a pad of tightly wrapped cloth soaked in ink.*

suburbs close to the Big Goose Pagoda, the museum, housed in a complex of striking Tang dynasty style pavilions, is an absolute must for every visitor to the city.

The exhibits here represent the very best of the museum's collection, the greater portion of which remain stored in its underground warehouse. The permanent exhibition on the ground and first floors is supplemented by touring exhibitions, usually two, in the basement. Included elsewhere in the museum are lecture theatres, conference rooms, a library, research laboratories and an extensive restoration centre. A new unit for restoration has been funded by an Italian Antiquities Department donation of US$4 million.

For security reasons, visitors to the museum must leave their bags in the cloakroom before entering the galleries. A spacious entrance hall greets visitors with its reproduction lion from Shun Ling, the tomb of Wu Zetian's mother. Pace yourself on the stunning marathon walk through a million years of Chinese history. You need about three hours in this museum to do it justice. For longer-stay visitors to Xi'an, a return visit after trips to outlying sites may help to put the sights that you have seen into context. The exhibits on the ground and first floors are arranged in chronological dynastic order.

PREHISTORY TO 2000 BCE

At the entrance to the first gallery a relief map of Shaanxi province shows the three main landscape divisions of the province, from north to south: the loess lands of the Yellow Earth Plateau, the Guanzhong Plain around the Wei River and the Qin mountain range. Most of the exhibits in this museum were unearthed from the Guanzhong Plain, one of the cradles of Chinese civilization. Relics in this room hail from Shaanxi's three main prehistoric sites—Lantian, Dali and Banpo. Fossilized remains of old Stone-Age man were discovered at Lantian and Dali, while at Banpo the foundations of a Neolithic village have been excavated (see page 79). Pottery with distinctive markings such as the fish design were among the most remarkable finds at Banpo.

XIA, SHANG, WESTERN AND EASTERN ZHOU DYNASTIES

The second gallery covers the 21st century BCE to 770 BCE, the dawn of the iron and bronze ages. By the Shang and Zhou dynasties, metalworking techniques had become highly sophisticated. Bronze was used in weapons for hunting as well as in battle, ritual implements, agricultural tools, and household and palace utensils. Particularly striking are the handsome cooking tripods (*ding*), some measuring up to one metre (3.3 feet) high. The Chinese government sent a replica of the largest tripod-cooking vessel on display as a gift to the United Nations headquarters. Also look out for the four-legged cooking vessel from the Shang dynasty, which is the only one of its kind. Elegant bulbous-based and thin-legged wine vessels (*jue*) were used for warming liquor. Weapons include daggers, halberds and spearheads, as well as stick-shaped scabbards with sawtooth edges.

Moving onto the relics from the Western Zhou and later the Eastern Zhou, one sees the same material, bronze, cast into more elegant, beautiful and practical wares. Extremely impressive are the bronze bells. There is a single Shicheng Bell, about the size of the largest of watermelons, a musical instrument used in the home of a nobleman or even at court. In a separate display case close-by is one of the museum's finest pieces, a set of chime bells (*bianzhong*). The set consists of eight bells suspended from a wooden beam and arranged according to size. Strangely enough, although their number corresponds to the eight notes of an octave, the fourth and seventh notes, 'fa', and 'ti', are absent. Discovered at Fufeng County, the bells were almost certainly used to entertain the courts established by the Zhou (see page 80). Other examples of aesthetic refinement in Zhou bronzeware include a fine ox-shaped wine vessel, an ornate incense burner, an artist's palette and a bronze vessel with a cover and handle.

SPRING AND AUTUMN PERIOD, THE WARRING STATES AND QIN DYNASTY 770 BCE–206 BCE

In the third gallery the exhibits highlight progress made during the Qin dynasty in the fields of construction, plumbing, metallurgy, agriculture and irrigation, weaponry and public works. However, rapid economic and technical development had already begun to take place in the pre-imperial period. Around 400 BCE, the casting of iron became widespread, as evidenced by the many remains of axes, spades and swords excavated in Shaanxi, a region rich in minerals.

The most important relics from Qin times are, of course, the terracotta warriors (four of which are on display here), but visitors are sure to go to the museum located at the excavations (see page 99). Look instead for a tiger tally. It is quite small, but this ingenious object was a symbol of imperial authority—its holder or recipient could be certain orders were genuine if both halves of the tally matched. Although not immediately apparent, the tally comes in two symmetrical parts split along the animal's backbone. There is also a very interesting exhibit demonstrating the standardization of weights, measures and coinage that took place at this time.

HAN DYNASTY 202 BCE–220 CE

An elaborate wooden map on the wall in this exhibition room, the first one upstairs on the left, highlights the expansion of Han China. The Silk Road became important during this period (see page 153). Travellers who have visited the Han tombs north of Xi'an will see fine examples of funerary objects, such as a gold incense burner discovered from the area of the tomb of the Han general, Huo Qubing (see page 155). Other excavated tombs in the north Guanzhong Plain have yielded tomb figurines which were on a more modest scale than Qin Shihuangdi's terracotta army, but which nevertheless provide much information about daily life at that time. To keep the deceased content in the afterlife a variety of models in pottery were produced, including water wells, pigsties, barns and domestic animals such as oxen, chicken and dogs. For those who cannot get to the Xianyang Museum, a couple of hundred

Portrait of Confucius on a stone tablet in the Forest of Steles Museum.

Tang-dynasty ox-head agate cup, unearthed at Hejia Village, Xi'an.
It was probably imported from Central Asia or Sassanian Iran.

of the miniature terracotta army are shown here. Finally, there are a number of exhibits to illustrate Han ingenuity. Paper making, one of the four great Chinese inventions—the others were gunpowder, printing and the compass—is generally attributed to the Han Wudi period of 140–87 BCE. This early paper was produced from hemp fibre mixed with ramie (fibre similar to flax and substitute for cotton and linen) by a process of pulping, boiling and drying. Another material unique to China was silk—there is an exquisite gilded bronze silkworm from this period that was used as a burial object. A third group of relics includes gear cogs, nuts and hinges.

WEI, JIN, NORTHERN AND SOUTHERN DYNASTIES 220–581 CE
A small room is devoted to the relics of this period, during which Chang'an lost its capital status and remained relatively unimportant until it regained its pre-eminence as a centre of imperial power and cultural influence under the Tang rulers.

SUI AND TANG DYNASTY 581–907 CE
This was a period that corresponds to Xi'an's restoration as the unified empire's capital. In particular, the brilliance of the mid-Tang period is reflected in the most extensive and spectacular collection of exhibits in this museum. A wooden map, similar to the one in the Han gallery, shows the expansion of Tang China, which capitalized on Sui unification and encompassed present-day Mongolia, Vietnam and parts of Kazakhstan as well as what we recognize as the People's Republic of China today. Beyond, one sees display cases full of markedly colourful relics, consisting in the main of tri-colour glazed pottery articles. Foremost amongst these

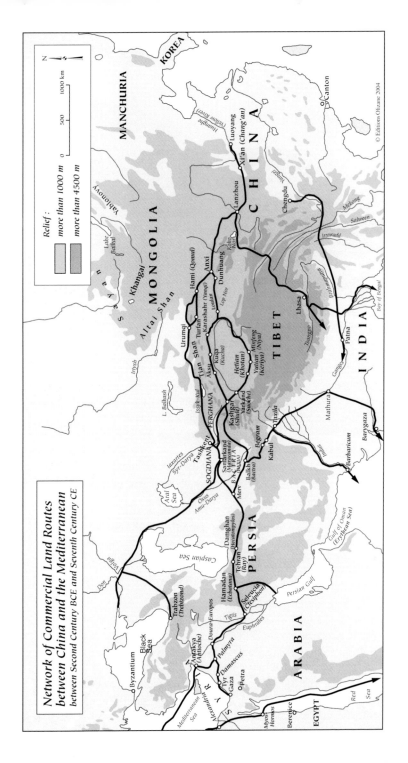

Network of Commercial Land Routes
between China and the Mediterranean
between Second Century BCE and Seventh Century CE

Relief :
more than 1000 m
more than 4500 m

© Editions Olizane 2004

are the handsome horses and camels, which bear witness to Chang'an's links to foreign lands by means of the Silk Road. Particularly outstanding is a band of musicians on a camel in tri-colour pottery. Other figures include heavenly gods stamping on evil and ugly beasts; gargoyle-like animals which were used as guardians of tombs; and Tang beauties with plump cheeks and bouffant hairstyles, shod in shoes with upturned toes. Tang dynasty women were ingenious in the variety of hairstyles they wore. One notable example wears a 'wild bird' coiffure. The mirrors on display highlight the leisured lifestyle of Tang women. These are of highly polished metal, but it is their ornately decorated backs that are of particular interest.

As a backdrop to these colourful relics, some replicas of murals removed from tomb passageways and chambers are displayed. The themes illustrated relate to recreation, fashion and court activities. Most striking are murals showing polo playing, hunting, ladies being attended by maidservants and court officials receiving foreign guests. The originals are so delicate and sensitive that they have to be stored in a special climate-controlled room in the museum and are only accessible to very special visitors.

SONG, YUAN, MING AND QING DYNASTIES

Chang'an was eclipsed with the collapse of the Tang in the early tenth century and neither Xi'an nor its environs ever dominated national affairs again. Although spanning a millennium, the relics from this period only occupy a small area. Particularly noteworthy, however, are the fine porcelain pieces, characteristically sea green or ivory in colour. There are also some examples of *mise*, or secret colour, porcelain plates. Pale olive green in colour, this material is so named because even today scientists are unable to replicate the manufacturing process. These particular examples are from the crypt of Famen Temple (see page 222). Another striking display relates to the Ming dynasty—an array of 300 colourfully painted miniature pottery figures unearthed at the tomb of a Shaanxi official.

THE BELL TOWER

Each Ming city had a bell tower and a drum tower. The bell was sounded at dawn and the drum at dusk. The two buildings still exist in many Chinese cities, but those at Xi'an are the best known in China.

The Bell Tower was originally built in 1384 at the intersection of Xi Dajie and Guangji Jie. This was the centre of the site of the old Tang Imperial City, where the government offices had been located. The tower was removed in 1582 and rebuilt in its present position in the centre of the southern section of the walled city, overlooking the four avenues which lead to the four gates. It was restored in 1739.

The Bell Tower is set on a square brick platform, each side of which is 35.5 metres (116 feet) long, with an arched gateway at ground level. The platform is 8.6 metres

Night view of Xi'an's imposing Bell Tower.

A line of drums sits at the top of Xi'an's Drum Tower.

(28 feet) high and on top is a triple-eaved, two-storey wooden structure, a further 27.4 metres (90 feet) high. There is a fine view in all directions from the parapet on the second floor. The inside is remarkable as an example of the very intricate roof truss system used in Ming and Qing wooden architecture. The original great bell no longer exists, but a small replica Ming-period bell is kept in a corner of the brick platform for visitors to strike. There is an exhibition of ancient instruments on the first floor, and traditional musical performances every hour from 9:00 am to 12:00 noon, and from 2:00 pm to 5:00 pm. On the second floor there are exhibitions of Chinese calligraphy, art and porcelain. The Bell Tower is open from 8:30 am to 6:00 pm

Traffic going around the Ming dynasty Bell Tower. In ancient times, the great bell was sounded at dawn each morning.

November–March, and 8:00 am to 10:00 pm from April–November. The entrance is via the underpass that can be entered at any of the intersections around the traffic circle surrounding the Bell Tower.

THE DRUM TOWER

The Drum Tower is quite similar to the nearby Bell Tower, except for its rectangular shape. It was first built in 1380, and restored in 1669, 1739 and 1853. The brick base, on which the wooden structure is built, is 52.6 metres (172 feet) long, 38 metres (125 feet) wide and 7.7 metres (25 feet) high. A road goes straight through it, under a vaulted archway. The triple-roofed, two-storey wooden building is a further 25.3 metres (83 feet) high off its brick platform. The second storey, which is surrounded by a parapet, is now splendidly restored like the Bell Tower, and is used as an antique shop and sometimes holds art exhibitions. It also houses a collection of a variety of drums in different shapes and sizes and made from different materials. There is an exhibition of Ming and Qing dynasty furniture on the third floor. A drum performance is given several times during the morning and the afternoon. The Drum Tower looks down on the irregular grey-tiled roofs of the Muslim quarter. It is open from 8:30 am to 6:00 pm November–March, and 8:00 am to 10:00 pm from April–November.

Mr. Zhang Goes to Washington

—Ann Dewi Mooney

Our van drives down the muddy paths of Beizhang Village in a light rain as we search for the house of a local paper maker. After we ask about half a dozen villagers, we finally found our way through the narrow alleyways to the humble house of Zhang Pengxue.

Zhang, who had been expecting our arrival, welcomed us into his dimly lit house with a big smile. As we entered his door, he began speaking immediately with great enthusiasm about his paper. He knows just two words in English, both important to his craft: 'mulberry' and 'pulp'. And he uses them over and over again in describing the process of papermaking. With a cigarette clamped in his mouth, he holds stalks of dried mulberry in his two gnarled hands, showing us one of his key ingredients.

The history of paper making in China goes back to the Han Dynasty. Cai Lun, a eunuch who served under Emperor Hedi, is credited with the invention of paper in 105 CE. Zhang's family has been carrying the same tradition of paper making for five generations, since the Qing Dynasty (1644–1911). He was taught to make paper when he was just a boy of ten and continues to make paper today at the age of 65.

There are signs of paper making all over Zhang's house. As you walk into the front yard, there is a big wooden press that keeps the paper flat. In the living room, mulberry stalks are strewn around, and there are a few stacks of paper ready to be sold. Upstairs, a small room is covered with paper drying on the walls. Baskets of pulp sit on the ground in the backyard, and there is a big vat of water under an open shed.

Once a year Zhang collects a truckload of mulberry at a nearby mountain. At home, the mulberry goes through a process of being soaked in water first, then beat down, then steamed, then rinsed off, and then finally chopped up into pulp. The pulp is then dumped into a vat of water. Next to the vat, is a deep pit, where Zhang stands whilst he vigorously stirs up the pulp in the water to get an even mix. A bamboo mat, sitting on a rack, is then dipped into the pool for an even layer of pulp. The bamboo mat is then picked up, flipped over, and rolled away carefully in order to peel the paper off and let it rest on top of the previous sheets. When he has a good stack, it is taken away for the drying process.

Artists use the mulberry paper as it is good for painting and calligraphy. Zhang claims, "the colours don't fade for 20–30 years," and some artists find it has special qualities in that the ink is absorbed differently on paper made with mulberry pulp. It's no surprise that nearby artists make the trek to this small village to buy stacks of the paper. It is also supposed to be much stronger than *xuanzhi*, or rice paper. The fibres are visible and give the paper an interesting texture. It is traditionally used for painting, or writing on, but it would make beautiful wrapping paper and it could also be used for paper crafts such as bookbinding.

We're surprised—almost doubtful—when Mr. Zhang, dressed in simple farmer's clothes spattered with mud, casually tells us that he visited Washington D.C. in 2002. He says he took part in an event at the Smithsonian Museum featuring folk artists living along the Silk Road. And as if to prove his claim, he proudly pulls out an envelope holding a few photos of his paper making demonstration and a soiled copy of a book on the exhibition titled *The Silk Road—Connecting Culture: The 2002 Smithsonian Folklife Festival*. Although he can't read what's written about himself, he beams as he tells us the page in the book where we see a small biography and photograph of the Shaanxi farmer. He then pulls out a small plastic card that he is also quite proud to display—the card key to his room at the Marriott Hotel, a memento of his two-week trip to America.

"Everyone applauded when I did my demonstration in Washington", he says, clapping his hands in imitation, and smiling broadly as he retells his story. "I was very well-received in Washington." In China, however, there is very little interest and this saddens Zhang. "No one values this here," he says shaking his head. "No one." He sighs when asked how much he makes, answering, "Gou yong," or "Just enough to get by."

His younger son is already carrying on the tradition, and while we chat with his father, he's hard at work in the backyard making sheet-after-sheet of paper. We ask him how old he is, and he responds, "I was born in the year of the Ox". Seeing the confusion on our faces, he adds, "I'm 31".

Mr. Zhang says the long family tradition could end with his 7-year-old grandson. The boy stands shyly behind him as he explains that the he will learn papermaking when he turns 15. He adds, with no apparent sadness that if the young boy can attend university, "we won't need to do this anymore."

"You can't make a living off paper", he says matter-of-factly. "Farmers are not afraid of bitterness. We're just afraid of not making money. If we can, we'll still make paper."

Sian-fu
The city wall and the west gate

The southwest corner of the city wall of Sian-fu (Xi'an) photographed by Osvald Siren c. 1920 and published in his milestone work The Walls and Gates of Peking *(Bodley Head, London, 1924). The structure in Xi'an is the only remaining complete Ming dynasty city wall in existence. Nanjing's wall was largely destroyed.*

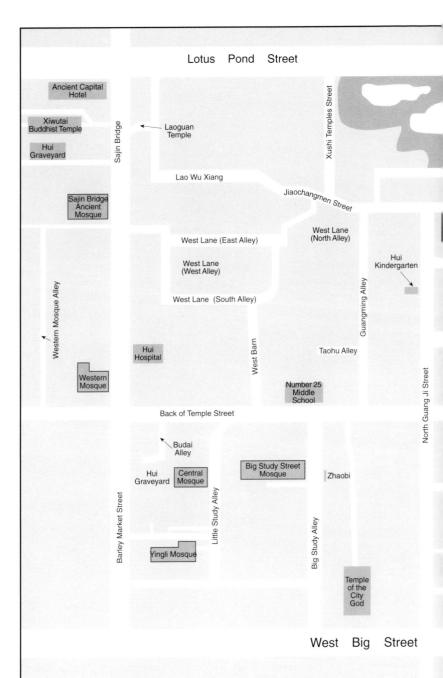

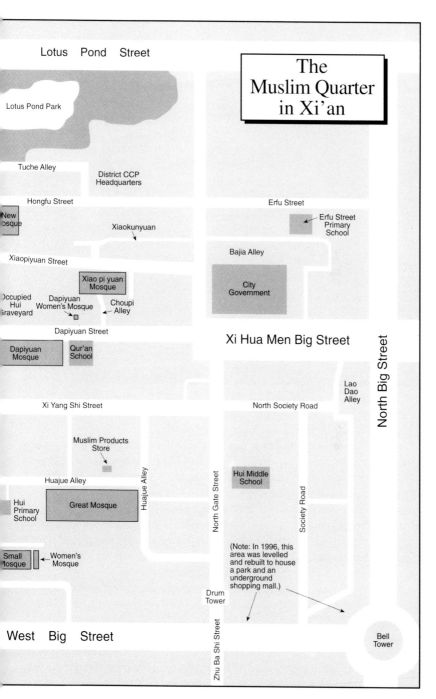

The Muslim Quarter in Xi'an

Lotus Pond Street

Lotus Pond Park

Tuche Alley

District CCP Headquarters

Hongfu Street

New Mosque

Xiaokunyuan

Xiaopiyuan Street

Xiao pi yuan Mosque

Occupied Hui Graveyard

Dapiyuan Women's Mosque

Choupi Alley

Dapiyuan Street

Dapiyuan Mosque

Qur'an School

Xi Yang Shi Street

Muslim Products Store

Huajue Alley

Huajue Alley

Hui Primary School

Great Mosque

Small Mosque

Women's Mosque

West Big Street

Erfu Street

Erfu Street Primary School

Bajia Alley

City Government

Xi Hua Men Big Street

Lao Dao Alley

North Society Road

Hui Middle School

Society Road

North Gate Street

North Big Street

(Note: In 1996, this area was levelled and rebuilt to house a park and an underground shopping mall.)

Drum Tower

Zhu Ba Shi Street

Bell Tower

Reconstructed Ming dynasty city walls and moat surrounding Xi'an.

THE MING CITY WALL AND GATES

Xi'an's 14th-century wall still stands, although today it is intersected by a few modern roads. It is one of the most important city walls in China and certainly one of the best examples from the Ming. Construction began during the reign of Hongwu, the first Ming emperor, on the remains of the Sui and Tang wall and took eight years to complete. Repairs and renovation have now been carried out by the local government to restore the wall to its original splendour and the structure is now once again completely connected. The circumference is 13.7 kilometres (8.5 miles), and it is 12 metres (40 feet) high, 12–14 metres (40–46 feet) wide at the top and 15–18 metres (49–59 feet) wide at the bottom. It is surrounded by a moat.

The Ming city gates face the four cardinal points, set off-centre in each of the sides of the rectangular wall. Originally each gate had two structures: the gate tower, a triple-eaved building 34.6 metres (114 feet) long, and beyond, on the city wall itself, was the massive archers' tower, 53.2 metres (175 feet) in length, with 48 openings on the outer face from which missiles could be fired on a potential enemy. Visitors are usually taken to the towers above the South Gate, which are well preserved; but instead of guardrooms and barracks you will now find souvenir shops and showrooms inside them.

Access to the top of the wall can also be gained at the North and West gates, and at all of the smaller gates along the south wall, where landscaping of the area between the wall and moat has provided a pleasant setting for a stroll. At the South Gate bicycles can be rented, and one can ride six kilometres along the wall, including the return trip. Motorized tourist vehicles are also available for the journey. It is open from 8:00 am to 10:00 pm and is attractively lit in the evening.

Xi'an's city wall detail.

THE MUSLIM QUARTER

The early Muslims in China came from what was known at Xiyu, or "the west", areas usually identified as Arabia or Persia. These people were much different from the Chinese in terms of their language, culture and physical appearance. Like other foreigners in China, they were labeled "foreign sojourners".

Islam was first introduced by Arab merchants during the Tang dynasty, and flourished during the Yuan (1279–1368). The Muslims gradually became concentrated in the northwestern part of the walled city, where they remain to this day. The community now numbers more than 60,000, or about one percent of the city's population. The residents, whose families have lived here for hundreds of years, are proud of their religion. They strongly identify with their mosque, frequently introducing themselves as "belonging" to this or that mosque. This is because the mosques play a key role in the daily lives of the Hui, or Muslims, filling a variety of spiritual and secular needs.

There were said to be 14 mosques open before the Cultural Revolution put a stop to Muslim privileges. But today, the community is regaining lost ground, and there are ten active mosques in the quarter, and chantlike Arabic calls can be heard throughout the area. All of the mosques have loudspeakers used to call people to prayer five times a day, a reminder that the residents' lives are also guided by Islamic time. Islam demands that each of the five daily prayer worships be preceded by a ritual washing of the hands, feet, face, nose, mouth, eyes and ears, and the mosques all provide ablution rooms with running water for washing. Although the Muslims generally work on Fridays, they do observe Ramadan, the month of fasting from sunrise to sunset. The men can often be distinguished from the Han Chinese by their white caps and long beards.

Many visitors to the quarter only visit the Great Mosque or stroll down Beiyuanmen Street, but there's a lot more to see here. Walk along the bustling side streets of the quarter for a closer look at life in the area (see map page 252). You'll walk past hundreds of small shops and restaurants (these are popular with the Han Chinese as well) as well as numerous stalls selling exotic spices and foods. Street names of the quarter, such as Western Sheep Market Street, Big Leather Yard, and Barley Market Street, are all indications of the long Muslim history of the area.

The Great Mosque

The beautiful mosque lies close to the Drum Tower in Huajue Xiang. It is surrounded by the old houses and narrow lanes of Xi'an's Muslim, or Hui, quarter. The mosque is still active: on ordinary days about 100 men pray there, with perhaps 1,000 on Fridays. Of the ten or so functioning mosques in the city this is the only one which is open to visitors, although non-Muslims are not admitted to the main prayer hall or at prayer times.

Islam has been the most enduring of all faiths in Xi'an. The Great Mosque survived the Cultural Revolution virtually unscathed and remains an outstanding Chinese re-interpretation of an Islamic place of worship. It was founded in 742 CE, according to a stone tablet in the mosque, but nothing from this Tang period survives. While some residents say the Great Mosque is the oldest mosque in China, others argue that the Big Study Street Mosque is older. The present layout dates from the 14th century. Restoration work was done in 1527, 1606 and 1768. The mosque occupies a rectangle 250 metres by 47 metres (820 feet by 155 feet), divided into four courtyards. Throughout there are walls with decoratively carved brick reliefs and the buildings are roofed with beautiful turquoise tiles.

The first courtyard, which was restored in 1981, has an elaborate wooden arch nine metres (29.5 feet) high dating from the 17th century. It contains a stone arch and two free-standing steles. One bears the calligraphy of a famous Song master, Mi Fu (1051–1107), the other that of Dong Qichang of the Ming.

At the entrance to the third courtyard is a Stele Hall with tablets of the Ming and Qing periods inscribed in Chinese, Arabic and Persian. The Stele of the Months, written in Arabic by an imam in 1733, bears information about the Islamic calendar.

In the middle of the third courtyard is the minaret, an octagonal pagoda with a triple roof of turquoise tiles, known as the Shengxin Tower. On either side are sets of rooms. In one section, next to the imam's living quarters, there is a fascinating Qing dynasty map of the Islamic world painted by Chinese Muslims with the black cube of the Kaaba at Mecca in the centre. In the same room is kept an illuminated, hand-written Koran dating from the Qing dynasty.

Muslim faithful walking to evening prayers.

The fourth courtyard, the principal one of the complex, contains the Prayer Hall. By the entrance is a small room with an upright stele recording in Chinese the foundation of the mosque in 742 CE. The stone itself is probably not original. In front of the entrance is the ornamental Phoenix Pavilion with a board proclaiming the 'One Truth of the One God', written during the Ming. Behind the Phoenix Pavilion are two fountains flanked by two small stele pavilions and behind them is the broad, raised stone terrace used for worship.

The large Prayer Hall dates from the Ming: the board outside the main door was bestowed by the Yongle Emperor (reigned 1403–24). The ornate woodwork inside is mainly of this period. There is a coffered ceiling, each panel containing different Arabic inscriptions. The mihrab at the far end has some fine carving.

To walk to the Great Mosque go north along the street that passes under the Drum Tower, and take the first left. A sign in English indicates the way. Along the way you'll pass numerous stalls selling souvenirs, the majority available throughout China. The Great Mosque is open from 8:30 am to 6:00 pm.

Temple of the City God.

THE TEMPLE OF THE EIGHT IMMORTALS

China's indigenous religion, Taoism, is best represented in Xi'an by the Temple of the Eight Immortals (*Baxian An*).

Located just east of the city wall, outside Zhongshan Gate, it housed 100 priests as recently as 20 years ago. But at the start of the Cultural Revolution in 1966 half the buildings were demolished by iconoclastic Red Guards, and those that survived were converted into a machine plant. Under a decade-long restoration programme initiated in 1981, the plant was moved out and the temple halls rebuilt and redecorated.

The temple is now functioning again as a place of worship and a centre for the training of priests. There are now more than 40 of them, easily distinguishable from other Chinese by their long hair, usually plaited and stuffed into one of nine different types of black hat according to their sect, sage-like long beards, white shirts, blue smocks, white gaiters and black canvas shoes.

Although no foundation steles exist, it is thought the temple was established during the Northern Song (960–1127 CE). It expanded during the Yuan and Ming, and became particularly important during the Qing. When the imperial court was in exile in Xi'an (1900–01), the Empress Dowager Cixi grew especially fond of the temple and used to go there to paint peonies.

The Temple of the City God

Within walking distance of the Bell Tower, this temple is now occupied by the bustling City God Temple Market (*Chenghuang Miao Shi*). Walk west from the Bell Tower along Xi Dajie and look for the entrance on the right, set back from the road. You'll first walk through a busy arcade of stalls selling all kinds of bric-a-brac and household items, including opera costumes, musical instruments, drums, swords, incense, Chinese toys, and clothing and accessories. One is amongst the temple buildings before realizing it. Some of the buildings are even used as storerooms or shops. The temple has not been well maintained, although renovation work was going on in the empty main hall at the beginning of 2005. Much of the paint on the woodwork has disappeared and grass is growing out of the roof tiles on top of the temple.

The temple dates back to 1389, but was moved to its present site in 1432. It has been rebuilt and restored many times since, notably in 1723, after a fire damaged the building, and when materials were utilized from the 14th-century palace of the Prince of Qin, Zhu Shuang. Parts of the structure were bombed in 1942. The main hall, built in 1723, survives with ornate carved doors and a roof of turquoise glazed tiles. In front of it is an elaborate wooden arch in good condition. The entrance ticket is 2 yuan and includes sticks of incense. Open from 9:00 am to 12:00 noon and from 2:00 pm to 4:00 pm.

Revolution Park

Revolution Park (*Geming Gongyuan*), in the northeast of the walled city, is the burial ground of those who died in the 1926 Siege of Xi'an. Anti-Nationalist forces laid siege to Xi'an on 15 May 1926 after the city had been occupied by a pro-Nationalist general, Yang Hucheng. Despite appalling starvation and a fierce bombing attack, the city held out until 28 November 1926, when the siege was finally lifted. Yang Hucheng wrote the funeral couplet for those 50,000 inhabitants and refugees who are said to have died during the siege:

> They led glorious lives and died a glorious death.
> Their merits are known throughout Shaanxi, as are their regrets.

The park contains a three-storey pagoda erected in 1927, and is very popular with the locals, especially on Sundays.

The Eighth Route Army Office Museum

Near Revolution Park at 1 Qixianzhuang, just off Beixin Jie, is the Eighth Route Army Office (initially called the Red Army Liaison Office) which is now a museum. It was founded immediately after the Xi'an Incident, which had resulted in the Nationalists and Communists joining forces against the Japanese (see page 192).

The office once linked the headquarters of the Communist Party in Yan'an (see page 286) in northern Shaanxi with the outside world in the struggle against the Japanese.

It obtained vital supplies for Yan'an, helped recruits make their way there, and publicized the polices of the party leadership. The office functioned until 10 September 1946. It is now preserved as it was during the Sino-Japanese War.

Occupying a series of plain, grey and white one-storey buildings set around four courtyards, the museum is a good deal more interesting than its name might suggest. There is an exhibition room with many fascinating photographs taken in Shaanxi during the 1930s and 1940s. Visitors are also shown where important Communist leaders, including Zhou Enlai, Deng Xiaoping, Zhu De and Liu Shaoqi stayed. The rooms are small and spartan with little more than a table, chair and a bed. The Canadian doctor Norman Bethune (see page 306), later to become almost a cult figure in China, was also once a visitor here. The museum houses the 'Snow Studies Centre' (see page 283), which was opened in 1992.

The office still has its 1939 Chevrolet, originally imported from Hong Kong and used for urgent missions to Yan'an. The radio room contains the old transmitter and receiver, and the well they had to draw their bitter water from still exists. The museum is open 9:00 am to 5:00 pm.

Qin Palace Film Set

This reproduction Qin Palace, a few minutes walk east of the Big Goose Pagoda, was built in 1988 for the IMAX film Qin Shihuang, a joint-venture production between Xi'an Film Studio and the Canadian State Film Bureau.

According to legend, the first emperor, Qin Shihuangdi, used the weapons he confiscated to make 12 monolithic copper statues. Replicas of these stand sentinel on the avenue approach to the palace. Climbing up the long flight of steps you reach the only hall of the palace, where dummies are dressed in Qin costume. The climb is worth the effort if only to stand and admire the view and imagine for a moment you are the emperor looking down on the giant statues.

On the right hand side of the hall is an exhibition room displaying stills of Xi'an Film Studio's most successful movies, notably *To Live*, *Red Sorghum* (filmed in Shandong), and *After the Final Battle*, a look at the re-education of Kuomintang officers in the post-Liberation years of the People's Republic.

A large dusty concourse in front of the elevated palace façade is dotted with a hotchpotch of redundant film-set props, including tanks, concrete horses and chariots. Just inside the entrance to the left is a mock Qin-dynasty street lined with shops used during the filming, however, these now sell tourist souvenirs.

CHIMERA

To this Tang capital, already old in refinement, Arabs and Persian arrived by the Silk Route or the southern ports. They came as merchants and mercenary soldiers, and the houses of their Muslim descendants, who call themselves Hui, still cluster in whitewashed lanes. Yet the people looked identical to Han Chinese, and when I ventured into the chief mosque I was surrounded by pagodas, dragon-screens and tilted eaves. Only when I looked closer did I notice that on some memorials Chinese characters gave way to the dotted swing of Arabic, and the prayer-hall enclosed no plump idol but an empty space, inviting a god only in the mind.

Outside, a few caretakers were sweeping leaves along the garden pathways. The chanting of the Koran sounded from a closed room. In one arcade an old man, the skin peeled white about his eyes, was singing in a high, weak voice, while a quorum of ancients seated round him quavered applause. Amongst them the imam of the mosque—a dark, lordly figure— exuded urbane authority. I sidled into talk with him. I was intrigued, I said, by the provenance of his people.

'We arrived in Xi'an as simple traders', he said, 'and nobody has any record of his ancestry except in his head. Our people came along the Silk Road during the Tang years.' His fingers made a little galloping motion in the air. 'But we stopped speaking Arabic long ago. Even I can only read the classical language of the Koran.'

'But you've been to Mecca?'

'I made the pilgrimage in 1956.'

He was dressed portentously in white cap and blue-grey robes. I played with the idea of his Arab-Persian descent for a while, studying his hirsute chin and tufted eyebrows. But nothing in his face—nor in that of anyone else—betrayed a trace of western Asia. 'You all look Chinese,' I said.

'Yes,' he answered bluntly. 'I can't tell any difference myself, not in any of us—and there are fifty thousand Hui in the city. But I suppose if we hadn't intermarried we would have died out. Still, it's a mystery.'

'In the Cultural Revolution…'

'Oh that.' He smoothed his hands resolutely over his robes. 'The Red Guards arrived planning to smash up the mosque, but I sat them down and *talked to them. I told them this was a historical place of great importance. Then...'—even now he looked surprised by the outcome—'then they just left. They simply went away.' A flicker of his fingers dispelled them. 'The mosque was closed down, of course, and we went into the fields.... But nobody touched it.'*

A lesser man would have called it a miracle.

Colin Thubron, *Behind the Wall: A Journey Through China*,
William Heinemann, 1987

Muslims at prayer in Xi'an.

Huashan

Introduction to Huashan

HUASHAN

Huashan is one of China's five holy Taoist mountains and since ancient times it has been the home of cave dwelling Taoist and Buddhist hermits searching for the Buddhist and Taoist tradition of solitary contemplation.

Taoists say that historic Taoism may have been born at the western end of the Qin Mountains on Loukuantai. However, it's said that the prehistoric form of Taoism flourished much earlier at the other end of the Qin Mountains on Huashan.

In his book *Road to Heaven – Encounter with Chinese Hermits*, writer and translator Bill Porter (see page 269) explains the mountain's significance for Taoists dates back even longer than prehistoric times to the time of creation.

According to Chinese legend, at creation Chaos split into yin and yang. When these divided again into a greater and lesser yin and a greater and lesser yang, the combined interaction produced a myriad of creatures, the first being Pan Gu. Upon birth, Pan Gu picked up a hammer and chisel and spent the remainder of his life knocking out the space between heaven and earth in which we live. But instead of working just seven days, it took him eighteen thousand years. And when Pan Gu finally died, his body was transformed into the five sacred mountains: his head became the eastern mountain; his arms the northern and southern mountains; his belly, the central mountain; and his feet, the western mountain. Then, after several millennia of weathering, Pan Gu's feet came to resemble a blossom rising from a foliage of stone, and the ancient Chinese named the western mountain Huashan, or Flower Mountain.

The climb was once a daunting venture, with several fatalities allegedly occurring each year on these narrow mountain trails and vertical cliff 'paths'. However, the addition of a cable car and ongoing improvements to the trails in recent years have made the hike considerably easier and safer.

A visit to the 2,200 metre tall granite peaks of Huashan can take one or two days. The North Peak is the stepping off point for visiting the other four peaks and there are several ways to reach this peak. For those who tire easily, a new state-of-the-art Austrian cable car whisks visitors up to the North Peak in 5–10 minutes, depending on the weather. From the cable car terminal, the top of the North Peak can be easily reached in less than 15 minutes.

If you decide to climb rather than take the cable car, one path begins at Huashan Village. From here it is a 6-kilometre walk up more than 3,000 steps in 2-4 hours, depending on your stamina. The first 4 kilometres is rather easy, but along the remaining 2 kilometres the steps become steeper and the walk can be very strenuous. But it's worth the effort. Along the way you'll see beautiful scenery and maybe some of the cave homes once inhabited by Taoist recluses—most of who have been driven away by encroaching tourism. You'll also pass by numerous stalls selling food and drinks.

The other four peaks are each about an hour's walk from each other, and the paths are well marked. In some areas, thick chains have been bolted into the hard rock to help one negotiate the steps that have been cut out of the mountain.

Visitors keen to see the sunrise can stay at a hotel on the East Peak and wake up in time for sunrise. Many visitors, however, begin their walk up the mountain at around 11:00 pm carrying torches, reaching the East Peak as the sun comes up.

April–May and September–October are the best seasons for a visit to Huashan. The walk can be slippery and dangerous in the winter months when snow covers the area.

The round-trip cable car ride costs 110 yuan, which is in addition to the 70 yuan entrance fee. The cable car runs from 7:00 am to 7:00 pm in the summer, and from 7:00 am to 5:00 pm in the winter. Huashan, 120 kilometres (75 miles) east of Xi'an, can be reached by bus or train in about two hours. The closest train station is at Mengyuan, which is 15 kilometres east of Huashan. Small buses shuttle to and from Huashan Village and the mountain.

The Beifeng Guest House sits precariously on a cliff atop the north peak of Huashan.

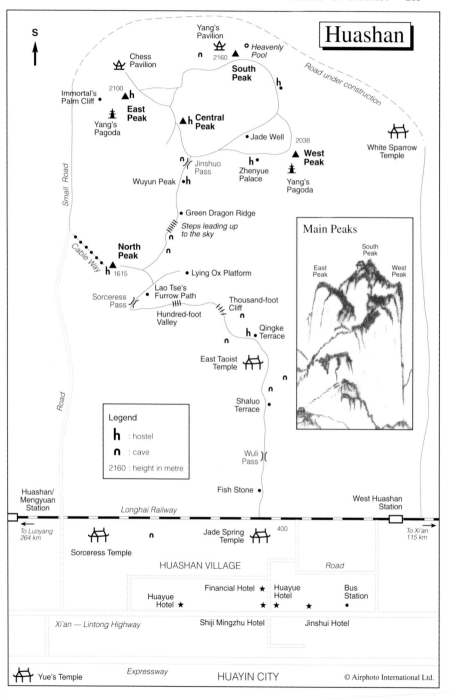

S

Huashan

Yang's Pavilion

2160 ▲ ○ *Heavenly Pool*

Road under construction

Chess Pavilion

South Peak

Immortal's Palm Cliff •

2100 ▲ h

East Peak

h •

Yang's Pagoda

▲ h **Central Peak**

• Jade Well

2038

▲ **West Peak**

White Sparrow Temple

Jinshuo Pass

h •
Zhenyue Palace

Wuyun Peak • h

Yang's Pagoda

Small Road

• Green Dragon Ridge

Steps leading up to the sky

Main Peaks

Cable Way

North Peak

h 1615

• Lying Ox Platform

South Peak

East Peak

West Peak

Lao Tse's • Furrow Path

Sorceress Pass

Thousand-foot Cliff

Hundred-foot Valley

h • Qingke Terrace

East Taoist Temple

Shaluo Terrace

Road

Wuli Pass

Fish Stone •

Legend

h : hostel

n : cave

2160 : height in metre

Huashan/ Mengyuan Station

Longhai Railway

West Huashan Station

← To Luoyang 264 km

Jade Spring Temple

400

To Xi'an → 115 km

Sorceress Temple

HUASHAN VILLAGE

Road

Financial Hotel ★ Huayue Hotel

Bus Station

Huayue Hotel ★

★ ★ ★ ●

Xi'an — Lintong Highway Shiji Mingzhu Hotel Jinshui Hotel

Yue's Temple *Expressway* HUAYIN CITY

© Airphoto International Ltd.

Steps hewn into the precipitous slopes of Huashan, 120 kilometres east of Xi'an, are ever-present reminders of the pilgrims' dangerous adventure walking the Thousand Foot Pillar (Qianchi) whilst in awe of the breathtaking views. (Top right) People wait for sunrise on East Peak.

The state-of-the art Austrian-built lift can make the steep, hold-your-breath,
1,610-metre ascent to the north peak of Huashan in just five minutes.

SOUND OF THE CRANE

On our first trip to China, we saw a picture of Huashan in a flight magazine. It was so dreamlike, we couldn't imagine actually being in such a place. But that was before we discovered hermits in the Chungnan Mountains and realized Huashan was at their eastern end. On our second trip, Steve and I decided it was time to climb P'an-ku's feet.

It was the middle of August and the middle of summer rains. After waiting for the sun in Xi'an for a week, we decided to take a chance. Four hours and 120 kilometres later, we were looking up Huashan's one muddy street into the mountains. We could see blue sky.

We dropped our gear in a cheap hotel and set out to explore. Past a gauntlet of tourist shops, we entered the main gate of Yuchuanyuan, or Jade Spring Temple. It was built in the middle of the eleventh century as a shrine to Ch'en T'uan, who had lived here as a hermit the century before. Besides inspiring early Neo-Confucian thinkers with his Wuqidu (Diagram of the Limitless), Ch'en cultivated Taoist meditation and was known for his ability to remain in a sleeplike trance for months at a time. His reclining figure can still be seen in a small cave on the west side of the grounds. For a small donation, the old lady in charge of the shrine let us inside. We ran our hands over Ch'en's stone figure. It had been touched by so many hands since it was carved in 1103, it looked and felt like polished black jade.

Nearby was a pavilion that Ch'en had built on top of a boulder. And in front of the boulder grew the lone survivor of four cuttings Ch'en planted from the tree beneath which the Buddha was born. According to one Taoist legend, after Lao-tzu joined the immortals, he was reborn as Shakyamuni. The Red Guards apparently thought they had destroyed the last of the four trees, but its gnarled stump was still sending forth shoots.

Just outside the entrance to the main shrine, a stele carved with a representation of Huashan caught our attention. It was cracked in the middle, but we studied it as best as we could through the protective bars and the dust on its surface. If the mountain was anything like the picture, Steve and I were going to lose some weight.

On the east side of the temple grounds, we stopped again at a stone marker next to another boulder. This was one of the many graves of Hua T'uo, China's greatest medical genius, who died in 207 CE at the age of ninety-seven. For many years Hua lived in a cave on Huashan and collected herbs. Among his accomplishments was the use of acupuncture and hemp-based anaesthetics to perform surgery. He is also credited with devising five forms of exercise that were later developed into the basic styles of Chinese martial arts.

Beyond Hua T'uo's grave and the eastern wall of Jade Spring Temple were two smaller Taoist monasteries. The first was Shihertung Temple, where most visiting monks stay. We walked past its rusted metal gate and after another hundred metres entered the brick and wooden doorway of Hsienku Temple. A Chinese friend in Xi'an had told us this was where Master Hsieh lived. We found him propped up in bed treating his arthritic knees with a heat lamp. Once renowned for his skill in martial arts, he now had trouble walking. His room included two plank beds pushed together and covered by a mosquito net, an arrangement I found in the rooms of other monks who used their beds for meditation and study as well as sleep. There were two chests containing books and clothes, a desk, two folding chairs, a new colour TV (presented by the provincial government for help in cultural preservation), and a scroll with the Chinese character for patience on the wall.

After exchanging introductions, I handed Master Hsieh a cigar and lit one myself. While we smoked, he told me about his life. He was born in Anhui Province and became a monk while he was still in his teens. After the standard three-year apprenticeship, he came to Huashan to practice. At the time of our meeting, he had just turned eighty and had been living at Huashan for sixty years.

Master Hsueh went into his bedroom and came out with a bag of pine seeds that he had collected from trees that grew at the summit. Huashan pines are a special species native to the summits of the higher peaks of the Chungnan Mountains. They're famous among tree growers throughout China, Korea, and Japan, and those that grow on Huashan's West Peak are the most famous of all. Their seeds, pollen, and even their needles were a staple in the diet of Taoists who lived on Huashan in the past. Ancient texts claim that after a thousand years the resin from the Huashan pine turns into amber and that eating it can transform a person into an immortal. Master Hsieh said to eat the seeds or plant them and grow trees. I told him I was an old friend of the pine family and would rather grow trees.

Later, as Steve and I walked back to our room under a bright moon, I wondered if Hsieh was among the last in the long line of Taoists who had been coming to Huashan for the past five thousand years, a line that included Mao Meng, who came to Huashan more than two thousand years ago. After he achieved immortality and disappeared on the back of a dragon in broad daylight, his descendants travelled to the eastern coastal province of Kiangsu, where they established on Maoshan one of China's most famous Taoist centres.

The next morning, Steve and I woke to sunlight for the first time in more than a week. We went back through the courtyard of Jade Spring Temple and began our hike up the gorge that led to the summit. It was the height of summer, and the morning sun was intense. We were glad to have the shade of the gorge as we began what turned out to be an eight-hour climb. After several kilometres, the main gorge opened up at Shaloping.

We continued along the gorge and paused again at the base of Maonudong Peak, named for a woman who cultivated the Tao. Her original name was Yu-chiang, and she once lived in a cave near the summit. When the first emperor of the Ch'in dynasty died in 210 BCE, a number of his concubines were chosen to join him in eternal repose. Yu-chiang was among those selected to play the heavenly zither. But the night before she was to be taken to the emperor's mausoleum near Lishan, an old eunuch helped her escape to Huashan.

Later, she met a Taoist master who taught her how to survive on a diet of pine needles and spring water, how to visualize the seven stars of the Big Dipper that connect a person's life force, and how to walk the shaman's Walk of Yu. Through such cultivation, her body became covered with long green hair, and people started calling her Mao-nu, down-haired Maiden. Since that time, hunters have periodically reported hearing the sound of her zither and seeing a flash of green near this peak where she once lived.

A few hundred metres past Maonudong, Huashan Gorge ended. We were at Chingkoping, the location of Tungtao Temple. Chingkoping is also the halfway point between the mouth of Huashan Gorge and the summit. It's 5.5 kilometres either way. But the next half is the hardest. The trail seems to go straight up, and in some places the gradient is, in fact, ninety degrees. Although shamans and Taoists had reportedly been climbing Huashan for centuries, if not millennia, it wasn't until the third century BCE that King Chao-hsiang of the state of Ch'in made the mountain accessible to ordinary mortals. In order to bring down an ancient pine from the summit to make into a huge chessboard, he had his workmen install a series of iron chains and ladders.

When he visited Huashan in the T'ang dynasty, the Confucian scholar and poet Han Yu got halfway across this ridge and became paralyzed with fear. Like all scholars, he never went anywhere without his writing kit. In desperation, he wrote a letter of farewell and dropped it over the edge. Help eventually arrived, and he was carried down the mountain. Since then, the path along the ridge has been made wider and lined with chains for safety.

A few minutes later, I reached the archway of Chisuokuan, the traditional entrance to the summit and the place where the trail finally divides. Master Hsieh had advised us to stay overnight at the lodge on East Peak, so I took the trail to the left. After a few minutes, I stopped to share a small watermelon with a porter who made his living carrying things up the mountain. Loads varied, he said, between forty and fifty kilograms, and the fee for one trip was 10 RMB, two dollars. I tried to heft his load. It felt like a ton.

Finally, I got up and climbed the rest of the way to Middle Peak. Middle Peak is also called Jade Maiden Peak after the daughter of Duke Mu of the state of Ch'in. The duke's daughter came to Huashan twenty-six hundred years ago with her husband, the flute master Xiao Shi. After living on the mountain for several decades, she and her husband drank an elixir of liquid jade and flew off to join the immortals. In honour of his daughter, the Duke built a shrine here. It's been rebuilt many times.

From Middle Peak, the main trail to East Peak leads down a long series of steps, then along the eastern edge of the summit's interior and up again to the peak. But there's a shortcut, and I needed a shortcut. I retraced my steps and took a side trail to Yinfeng pavilion, where the Duke's daughter often played pan-pipes and her husband the flute, and the wind carried their music all the way to her father's palace on the plains. Looking south from the pavilion, I could see the handprint on East Peak left by the giant who shoved Huashan and Shouyangshan apart so that the Yellow River could turn east and flow to the sea.

I pulled myself up the final series of chains and arrived at the back gate of the temple that now serves as a lodge, just below the summit of East Peak. I sat down outside the front gate and drank one of the beers that came up the mountain along with other necessities of life on the shoulders of local porters. Steve arrived during the second bottle and joined me in a third.

We were sitting in the spot where the picture in the flight magazine had been taken. I was amazed: the scene was real, and we were actually sitting there. Directly below us the same magic pavilion perched on the same magic promontory. The pavilion, its stools, and its chessboard-table had all been recently rebuilt, hewn from white granite. More than two thousand years ago, during the reign of Emperor Wu, a Taoist by the name of Wei Shu-ch'ing was seen playing chess on this promontory with several immortals.

East Peak is also known as Sunrise Peak, and we joined a hundred other visitors shivering outside before dawn. The sun rose and a hundred cameras clicked. It rose from behind a mountain where the Shanhaiching says a black pheasant lives that can be used to cure boils. The shaman's guide to the mountains also claims: "There are no birds or animals on Huashan, except for a serpent called the fei-yi, which has six feet and four wings and causes great droughts whenever it appears," and which we didn't see.

After a breakfast of noodles, Steve and I began our tour of the rest of Huashan's flower-shaped summits. On the way to South Peak, we passed through the gate of a small temple at Nantianmen and came out on the peak's southern face. Along the cliff, a trail of chains and planks lead down and across to Holao Cave, one of several hermitages carved into the mountain's sheer face by the thirteenth-century Taoist Ho Yuan-hsi. A caretaker said that someone falls almost every month but added that the awareness of danger has a way of concentrating a person's abilities.

South Peak is also known as 'Wildgoose Landing'. It's the highest point on Huashan, slightly under 2,200 metres . Standing here in the eighth century, the poet Li Bai remarked, "From this highest of places, my breath can reach the throne of Heaven. I regret that I didn't bring with me the profound poems of Hsieh T'iao. I had some questions for the blue sky."

From South Peak the trail winds down and across another dragon spine to West peak. At the edge of the peak there's another thousand-metre drop-off into Hsienyu Gorge. We peered over the precipice, and then retraced our steps to Tsuiyun Temple, which huddles against the inside of the dragon spine.

When the Buddhist travel-diarist Kao Ho-nien visited the mountain in 1904, he marvelled at how the Taoists on Huashan were able to get by on so little. He also commented on the serenity of Huashan and the dedication to seclusion of those who lived here. He said this was not true for other Taoist mountains—and he had visited them all.

On the way down, we rested again at Shaloping. I remembered what Master Hsieh had said about Master Su moving a disciple to a cave on the summit of Dashangfang. Dashangfang was somewhere up there in the clouds. I looked at the cliff across the gorge and wondered out loud how far up it was to Master Su's cave. A man who was selling slices of watermelon said he knew Master Su. He said Dashangfang wasn't far, and he offered to guide us.

We accepted his offer and followed him across the stream. On the other side, he showed us where the trail began. We stared in disbelief. The trailhead was an iron chain hanging about thirty metres down the face of the cliff. Our guide pulled himself up, then waved for us to follow. Steve and I looked at each other with dismay, but what respectable excuse could we offer? So we followed. The next part was even more frightening: finger and toe holds up a seventy-degrees slope made slick by a seeping spring. And no chain. Terrified to look down, we just kept climbing so that we wouldn't think about the drop.

After about a hundred metres, we reached the ruins of an ancient hermitage, then started up an even steeper cliff. Halfway up, legs wobbling from exhaustion and fright, I asked our guide how much farther it was. He said two hours and pointed to the top of a cliff just below the clouds. When he'd told us Master Su's cave "wasn't far," I had neglected to ask him what that meant. Now that I knew, I realized we couldn't possibly make it. We had less than two hours of daylight *and practically no strength. We decided to visit Master Su another day, and descended slowly to the main trail.*

That should have been the end of this chapter, but seven months later I visited Huashan again. It was late March, and everything had changed. There was almost no water in the stream, the walls of the gorge were sere, except for an occasional wild peach tree in bloom. When I reached Shaloping, I stopped to talk with our former guide. He said Master Su and his disciple had come down from Dashangfang for a few days and were staying at Chaoyuangtung Temple at the mouth of the gorge. I smiled, happy in the thought that I wouldn't have to climb that cliff again.

I returned to Jade Spring Temple and headed toward Shihetung. As I walked across the grounds, I ran into old Master Hsieh. On West Peak, he lived alone. Here, at the bottom of the mountain, he was surrounded by a dozen young disciples. He asked me if I had planted the pine seeds. I told him I had given them to friends of the forests of Taiwan, Japan, and America. When I asked him about Master Su, he disappeared into what looked like a temporary mess tent and returned with a tall monk who looked about forty.

Hsieh introduced the monk as Su's disciple. His name was Chou. When I said I had tried to visit him and his master the previous Fall, he said if I waited another year or two I might have an easier climb. Taiwan's Tien Ti Association, he said, had offered to finance construction of a safer trail. It was obvious he didn't welcome the offer. Just then, another monk came out of the tent. Chou said this was Master Su. I bowed and introduced myself. Without pausing, Su said I had the wrong man, that his name was Hua, as in Huashan. Then he walked off, flapping his long sleeves as if he were about to fly away. [Source: Bill Porter, *Road to Heaven: Encounters with Chinese Hermits*, Rider, London, 1993]

In 1989, Bill Porter, a writer and translator of ancient Chinese poetry, and photographer friend Steven Johnson, roamed the Qin Mountains to see if the centuries old tradition of hermits continued in China. They found the answer to their question on Huashan. Porter has lived in Taiwan for more than 20 years, including four years in a Buddhist monastery. He now lives near Seattle, Washington. His other works, published under the pen name 'Red Pine', include *The Collected Songs of Cold Mountain* and *The Mountain Poems of Stonehouse*. Bill's latest book is *Poems of the Masters: China's Classic Anthology of Tang and Sung Verse*, Copper Canyon Press, USA, 2003.

Towers of the Great Wall, north of Yulin, Shaanxi, 1911.

View of the Great Wall showing encroaching sands, 1911.

Great Wall in Shaanxi Province

—William Lindesay

The words of Chairman Mao Zedong etched facsimile on stone in his cursive calligraphic style are a common sight at every Great Wall tourist location. Yet these words, actually a line from his poem *Liupanshan*, are so badly twisted in their modern and now-accepted Mandarin meaning, and English translation, that few can now appreciate what and where, he was originally writing about.

Nowadays, *Bu dao chang cheng fei hao han* is typically turned into 'We are not heroes unless we have climbed the Great Wall', in order to boost domestic tourism. But the accurate meaning in 1934 was issued by Mao as a challenge to his war-torn army: Who are we if we cannot reach the Great Wall?

Mao is believed to have penned his poem *Liupanshan*, the name of a mountain in southern Ningxia, while atop its 2,928 metre summit. With a clear vista ahead towards Shaanxi province, he envisaged that the incised loess plateau that lay beyond the horizon in the northwest would serve as the new revolutionary base for his Communist army. And so he spurred his followers on with the immortal, poetic line demanding a final effort on their 12,000 kilometre journey that became known as the Long March.

The Zhenbei Terrace at Yulin, painted by naturalist Arthur de C. Sowerby who passed through the area in 1908.

The Ming Dynasty Great Wall writhes its way across nine provinces and regions of northern China, from the desert to the sea. Mao Zedong led his army through seven provinces and regions, from the southeast to northwest. The Wall and the leader 'met' in northern Shaanxi, just south of ramparts built five centuries before to defend China from Mongol incursions.

The Great Wall here looks very different from the familiar image that lies far away to the east, in the suburbs of Beijing. In northern Shaanxi the ramparts were made of rammed earth, a process that involved ramming wet earth, layer upon layer, into wooden frames. Using large stones, hollowed on their top surfaces at centre and affixed to the ends of poles, the builders of the Wall pummelled down some 40 layers in succession to achieve a maximum height of up to 9 metres—still a formidable physical barrier to cavalry invaders.

Against the march of time however, such Wall has faired less well than its stone and brick built counterpart in the east around Beijing, being easily washed by heavy rains and degraded by loess-laden winds, let alone by the physical assault of migrating sand dunes. Now the ramparts of the area remain as crumbling, amorphous mounds, nevertheless a distinct and impressive landscape linearity stretching far.

In analyzing the conflict between the sedentary society of China and the nomadic society of the steppe during the Ming Dynasty, military strategists are surprised that, in this part of the country, the line of border defences were eventually routed across, rather than around, the great loop of the Yellow River.

Earlier Great Walls had completely incorporated the mighty river's channels, which served not only as a natural psychological demarcation but also a physical barrier to hinder the advance of invaders. The Zhao State Great Wall, built circa 300 BCE, was well to the north of the Yellow River, and this structure was later included within the Qin Dynasty Great Wall, part old Wall part new, circa 214 BCE. However, just south of the river, in the northern part of its great loop, was a great tract of desert, the Mu Us Shamo.

The sandy, windswept Ordos (as it is known in English) was considered a hostile land to the Chinese, lying beyond the limits of what they considered to be cultivable. Yet for nomads who had much worse to deal with further north, this was seen as good land, edged by a massive river. Effectively the Ordos was part of the great northern steppe that protruded south, piercing the geographical line of China's northern border. Occupation of the region by the Chinese required so-called forward garrisoning—outposts—beyond the natural demarcation line. Some emperors attempted the strategy, but repeatedly failed, for the same reasons. Governments could never successfully and permanently colonize such poor land, and such a change was an essential security backup to any defence line, otherwise the defence line was isolated and vulnerable.

Hence, during the Ming Dynasty, the border defences were routed just south of the Ordos. This apparent concession of useful-to-the-enemy territory was matched with the construction of elaborate earthworks in the area of today's northern Shaanxi. Two lines of Wall were built as a belt and braces security measure, while the worst scenario of an eventual breach of the defences in the region led to the southerly extension of the inner Great Wall in neighbouring Shanxi province to the east, to block the enemy's potential advance through mountain passes that would lead them onto the North China Plain and toward the imperial capital of Beijing located on its northern edge.

The evolution of such a complex system of border defences eventually saw the Ming Dynasty leaving behind some 6,700 kilometres of Great Wall when the Manchus established the Qing Dynasty in 1644. Since then, both man and nature have combined to damage the Wall, so much so that conservationists now estimate only two-thirds, or 4,500 kilometres, of the original length to be extant.

Of the "disappeared" 2,200 kilometres, much has been lost to desertification. In the autumn of 1908, Robert Clark and Arthur de C. Sowerby organized an expedition through Shaanxi, inspecting the Wall near Yulin, (known as Yansui during Ming times, since the seat of the military region lay between the towns of Yan'an and Suide):

"Just within the Great Wall, and about three miles north of the city, stands a large fort originally built to guard the entrance, through which runs the main road from the Ordos. It is some ninety feet in height and surrounded by a high wall. There are three storeys: the first a solid block of masonry about thirty feet square; the second and third similar, but lessening in size."

Clark and Sowerby were standing on the largest structure on the whole length of the Ming Great Wall, the Zhenbei Terrace (now restored). Built over a three-month period in the spring of the 35th year of the Wanli Emperor (1607), the terrace is regarded architecturally as a watchtower and as such is the largest of its kind on the whole length of the Ming Wall. It was built on the orders the governor of the Yansui military region—one of 11 border defence regions—to protect the horse-tea markets that were organized annually outside the city during the late Wanli period as a policy aimed at pacifying the Ordos nomads by offering them guaranteed trading rights.

Continuing from their standpoint atop the Zhenbei Terrace, Clark and Sowerby wrote:

"From here a splendid bird's-eye view of the desert is obtainable—countless sand dunes stretching north and south to the horizon.... The Great Wall at this point, and indeed the whole boundary-line between the Ordos and Shensi [Shaanxi], is little more than a low ridge of earth. Its course however is easily distinguishable by the watch towers still existing at intervals of about three hundred yards. In many cases these are in admirable states of preservation, leading to the supposition that the Wall in this part was not faced with brick or stone." *

Sadly, those fine towers have themselves since vanished, ransacked for building material, mainly between 1958 and 1976 when Mao advocated "letting the past serve the present". Yet to the west of Yulin, strung out between the towns of Jingbian, Anbian and Dingbian, many long sections of rammed-earth Great Wall can still be seen, while the names of these places—Jing, An and Ding—being characters for calm, peaceful and stable, preserve geographically the historical hope that inhabitants nurtured for a life without conflict on this ancient *bian*, border. [Extracts are from *Through Shen-Kan, The Account of the Clark Expedition in North China* by Robert Clark and Arthur de C. Sowerby; published by T. Fisher Unwin, London, 1912.]

William Lindesay travelled alone and on foot for a distance of 2,470 kilometres along the route of the Ming Great Wall between Jiayuguan and Shanhaiguan in 1987. He recounted his journey in Alone on the Great Wall *(Hodder, UK 1989; Fulcrum USA 1991). Remaining in China since his adventure to research he became concerned about the physical and spiritual destruction of the Great Wall cultural landscape and established the conservation group* International Friends of the Great Wall *(www.friendsofgreatwall.org) in 2001. Lindesay now works with the Beijing Bureau for Cultural Relics, UNESCO Beijing Office and the US-based World Monuments Fund to preserve the authenticity of Great Wall. His latest book is* Images of Asia: The Great Wall *(Oxford Univ. Press, Hong Kong, 2003).*

'Warm guidance'

'Chairman Mao's heart and ours beat as one'

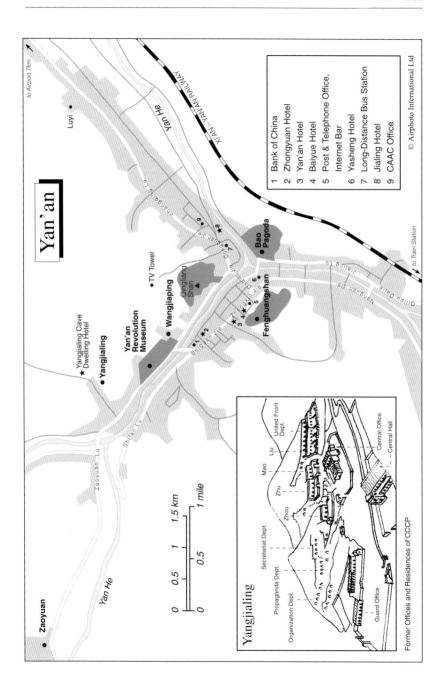

Yan'an

to Airport 7km

Luyi

XIAN-YAN'AN RAILWAY

Yan He

Changqing Lu

to Train Station

1 Bank of China
2 Zhongyuan Hotel
3 Yan'an Hotel
4 Baiyue Hotel
5 Post & Telephone Office,
   Internet Bar
6 Yasheng Hotel
7 Long-Distance Bus Station
8 Jialing Hotel
9 CAAC Office

© Airphoto International Ltd

Bao Pagoda

TV Tower

Qingliang Shan

Wangjiaping

Fenghuangshan

Yan'an Revolution Museum

Yangjialing Cave Dwelling Hotel

Yangjialing

Zaoyuan

Yan He

Zaoyuan Lu

Shibai Lu

Beiguan Jie

Daqiao Jie

Zhongxin Jie

Air union Jie

Daqiao Beilu

Jiefang Lu

Yanguan Jie

Nanguan Lu

Qilipu Dajie

0   0.5   1   1.5 km

0   0.5   1 mile

Yangjialing

Former Offices and Residences of CCCP

Secretariat Dept.

Propaganda Dept.

Organization Dept.

Mao
Liu
Zhu
Zhou

United Front Dept.

Central Office

Central Hall

Guard Office

Lost Luggage in Sianfu —Simon Hollege

In June 1936, the American correspondent Edgar Snow left the peaceful campus of Yanjing University in Beijing, where he had been teaching in the school of journalism, to travel to the war-torn hinterland of China on his toughest mission to date. Five years previously the Japanese had annexed Manchuria. Further incursions by the Japanese went unchecked as civil war between Nationalists and Communists kept the armies occupied. Just eight months before, Mao Zedong had led the Communist retreat—later called the Long March—from soviet areas in the southeastern province of Jiangxi to a new base in northern Shaanxi. Edgar Snow wanted to find the Red Bandits, as the Communists were called, interview their leader Mao, and report their manifesto for China to the world.

Inoculated against smallpox, cholera, typhus, plague and typhoid and armed with a letter written in invisible ink testifying his credentials as a trustworthy journalist, Snow boarded the night train to Zhengzhou where he would change for Sianfu (present-day Xi'an). Later he disclosed that the introduction was written by Soong Chingling, widow of Sun Yat-sen.

Sianfu—Prefecture of Western Peace—was the headquarters of two warlords and their own troops: General Yang Hucheng and Marshall Zhang Xueliang. Both were poised to implement what Generalissimo Chiang Kai-shek hoped would be the final suppression of the Red Bandits in the north.

On arrival at Sianfu's 'new and handsome railway station', Edgar Snow took a room, as he had been instructed, in the Xijing Hotel on the west side of present-day Jiefang Lu (the building now houses the Provincial Travel Bureau). There he waited patiently for a man who would identify himself as 'Wang'. A few days later, a pastor of that name, fluent in English thanks to his missionary education in Shanghai, came to the hotel. He was to be the go-between responsible for arranging Snow's onward travel to the Communists' capital of Bao'an, 350 kilometres (217 miles) away in the north.

A few day later Snow, escorted by troops from Zhang Xueliang's army, passed through the high wooden gates of the walled city in the half light of dawn. After crossing the Wei River by ferry and passing through a strip of no man's land, he reached 'Red' territory. From a village within this territory, where he met Zhou Enlai, he was escorted at last into the presence of the Communist leader.

What happened in the ensuing few months is journalistic history. Snow interviewed Mao Zedong over many nights, taking notes which in the end totalled about 20,000 words. From these and talks with other leaders Snow was able to write the first authentic account of the life and conditions of the northwestern Communist enclave, the revolutionary struggles of Mao and his comrades, and the fundamental policies of the People's Soviet Republic.

In mid-October 1936, Snow bid farewell to his Communist hosts, and about a week later crossed safely behind Nationalist lines again. He rode on to a town where a truck waited to take him back to Sianfu. As he prepared to disembark near the Drum Tower, he asked one of his escorts to toss down his kitbag. To his horror, it could not be found. In the bag were a dozen diaries and notebooks, 30 rolls of film and many magazines, newspapers and documents he had collected during his time in 'Red' territory. It then dawned on the travellers that Snow's bag had been stuffed into a gunnysack amongst broken rifles and guns, which had been offloaded at Xianyang 30 kilometres (18 miles) back.

The truck driver proposed they waited till the next day to retrieve the bag, but Snow insisted on the search being made without delay. The driver returned to Xianyang and the precious bag was recovered. Snow's sense of urgency proved justified. The next day much of Sianfu was cordoned off and traffic was cleared from the roads, for Chiang Kai-shek had decided to pay a sudden call on the city.

The manuscript of *Red Star over China* was completed within an astonishing eight months in Beijing, where Snow returned to live. The 500-page epic was first published in England in 1937 and has since become a classic.

In Xi'an, Edgar Snow's contribution to the world's understanding of Chinese Communism is remembered by the Snow Studies Centre, based at the Eighth Route Army Office Museum (see page 259). The centre was established in February 1992, the 20th anniversary of Snow's death. Many of the journalist's belongings, including his khaki uniform, knapsack and grass sandals, were donated to the centre by his family.

(Above) *Row of rustic Communist Party cave residences built into a mountainside.*

(Left) *Mao Zedong addressing cadres in Yan'an, 1942. It was at this far-flung base that he transformed his movement and planned his comeback .*

Yan'an

Introduction to Yan'an

The dusty city of Yan'an looks like anything but the holy land of the Chinese revolution. But this small city, nestled beneath the loess hills of northern Shaanxi along the Yan River, played an important role in the resurrection of the Chinese Communist Party (CCP) which arrived in the city with the bulk of its organization destroyed. Yan'an served as the general headquarters for the Communists from 1936 to 1947—a period during which the Party leadership reorganized itself, and set the stage for its final victory over the Nationalist forces (KMT). Today, the city is one of the most popular stops along the Communist pilgrimage trail, second only to Mao's birthplace of Shaoshan, in Hunan province.

The remnants of the Eighth Route Army crawled into the city in 1936 at the end of the famous 8,000-mile Long March through central and western China. Only 8,000 to 9,000 of the 80,000 troops who left Jiangxi in eastern China two-and-a-half years earlier were still with Mao when he arrived in Shaanxi province. Reflecting on this experience, Mao said that the Long March "has proclaimed to the world that the Red Army is an army of heroes, while the imperialists and their running dogs, Chiang Kai-shek and his like, are impotent." Mao's brave words could not disguise the reality that his battered forces had suffered a major defeat.

However, it was at this far-flung base that Mao Zedong transformed his movement and planned his comeback. This was Mao's most creative period. During the stay in Yan'an, he spent much of his time reading, thinking and writing, and it was in these spartan surroundings that he penned some of his most famous political treatises, which were of major importance to the rise of Chinese Communism. He worked 14 hours a day, often staying up until the early morning hours. It's said that in 1938 he once worked without stop for nine days and nights to finish his essay *On Protracted War*.

After arriving in Yan'an, the CCP immediately set to restructuring the Party, government and army. Party membership soared from about 40,000 in 1937 to around 800,000 in 1940, due to intense recruiting efforts and the popularity of the Communist's united front policies. The Party forbid the expropriation of land and implemented a systematic policy of rent reduction. The graded taxation system made it unfeasible for the wealthy to maintain large land holdings, but in turn made it possible for poor peasants to boost their land holdings. It was thus easy to rally villagers to the anti-Japanese and anti-KMT cause. The CCP also prohibited Red Army soldiers from exploiting local farmers, and ensured that they paid for food and supplies they took. They were also careful to prevent the soldiers from molesting local women.

It was this idealism that attracted the interest of foreign journalists who braved many dangers to make their way to the 'Red' area for a first-hand look. These included Agnes Smedley, Anna Louise Strong, Theodore White, Edgar Snow, his wife Helen, and several others. Edgar Snow was the first to break through the Nationalist blockade, and his reports arguing that the CCP was a unique and indigenous brand of communism, and not a puppet of Moscow, changed American notions about Red China (see page 281). Snow's wife, who visited Yan'an in 1937, heaped praise on the CCP, and concluded that the Chinese Communists "belonged to the same human race as myself". Another foreign visitor dubbed the Chinese Communists "Prince Valiants in Straw Sandals". In retrospect, many of these foreign journalists, who were disillusioned with the corruption and inefficiency found in the Nationalist controlled areas, were blind to the problems and injustices that existed in Yan'an.

There was also a steady parade of U.S. military and government officials who were also quite taken with the ideals espoused by the Communist leadership. The first American officer to arrive in Yan'an was U.S. Marine Corps. Captain Evans F. Carlson, who was impressed with the moral conduct and democratic camaraderie between soldiers and officers. In July 1944, the Dixie Mission (see page 302) flew to Yan'an for a look around. The U.S. Army Mission in Yan'an predicted in 1944 the possibility of an ultimate victory for the Chinese Communists in the war against the Nationalists. And during a visit to Yan'an in November that year, Patrick Hurley, Roosevelt's special emissary to China, said that the Communists were "the only real democrats in China".

The Nationalists launched a major offensive in December 1946, and succeeded in taking the Communist capital of Yan'an three months later, forcing the CCP to evacuate the city. Two years later, however, the Communists overthrew the Chiang Kai-shek government, which retreated to the island of Taiwan.

YAN'AN REVOLUTION MUSEUM

Although there are no English signs at this museum, visitors may want to come here before visiting Yan'an's revolutionary sites. The museum has an extensive collection of interesting photographs and other memorabilia from the Yan'an period, much of which will be self-explanatory.

Interesting are the weapons used by the Red Army, from an old wooden cannon and grenades with wooden handles to a mish mash of rifles, swords and spears. One photo exhibition introduces smiling American soldiers and government officials who visited the Communist base as well as well-known Western journalists. Another section illustrates the self-sufficient nature of the Communists, displaying looms used to make clothing, and homemade pottery bowls, cups and bottles.

A simple cave dwelling on the outskirts of Yan'an.

Chilli peppers hung on a cave window to dry in the sun.

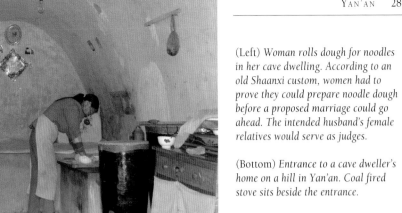

(Left) *Woman rolls dough for noodles in her cave dwelling. According to an old Shaanxi custom, women had to prove they could prepare noodle dough before a proposed marriage could go ahead. The intended husband's female relatives would serve as judges.*

(Bottom) *Entrance to a cave dweller's home on a hill in Yan'an. Coal fired stove sits beside the entrance.*

Mao's loyal steed is also on display. A sign in front of the stuffed horse explains that the horse was transplanted to the Beijing Zoo after the Communist victory in 1949. Just before it died in 1962, goes the official explanation, the horse turned in the direction of the Communist headquarters at Zhongnanhai in Beijing, and cried three times, as if bidding farewell to its former master.

The Four Former Residences of the CCP

The Communist leadership had four bases in Yan'an, each set up in cave homes. The four sites have become important sites for Chinese making this pilgrimage to the Communist "holy land." Smiling Chinese tourists experience the past by dressing up in the light grey uniforms of the Red Army, posing for photographs while holding a wooden rifle, or sitting on the ground in front of a spinning wheel. The cave homes at each place are quite similar. The arched rooms, built into the side of the loess hills, have a Spartan and monastic look to them, decorated with simple kang beds and wooden desks. The cave dwellings, said to be somehow warm in the winter but also cool in the summer, have bright sunlight shining through the horse-shoe shaped latticed windows. Many of the rooms display photographs of the former Communist occupants—and their foreign visitors—who spent time here.

Public buses 7, 8 and 13 stop at the main revolutionary sites. It's also possible to hire a private car to visit all these sites for about 100 yuan.

FENGHUANSHAN

Former home of Mao Zedong, Zhou Enlai and Zhu De. This was the first site occupied by the Communists after their arrival in the city. The CCP Central Committee moved here from Baoan (now Zhidan) on January 13, 1937. It was here that the Communists discussed plans for the anti-Japan united front following the Xi'an Incident. Mao wrote *On Protracted Warfare* while living here. Japanese air raids forced the Chinese leadership to move to Yangjialing in November 1938.

This site has an exhibition of photos of Norman Bethune, the Canadian doctor who died while working in Yan'an (see page 306).

ZAOYUAN REVOLUTIONARY HEADQUARTERS

Zaoyuan, or Date Garden, was the workplace of the CPC Central Secretariat from 1945 to 1947. Zhou Enlai moved to Wangjiaping in March 1947, just a few days before the Communists fled the city as Chiang Kai-shek's forces attacked. Zhu De, the commander-in-chief of the Red Army, also lived here. A stone chessboard where Zhu played with workers, remains in front of Zhu's cave dwelling.

IN THE HOSPITAL

While foreign visitors to the 'Red' capital were infatuated with the idealism of the Yan'an spirit, all was not well in the Communist base. In her novel *In the Hospital*, popular writer Ding Ling made a veiled criticism of the Party's treatment of women in Yan'an and the double standards they faced.

She argued, saying that she didn't have the right disposition for such work, and that she would do anything else, no matter how significant or insignificant. She even dropped a few tears, but there arguments weren't enough to shake the chief's determination. She couldn't overturn this decision, so she had no choice but to obey.

The party branch secretary came to talk to her and the section leader wouldn't leave the subject alone. Their tactics irritated her. She knew the rationale behind all this. They simply wanted her to cut herself off from the bright future which she had been dreaming of for the past year and to return to her old life again. She knew she could never become a great doctor and was nothing more than an ordinary midwife. Whether she was there or not made no difference at all. She was full of illusions about her ability to break out of the confines of her life. But now that the iron collar of 'party' and 'needs of the party' was locked about her neck, could she disobey party orders? Could she ignore this iron collar which she had cast upon herself?

The realities of life frightened her. She wondered why many people had walked by her that night, yet not a single one of them had helped her. And she thought about the fact that the director of the hospital would endanger patients, doctors, and nurses just to save a little money. She looked back on her daily life. Of what use was it to the revolution? Since the revolution was for the whole of mankind, why were even the closest of comrades so devoid of love? She was wavering. She asked herself: "Is it that I am vacillating in my attitude toward the revolution?" The neurasthenia which she had of old gripped her once again. Night after night she could not sleep.

People in the party branch were criticizing her. They capped her with labels like "petty-bourgeois consciousness," "audacious and liberal intellectualism," and many other dangerous doctrines; in short, they said that her party spirit was weak. The director of the hospital called her in for a talk.

Even the patients were cool and distant toward her, saying she was a romantic. Yes, she should struggle! But whom should she struggle against? Against everyone?

Excerpt from Ding Ling's *In the Hospital*,
within *The Gate of Heavenly Peace: The Chinese and their Revolution 1895-1980*
by Jonathan Spence. Penguin, New York, 1982.

YANGJIALING REVOLUTIONARY HEADQUARTERS
This was the former residence of Mao, Zhu De, Zhou Enlai and Liu Shaoqi. The large auditorium here was the site for large party activities. It was also here that Mao held the Yan'an Forum on Literature and Art in May 1942. Mao spoke at the forum, insisting that literature and art should be a reflection of the views of workers, peasants and soldiers, and denouncing the concept of art for art's sake. This speech set the CCP line toward writing and art for decades to come. Fresh cigarettes, left by visitors, are strewn across the bed allegedly once used by Mao, an avid smoker. A sign on the wall says "No Smoking". Liu Shaoqi met American writer Anna Louise Strong here in November 1946.

WANJIAPING REVOLUTIONARY HEADQUARTERS
This is the headquarters of the CPC Central Military Committee and the General Headquarters of the Eighth Route Army. It was from here that Mao and Zhou retreated to northern Shaanxi following the Nationalist attack on Yan'an in March 1947.

BAO PAGODA
This 44-metre pagoda, originally built during the Song dynasty in 766–78, was restored in the 1950s. The pagoda, which is now a national symbol of China, sits on a hill on the southeast side of the Yan River, and provides good views of the surrounding area. The Bao Pagoda is a short walk from the downtown area of Yan'an.

Austere interior of a Red Army leader's cave home in Yan'an,
with latticed windows and brick, kang-heated bed.

延 安 的 曙 光

'*Mao Zedong: the shining light of Yan'an.*'

CONVERSATION WITH RED PEASANTS

As I travelled beyond Pao An, toward the Kansu border and the front, I stayed in the rude huts of peasants, slept on their mud kang (when the luxury of wooden doors was not available), ate their food, and enjoyed their talk. They were all poor people, kind and hospitable. Some of them refused any money from me when they heard I was a 'foreign guest.' I remember one old bound-footed peasant woman, with five or six youngsters to feed, who insisted upon killing one of her half-dozen chickens for me. We can't have a foreign devil telling people in the outer world that we Reds don't know etiquette," I overheard her say to one of my companions. I am sure she did not mean to be impolite. She simply knew no other words but 'foreign devil' to describe the situation. I was traveling then with Fu Chin-kuei, a young Communist who had been delegated by the Red Foreign Office to accompany me to the front. Like all the Reds in the rear, Fu was delighted at the prospect of a chance to be with the army, and he looked upon me as a godsend. At the same time he regarded me frankly as an imperialist, and viewed my whole trip with open skepticism. He was unfailingly helpful in every way, however, and before the trip was over we were to become very good friends. One night at Chou Chia, a village of north Shensi near the Kansu border, Fu and I found quarters in a compound where five or six peasant families lived. A farmer of about forty-five, responsible for six of the fifteen little children who scampered back and forth incessantly, agreed to accommodate us, with ready courtesy.

He gave us a clean room with new felt on the kang, and provided our animals with corn and straw. He sold us a chicken for twenty cents, and some eggs, but for the room would take nothing. He had been to Yenan and he had seen foreigners before, but none of the other men, women, or children had seen one, and they all now came round diffidently to have a peek. One of the young children burst into frightened tears at the astonishing sight. After dinner a number of the peasants came into our room, offered me tobacco, and began to talk. They wanted to know what we grew in my country, whether we had corn and millet, horses and cows, and whether we

(Left) *The People's Militia preferred sabotage and surprise when fighting the Japanese (1937–1945).*

used goat dung for fertilizer. (One peasant asked whether we had chickens, and at this our host sniffed contemptuously. "Where there are men, there must be chickens", he observed.) Were there rich and poor in my country? Was there a Communist Party and a Red Army? In return for answering their numerous questions, I asked a few of my own. What did they think of the Red Army? They promptly began to complain about the excessive eating habits of the cavalry horses. It seemed that when the Red Army University recently moved its cavalry school it had paused in this village for several days, with the result that a big depression had been made in the corn and straw reserves. "Didn't they pay you for what they bought?" demanded Fu Chin-kuei. "Yes, yes, they paid all right; that isn't the question. We haven't a great amount, you know, only so many tan of corn and millet and straw. We have only enough for ourselves and maybe a little more, and we have the winter ahead of us. Will the cooperatives sell us grain next January? That is what we wonder. What can we buy with soviet money? We can't even buy opium!" This came from a ragged old man who still wore a queue and looked sourly down his wrinkled nose and along the two-foot stem of his bamboo pipe. The younger men grinned when he spoke. Fu admitted they couldn't buy opium, but he said they could buy in the cooperatives anything else they needed. "Can we now?" demanded our host. Can we buy a bowl like this one, eh?" And he picked up the cheap red celluloid bowl (Japanese-made, I suspect) which I had brought with me from Sian. Fu confessed that the cooperatives had no red bowls, but said they had plenty of grain, cloth, paraffin, candles, needles, matches, salt. What did they want? I hear you can get more than six feet of cloth per man; now, isn't it so?" demanded one farmer. Fu wasn't sure; he thought there was plenty of cloth. He resorted to the anti-Japanese argument. "Life is as bitter for us as for you," he said. "The Red Army is fighting for you, the farmers and workers, to protect you from the Japanese and the Kuomintang. Suppose you can't always buy all the cloth you want, and you can't get opium, it's a fact you don't pay taxes, isn't it? You don't go in debt to the landlords and lose your house and land, do you? Well, old brother, do you like the White Army better than us, or not? Just answer that question. What does the White Army give you for your

(Left) Shaanxi farmers normally have little time for relaxation, producing as they do, two main crops per year in their fields—one of maize and the other of winter wheat—together with chillies and fruit, including pomegranates, persimmons, apples and pears.

crops, eh?" At this, all complaints appeared to melt away, and opinion was unanimous. "Certainly not, Old Fu, certainly not!" Our host nodded. "If we have to choose, we take the Red Army. A son of mine is in the Red Army, and I sent him there. Does anyone deny that?" I asked why they preferred the Red Army. In answer the old man who had sneered at the cooperatives for having no opium gave a heated discourse. "What happens when the Whites come?" he asked. "They demand such and such amounts of food, and never a word about payment. If we refuse, we are arrested as Communists. If we give it to them we cannot pay the taxes. In any case, we cannot pay the taxes! What happens then? They take our animals to sell. Last year, when the Red Army was not here and the Whites returned, they took my two mules and my four pigs. These mules were worth $30 each, and the pigs were full grown, worth $2 each. What did they give me? Ai-ya, ai-ya! They said I owed $80 in taxes and rent, and they allowed me $40 for my stock. They demanded $40 more. Could I get it? I had nothing else for them to steal. They wanted me to sell my daughter; it's a fact! Some of us here had to do that. Those who had no cattle and no daughters went to jail in Pao An, and plenty died from the cold..." I asked this old man how much land he had. "Land? " he croaked. "There is my land," and he pointed to a hilltop patched with corn and millet and vegetables. It lay just across the stream from our courtyard. "How much is it worth?" "Land here isn't worth anything unless it's valley land," he said. "We can buy a mountain like that for $25. What costs money are mules, goats, pigs, chickens, houses, and tools." "Well, how much is your farm worth, for example?" He still refused to count his land worth anything at all. "You can have the house, my animals and tools for $100—with the mountain thrown in," he finally estimated. "And on that you had to pay how much in taxes and rent?" "Forty dollars a year!" "That was before the Red Army came?" "Yes. Now we pay no taxes. But who knows about next year? When the Reds leave, the Whites come back. One year Red, the next White. When the Whites come they call us Red bandits. When the Reds come they look for counterrevolutionaries.""But there is this difference, " a young farmer interposed, "If our neighbours say we have not helped the Whites that satisfies the Reds. But if we have a hundred names of honest men, but no landlord's name, we are still Red bandits to the Whites! Isn't that a fact?" The old man nodded. He said the last time the White Army was here it had killed a whole family of poor farmers in a village just over the hill. Why? Because the Whites had asked where the Reds were hiding, and this family refused to tell them. After that we all fled from here, and took our cattle with us. We came back with the Reds." "Will you leave next time, if the Whites return?" "Ai-ya!" exclaimed an elder with long hair and fine teeth. "This time we will leave, certainly! They will kill us!" He began to tell of the villagers' crimes. They had joined the Poor People's League, they had voted for the district soviets, they had given information to the Red Army about the White Army's movements, two had sons in the Red Army, and another had two daughters in a nursing school. Were these crimes or not? They could be shot for any one of them, I was assured. But now a barefoot youth in his teens stepped up, engrossed in the discussion and forgetful of the foreign devil. "You call these things crimes, grandfather? These are patriotic acts! Why do we do them? Isn't it because our Red Army is a poor people's army and fights for our rights?" He continued enthusiastically: "Did we have a free school in Chou Chia before? Did we ever get news of the world before the Reds brought us wireless electricity? Who told us what the world is like? You say the cooperative has no cloth, but did we ever even have a cooperative before? And how about your farm, wasn't there a big mortgage on it to landlord Wang? My sister starved to death three years ago, but haven't we had plenty to eat since the Reds came? You say it's bitter, but it isn't bitter for us young people if we can learn to read! It isn't bitter for us Young Vanguards when we learn to use a rifle and fight the traitors and Japan!" This constant reference to Japan and the 'traitors' may sound improbable to people who know the ignorance (not indifference) of the mass of the ordinary Chinese peasants concerning Japanese invasions or any other national problems. But I found it constantly recurring, not only in the speech of the Communists but among peasants like these. Red propaganda had made such a wide impression that many of these backward mountaineers believed themselves in imminent danger of being enslaved by the 'Japanese dwarfs'—a specimen of which most of them had *yet to see outside Red posters and cartoons. The youth subsided, out of breath. I looked at Fu Chin-kuei and saw a pleased smirk on his face. Several others present called out in approval, and most of them smiled. The dialogue went on until nearly nine o'clock, long past bedtime. It interested me chiefly because it took place before Fu Chin-kuei, whom the farmers appeared to hold in no awe as a Red 'official'. They seemed to look upon him as one of themselves—and indeed, as a peasant's son, he was. The last one to leave us was the old man with the queue and most of the complaints. As he went out the door he leaned over and whispered once more to Fu. "Old comrade," he implored, "Is there any opium at Pao An; now, is there any?" When he had left, Fu turned to me in disgust. "Would you believe it?" he demanded. "That old defile-mother is chairman of the Poor People's Society here, and still he wants opium. This village needs more educational work."*

Edgar Snow, Red Star Over China (*Random House, USA, 1938*)

Mao Zedong with Zhou Enlai (left), who went on to become China's premier from 1949 until his death in 1976, and Bo Gu (right), founder of the Liberation Daily and the New China News Agency, who died in an air crash in 1946.

*Visitors to the Date Orchard (Zao Yuan) Revolutionary Base get into
the Yan'an spirit by posing for photos dressed in the Red Army garb.*

SATURDAY NIGHT FEVER

—John Colling, from Spirit of Yenan

On July 22, 1944, a C-47 carrying American soldiers and officials flew over the loess hills of Yan'an and landed with a jarring halt at the Communists' primitive airfield. Mao Zedong rode out in his ambulance-cum-limousine to greet the American Military Observers Mission, which included John Colling. The mission was also known under the name Dixie—for the rebel side and for the song "Is It True What They Say About Dixie." General Joseph Stilwell was frustrated with the Generalissimo's corrupt and inefficient regime. Vinegar Joe, as Stilwell was affectionately known, was impressed by the Red Army and wanted to know if the Communists' had the ability—if armed with American equipment—to stand up against the Japanese forces. The Dixie Mission,

John Colling, member of the Dixie Mission,
seen during his participation in the Burma Campaign.

under the command of Colonel David Barrett, a former Chinese language officer and military attaché in Peking, called the Communist area "a different country," and Yan'an "the most modern place in China." The Americans noted the strong nationalism and pragmatism of the Communists and in the fall of 1944 predicted the real possibility that they would win the civil war with the Nationalists. After U.S. Naval Intelligence, which had close ties with the Nationalist secret police, leaked to Chiang Kai-shek the American plan to arm 25,000 Communist guerrillas to fight the Japanese, Barrett took the blame for the incident, and the Dixie Mission was recalled. During the McCarthy period in the U.S. after the war, which led to a vicious Communist witch-hunt in America, many of the Americans affiliated with the Dixie Mission lost their jobs.

In our leisure time, sports were a high priority. We played American softball, ping pong, volleyball, and basketball. Zhou En-lai, a good outfielder who liked baseball tremendously, would play whenever time permitted. Further entertainment included movies that were brought up with the supply flights from Chongqing. The usual GI fare, which included the introduction of Mickey Mouse (better known in Chinese as Mickey Lau Shu, was the first opportunity many of the peasant people had to see the silver screen.

In confusion over what the screen was, many of the peasants when they first saw it would come up, touch the screen and look behind to see if it was real.

Yenan's 'Pear Orchard', featured Saturday night dancing and entertainment. Everyone was invited, including the members of the Japanese Emancipation League (JEL) who readily mingled with the Chinese men and women. This was the centre of all relaxation and small talk. It was here, between dances and presentations, that we heard most clearly about the Communist dream.

Local musicians, although in short supply, usually played Chinese stringed instruments. Music that rasped and spluttered out of an old phonograph machine included 'Yankee Doodle Dandy', and American folk music. We danced the foxtrot and other Western ballroom styles, but most frequently swayed to the 'yang ke', or rice sprout dance, which closely resembled a conga.

Theatre was an important propaganda tool of the Communists, and the most memorable events in the Pear Orchard were the folk drama adaptations. Young soldiers would comb the countryside for authentic songs and dances, which contained political messages and resistance propaganda, which they would then take back to Yenan to rework into skits. Themes included tilling the soil and hiding Chinese soldiers from the Japanese. Taxes were either paid in kind, or with paper currency, which was illustrated in the play with a paper drawing and an actual piece of millet.

The leaders moved easily among their people, and danced often and with anyone who asked. Accompanying these leaders, on and off the dance floor, were their wives—all of whom were important. Prior to Yenan, Zhou Su-fei (Madam M Haide) and Jiang Qing (Madam Mao Zedong) were movie actresses. Kang Ke-ching (Madam Zhu De) was a peasant guerrilla fighter and Deng Ying-chao (Madam Zhou Enlai), an educated Hunanese, was a national leader of women's organizations.

'Saturday Night Fever' in the Pear Orchard, Yan'an's local weekly disco.

(Right) A common sight in the courtyards of many homes in the Shaanxi countryside—red chillies and maize drying in the autumn sunshine.

Where The Twain Met —Gerald Hatherly

Comrade Bethune and I met only once ... I am deeply grieved over his death. Now we are all commemorating him, which shows just how profoundly his spirit inspires everyone. (Chairman Mao Zedong)

Jonathan Spence's *To Change China* (Penguin Books, 1980) is an interesting profile of Westerners who had exerted some influence within China. The most compelling chapter tells the story of the Canadian physician and humanitarian, Norman Bethune (1890–1939). While there are many examples of foreign adventurers, explorers, scholars and dreamers making their mark on the country, Norman Bethune stands out—above all others—for the utter selflessness and deeply measured love he held for China and the Chinese. As every middle school child can tell you, Bai Qiuen (Bethune's Chinese name) loved China so much that he died in its quest for freedom and liberation. This is a deeply felt love and respect, despite the fact that Bethune lived less than two years in China, and then only in a remote region of the country's wild northwest.

Born into a deeply religious family in quiet Gravenhurst, Ontario (approximately 100 miles to the north of Toronto) in March, 1890, Norman Bethune was raised to consider the condition of his fellow man. He studied medicine at the University of Toronto but broke his studies on two occasions in order to work as a stretcher-bearer and medical aid during World War I. Badly wounded, he convalesced in France and England and upon his recovery completed his medical studies. He then served his internship at the Hospital for Sick Children and the Fever Hospital in London, where he met and married Frances Campbell Penny. The couple moved to Detroit in 1924, where Bethune encountered the plight of the poor and began to provide free medical care for those in the direst need. During his time in Detroit he contracted tuberculosis and was sent to a sanatorium in upstate New York. His recovery, partly aided by an advanced form of surgery, spurred his interest in thoracic surgery and over the next several years —in the United States and in Montreal—he became a leading expert in new surgical techniques.

The outbreak of the Spanish Civil War appealed to his altruistic nature and he went to Spain to serve as a medical doctor. He set up the first portable mobile blood units that enabled wounded soldiers to receive blood transfusions on the battlefield. "Spain", he wrote, "is a scar on my heart". The misery and suffering of the anti-fascist forces touched him and deepened his resolve to serve those in the greatest need.

Upon his return to Canada he set about on a cross-country lecture tour to raise money for medical causes, and it was then that he learned of the Japanese invasion of China. Bethune had more than a passing interest in China, having read extensively of the country's ongoing problems and the suffering of her people. He left Vancouver in January, 1938 bound for Hong Kong. He then crossed into China, making his way up to Yan'an, Shaanxi province, where he joined Mao's Communist Red Army. From here he set off into some of the most hostile territory, some 300 kilometres north of the main communist bases.

The region had more than 13 million people and less than a handful of properly trained doctors, and so Norman Bethune established 20 teaching and nursing hospitals and trained young doctors and nurses, often without the aid of any text materials or proper equipment. He treated, without any compensation, sick and wounded soldiers and peasant farmers. He operated, often for long periods at a time, driven by the urgency of the situation. In one instance he operated for 69 hours non-stop treating some 115 individuals.

It was not long before the tales of this quiet Canadian—a man who shared his food rations, clothing, limited medicines, and even his blood—circulated among the population, which was moved by the selfless gesture of a doctor from across the ocean who was fighting for the cause of a New China.

In October 1939, during another marathon operating session, Dr. Bethune cut his hand during an operation (he had no operating gloves) and developed blood poisoning. Knowing that he had little time, he ordered the recording of his will in which he instructed that money be given to his wife and the rest used to buy medical supplies. He closed with this statement which best describes a remarkable individual who brought together the twain of East and West:

"The last two years have been the most significant, the most meaningful years of my life ... I have found my highest fulfillment here among my beloved comrades".

On November 12, 1939, Bethune died and became a folk hero throughout China. Chairman Mao wrote a moving essay, which every Chinese student is required to learn, in memory of his selfless sacrifices for China.

Physician, teacher, humanitarian and advocate for those in need, Norman Bethune has become the symbol of a cross-cultural friendship that tied together two very different worlds.

THE LONG LONGING

Endless is my longing—longing for Chang'an.
When autumn crickets hum by the golden edge of the well,
A light frost casts cold colours on my mat,
The solitary lamp is dim; my longing near despair.
I furl the curtain and look upon the moon,
In vain, I sigh...
Like a flower is my fair one, sever'd by cloud and mist.
Above, the faint blue sky,
Beneath, the green water wave...
High is heaven, wide is earth;
Neither can my spirit fly,
Nor my dreams carry me over the grim mountain pass.
Long is the longing that crushes my heart!

Li Bo (688–762), translated by Moon Kwan

长相思　李白

长相思
在长安
络纬秋啼金井阑
微霜凄凄簟色寒
孤灯不明思欲绝
卷帷望月空长叹
美人如花隔云端
上有青冥之高天
下有渌水之波澜
天长路远魂飞苦
梦魂不到关山难
长相思
摧心肝

RECOMMENDED READING

HISTORY AND RELIGION

Barrie, David, *Dixie Mission: The United States Army Observer Group in Yenan, 1944* (Berkeley, University of California Press, 1970)

Bertram, J, *First Act in China: The Story of the Sian Mutiny* (1938, reprinted by Hyperion Press, Westport, Conn, 1973)

Ch'en, K, *Buddhism in China, Historical Survey* (Princeton University Press, Princeton, New Jersey, 1964)

Hopkirk, Peter, *Foreign Devils on the Silk Road* (Oxford University Press reprint, 1986)

Porter, Bill, *Road to Heaven-Encounters with Chinese Hermits* (Rider, London, 1993)

Reischauer, E, *Ennin's Diary* (Ronald Press Company, New York, 1955)

Selden, Mark, *The Yenan Way in Revolutionary China* (Cambridge, Harvard University Press, 1971)

Snow, Edgar, *Red Star Over China* (Random House, USA, 1938)

Temple, Robert, *The Genius of China: 3,000 Years of Science, Discovery and Invention* (Prion Books, Ltd., 1991)

Zanchen, M, (translated by Wang Zhao), The Life of General Yang Hucheng (Joint Publishing Company, Hong Kong 1981)

ARTS AND ARCHAEOLOGY

Laufer, B, *Chinese Pottery of the Han Dynasty* (1909, reprinted by Charles E Tuttle, Vermont and Tokyo, 1962)

Li, Hui, *Xi'an: The Famous Ancient Capital of China* (Shaanxi Tourism Bureau, 1990)

Luo, Zhewen and Shen, Peng (Compilers), *Through the Moon Gate: A Guide to China's Historic Monuments* (Oxford University Press, 1986)

The Pick of Prehistoric Cultural Relics of Ban Po Museum (Shaanxi Tourism Publishing House, 1995)

The Subterranean Army of Emperor Qin Shi Huang (China Travel and Tourism Press, 1999)

Wang, Xueli, *The Coloured Figurines in Yang Ling Mausoleum of Han in China* (China Shaanxi Travel and Tourism Press, 1992)

Watson, W, *Ancient China, The Discoveries of Post-Liberation Archaeology* (BBC, London, 1974)

Xi'an: World Ancient Chinese Capital for over a Thousand Years (Shaanxi People's Fine Arts Publishing House, 1990)

Geography

Liu, Tungshen, *Loess in China* (China Ocean Press, Beijing/Springer-Verlag, 1985)

Zhang, Zonghu, Zhang, Zhiyi and Wang, Yunsheng, *Loess Deposits in China* (Geological Publishing House, Beijing, 1991)

Zhao, Songqiao, *Physical Geography of China* (Science Press and John Wiley & Sons, 1986)

Literature

Cooper, Arthur, *Li Po and Tu Fu* (Penguin Books, Harmondsworth, 1979)

Hughes, E R, *Two Chinese Poets, Vignettes of Han Life and Thought* (Princeton University Press, Princeton, New Jersey, 1960)

Inoue, Y, (translated by J T Araki and E Seidensticker), *Lou-lan and Other Stories* (Kodansha International Limited, New York and San Francisco, 1979)

Waley, Arthur, *The Life and Times of Po Chü-i 772–846* (George Allen & Unwin, London, 1949)

Translated by Yang Xianyi and Gladys Yang, *Poetry and Prose of the Tang and Song* (Panda Books, Beijing, 1984)

Twentieth-century Travellers

Clark, R Stirling and Sowerby, A de C: *Through Shen-Kan: The Account of the Clark Expedition in North China 1908–09* (T Fisher Unwin, London, 1912)

Cressy-Marcks, Violet, *Journey into China* (Hodder and Stoughton, London, 1940)

Crow, Carl, *Handbook for China* (Oxford University Press, 1984)

Eliasson, S, (translated by K John): *Dragon Wang's River* (Methuen and Company Limited, London, 1957)

Farrar, R, *On the Eaves of the World* (E Arnold, London, 1917)

Fleming, Peter, *News from Tartary* (1936, reprinted by Futura Publications, London, 1980)

Lindesay, William, *Alone on the Great Wall* (Hodder & Stoughton, London, 1989 and Fulcrum Publishing, Colorado, USA, 1991)

Nichols, F H, *Through Hidden Shensi* (Charles Scribner's Sons, New York, 1902)

Pan, Lynn, *China's Sorrow—Journeys Around the Yellow River* (Century, London, 1985)

PRACTICAL INFORMATION

HOTELS

Xi'an did not have a Western-style hotel until the 1950s. In the early part of the century Chinese inns were open to foreigners, but many Western travellers arriving in Xi'an stayed with the European missionaries of the Scandinavian Alliance, the English Baptist Mission and the China Inland Mission.

Since the city's first joint-venture hotel, the Golden Flower, opened in 1985, many new international-standard hotels have been built. Now Xi'an has a surplus of quality accommodation, so that even in the peak seasons of spring and autumn many hotels still have a large percentage of their rooms vacant. In the winter, from mid-November until the end of March, these hotels offer various bargain packages whereby tariffs are reduced, sometimes by up to 50 percent. Check with individual hotels directly.

Shangri-La Golden Flower Hotel (Xiang Ge Li La Jinhua Fandian)
8 Changle Xilu. Tel. (029) 83251000-4720; fax. (029) 83235477
e-mail: slx@shangri-la.com; www.shangri-la.com,
visit www.virtual-tour.shangri-la.com/six for a virtual tour.
香格里拉金花饭店　长乐西路8号
Five-star hotel situated outside the city wall on the road to the Terracotta Warriors. The Golden Flower has 446 of the largest rooms in Xi'an, and the largest swimming pool. Restaurants serve Cantonese, Shaanxi and international cuisine (see Restaurant section on page 318).

Prince International Hotel (Wangzi Guoji Jiudian)
32 Nan Dajie. Tel. (029) 87632222; fax (029) 87632188
e-mail: xian-hotel@prince-catering.com
王子国际酒店　南大街32号
Four-star hotel located just south of the Bell Tower. 170 luxurious rooms. Various restaurants serving Western food, Chinese cuisine and seafood hotpot. Business centre, conference room and shopping centre.

Sheraton Xi'an Hotel (Xi'an Xi Lai Deng Dajiudian)
262 Fenghao Donglu. Tel. (029) 84261688; fax. (029) 84262983
www.sheraton.com
喜来登大酒店　沣镐东路262号
Five-star hotel conveniently located to the west of the city wall. 438 luxuriously equipped rooms.

ANA Grand Castle Xi'an (Chang'an Chengbao Dajiudian)
12 Xiduan Huancheng Nanlu. Tel. (029) 87231800; fax. (029) 87231500
e-mail: sales@anahotelxian.com; www.anahotelxian.com
长安城堡大酒店　西段环城南路12号
Modern five-star hotel conveniently located facing the south gate of the city wall. 340
rooms and suites. Spacious atrium lobby lounge, Sky Lounge, Chinese and Japanese
restaurants, banqueting hall and coffee shop. Business centre, beauty salon and
shopping centre.

Hyatt Regency Hotel (Kaiyue Fandian)
158 Dong Dajie. Tel. (029) 87231234; fax. (029) 87216799
凯悦饭店　东大街158号
Situated within the city walls and close to the business and shopping districts. 404
luxurious rooms. Various restaurants serving both international and Chinese cuisine,
public bar and pizzeria. Business centre, health club, beauty salon and shopping
facilities.

Grand New World Hotel (Gudu Xin Shijie Jiudian)
172 Lianhu Lu. Tel. (029) 87216868; fax. (029) 87210708
e-mail: gnwhbc@pub.xaonline.com; www.gnwhxian.com
古都新世界酒店　莲湖路172号
Conveniently located within the walled city. 493 rooms. Fully equipped meeting
facilities with 1,130-seat theatre and 12 meeting rooms. Four restaurants serving
local, Cantonese, continental, American and Southeast Asian specialties. Indoor
swimming pool, open tennis court, sauna and gymnasium.

Hotel Royal Xi'an (Xi'an Huangcheng Binguan)
334 Dong Dajie. Tel. (029) 87235311; fax. (029) 87235887
e-mail: huangchengbz@royalxa.com; www.royalxa.com
皇城宾官　东大街334号
Four-star hotel located within the city walls, managed by Nikko Hotel International.
439 rooms, including two royal suites, and business and deluxe suites. Chinese and
Western restaurants, banquet halls, tea lounge, bar and business centre.

Xi'an Garden Hotel (Xi'an Tanghua Binguan)
4 Yanyin Lu, Dayan Ta. Tel. (029) 85261111; fax. (029) 85261778/85261998
e-mail: tanghua@pub.xaonline.com; www.xagarden-mitsuihotel.com
唐华宾官　大雁塔 雁引路4号
Four-star joint-venture hotel located adjacent to the Big Goose Pagoda in a spacious
garden setting. 292 rooms. Chinese, Japanese and Western restaurants. Tang Theatre

*(Left) One of the massive stone guardians that line the 'Spirit Way' of Qian Ling,
the mausoleum of Emperor Gaozong and his empress Wu Zetian.*

Restaurant serving French cuisine also equipped as a conference hall. Sauna, fitness centre and massage facilities.

Bell Tower Hotel (Zhonglou Fandian)
1 Nan Dajie (southwest corner of Bell Tower)
Tel. (029) 87600000; fax. (029) 87218767; www.belltowerhtl.com
钟楼饭店 南大街1号
Good central location overlooking the Bell Tower and a short walk from the Drum Tower and Great Mosque. 321 fully appointed rooms. Chinese and Western restaurants, meeting and banquet rooms.

Jianguo Hotel (Jianguo Fandian)
2 Hu Zhu Road. Tel. (029) 83238888; fax. (029) 83237180/83235145
e-mail: jgsale@pub.xaonline.com
建国饭店 互助路2号
Located just east of the city wall, near the zoo. Its 800 rooms are equipped with satellite TV. Banquet hall, conference rooms, a variety of restaurants, swimming pool, sauna, beauty salon, gym and bicycle rental.

Orient Hotel Xi'an (Dongfang Dajiudian)
393 Zhuque Street. Tel. (029) 85262211; fax. (029) 8526 1768
东方大酒店 朱雀路393号（小寨西路）
Four-star hotel located on the south side of the town. 299 rooms. Serving Western and Chinese food.

Le Garden Hotel (Li Yuan Jiudian)
8 Laodong Nanlu. Tel. (029) 84263388; fax. (029) 84263288
e-mail: legarden2001@sinlang.com; www.legardens.com
骊苑酒店 劳动南路8号
Four-star hotel located on the ring road to the southeast of the walled city. 298 rooms with executive and non-smoking floors and meeting rooms. Two Chinese restaurants serving Cantonese and southeastern cuisine, a Western-style coffee shop, bar and disco. Health club with gymnasium, sauna, steam bath and Jacuzzis, and beauty salon.

Xi'an Hotel (Xi'an Binguan)
36 Chang'an Lu. Tel. (029) 87666666; fax. (029) 87666333; www.xahotel.com
西安宾馆 长安路36号
Four-star, 545-room hotel located close to the Little Goose Pagoda south of the city wall. Restaurants serve Chinese, Japanese and Western cuisine. Health and recreation centre including swimming pool and gymnasium. Business centre.

Tangcheng Hotel (Tangcheng Binguan)
3 Hanguang Nanlu. Tel. (029) 85265711; fax. (029) 85261041
e-mail: csxtch@public.xn.sn.cn; www.xiantangchenghotel.cn
唐城宾馆　含光南路3号
Modern three-star hotel, located south of the walled city. 406 rooms and suites,
conference rooms, business centre, Chinese and Western restaurants, bars, coffee
shop and recreational facilities.

Wannian Hotel (Wannian Fandian)
93 Changle Zhonglu. Tel. (029) 82596666; fax. (029) 82596668
e-mail: wnhotel@wnhotel.com, www.wnhotel.com
万年饭店　长乐中路93号
Located outside the city wall on the road to the Terracotta Warriors. 170 rooms.
Chinese and international restaurant, lounge bar, health centre, sauna, massage
parlour and beauty salon.

Xi'an Melody Hotel (Xi'an Meilun Jiudian)
86 Xi Dajie. Tel. (029) 87288888; fax. (029) 87273601
西安美伦酒店　西大街86号
Located facing the Drum Tower and Century Ginwa Shopping Square. 158 rooms
equipped with internet, IDD/DDD, satellite TV, sauna, fitness centre, KTV rooms,
mini bar and beauty salon. Chinese restaurant serving traditional food and seafood.

Dynasty Hotel (Qindu Jiudian)
55 Huancheng Xilu. Tel. (029) 88626262; fax. (029) 88627728
e-mail: dynasty@pub.xaonline.com; http//:www.dynastyhotel.com
秦都酒店　环城西路55号
Conveniently located alongside the west city wall. Modern facilities in ancient
Chinese palatial style architecture with 200 rooms. Restaurants and 300-seat
banquet room offering hot-pot, Cantonese, Shanghainese, and Western cuisine.
Meeting rooms and business centre. Sauna and fitness room, beauty salon, bar,
nightclub and shopping arcade. Air-ticketing service.

Empress Hotel (Huanghou Jiudian)
45 Xingqing Lu. Tel. (029) 83232999; fax. (029) 83236988
皇后酒店　兴庆路45号
Located east of the walled city, not far from the zoo. 259 spacious rooms.
Comprehensive business, entertainment and dining facilities.

Longhai Hotel (Longhai Dajiudian)
306 Jiefang Lu. Tel. (029) 87416090; fax. (029) 87416580
陇海大酒店　解放路306号

Fengxiang county painted clay tiger.

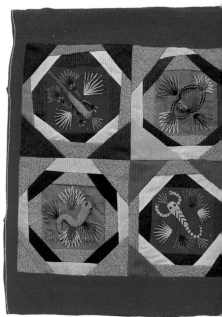

*Child's appliquéd vest featuring
four of the 'five poisonous creatures'.*

International standard three-star hotel, located in the northeast of the walled city, not far from the railway station. 308 rooms.

Huaqing Guesthouse (Huaqing Chi Binguan)
Lintong County. Tel. (029) 83812002
华清池宾馆 临潼县
Part of the hot springs complex, with 23 rooms. On the road to the Terracotta Army Museum.

XIANYANG 咸阳

Imperial Hotel (Qinbao Binguan)
60A Weiyang Xilu. Tel. (0910) 3313388; fax. (0910) 3313366
e-mail: qingbao@public.xa.sn.cn

秦宝宾馆 渭阳西路甲60号
Located in the centre of Xianyang, 15 minutes drive from the international airport. 220 rooms, conference rooms, Chinese and Western restaurant, coffee shop and business centre.

FAMEN 法门

Famen Temple Hotel (Famen Si Binguan)
Zhongzheng Lu. Tel. (0917) 5254141; fax. (0917) 5255489
法门寺宾馆　中正路
A small but new 36-room hotel close to the Famen Temple.

HUASHAN 华山

Huashan Lotus Hotel (Huashan Lianhua Shanzhuang)
Huayinshi, Huashan Donglu Dongduan. Tel. (0913) 4368888; fax. (0913) 4362961
华山莲花山庄　华阴市华山东路东段

Huashan Financial Hotel (Huashan Jinrong Binguan)
Huayinshi, Huashan Yuquanlu Zhongduan. Tel. (0913) 4363120 and 4363123
fax. (0913) 4363124
华山金融宾馆　华阴市华山玉泉路中段

Beifeng Fandian
Tel. (0913) 4300062
北峰饭店
Small guest house located on the North Peak of Huashan.

YAN'AN 延安

Yan'an Hotel (Yan'an Binguan)
Yan'an Shi Dajie No. 56. Tel. (0911) 2113122; fax. (0911) 2114297
延安宾馆　延安市大街56号
Four-star hotel, founded in 1965. In the last 40 years, it has received government leaders, including the late Premier Zhou Enlai. Foreign national leaders have also stayed here, including Ho Chi Minh, Ferdinand Marcos and Norodom Sihanouk. 210 guestrooms. Conference hall, business centre, banquet hall, entertainment centre, gym facilities and swimming pool.

Yangjialing Shiyao Binguan
Yangjialing Geming Jiuzhi Tel. (0911) 2330836; fax (0911) 8261203
杨家岭石窑宾馆　杨家岭革命旧址
This cave hotel is located in Yangjialing village, about 500 metres from the cave houses used by Mao Zedong and other revolutionary veterans between 1936 and 1948. There are 248 cave dwellings in this hotel. Built to modern three-star hotel standards, the Yangjialing Shiyao Binguan features unusual architecture and offers visitors the chance to experience traditional furnishings such as a Chinese *kang*, or heated brick beds.

Silver Seas International Hotel (Yinhai Guoji Dajiudian)
Daqiao Street. Tel. (0911) 2139999; fax. (0911) 2139666
银海国际大酒店 大桥街
Five-star hotel located in the centre of the city. 212 rooms. Business centre, gym
facilities, swimming pool, bar, and karaoke lounge.

Restaurants

Shangri-La Golden Flower Hotel (Xiang Ge Li La Jinhua Fandian)
8 Changle Xilu. Tel. (029) 83232981
香格里拉金花饭店 长乐西路8号
The Shang Palace is regarded by the most critical of locals as one of the best
restaurants in the city. The menu features Sichuanese and Cantonese home-style
cooking. Some items on the menu are available only in season. Particularly
recommended is the Sichuan roast duck, a variation of the more famous Beijing
counterpart.

Qianzhou Shifu
134 Youyi Xilu. Tel. (029) 87810767
A26, Kejilu, Gaoxinqu. Tel. (029) 88228166
乾州食府 友谊西路134号；高新区科技路甲字26号
The first page of the menu introduces a set meal offering a variety of snack specialties
from Qian county in Shaanxi province. The set meal, called *qianzhou xiaochi* in
Chinese, includes a small bowl of *doumian hu* (a paste made of peas), a small bowl
of *douhuanao* (soft beancurd in spicy sauce), *guokui* (toasted flat bread with a soybean
spread), *chasu* (sweet fried dough filled with sugar, crushed nuts and almond
flavour). The final dish is a special noodle from Qian county served in a tasty broth.
The noodles are cooked at your table, with diced cilantro and minced meat added to
the boiling broth, which is seasoned with a drop of vinegar and chili oil.

Lan Hua Hua Shifu
76 Renhouzhuang, Jinhua Nanlu (East Second Ring Road, 200 meters south of the
Jianguo Hotel). Tel. (029) 83252897
兰花花食府 金花南路76号
The front façade of the restaurant resembles a cave house. This restaurant specializes
in traditional Shaanxi dishes, such as *yangyu chacha* (stir-fried noodles made of
potatoes and flour), *qiaomian hele* (cold noodle made of buckwheat flour), *zhurou
qiao banmian* (stir fried bean-starched noodle with spiced pork), *youbing* (like a
doughnut without the hole, made of millet), *juanbing* (meat filling steamed in a
paper-thin wrapper and dipped in vinaigrette sauce).

Wenhao Zaliang Shifu
2 Nan Erhuan Zhongduan, Provincial Sports Stadium, South Building
Tel. (029) 85215555
文豪杂粮食府 南二环中段2号
This restaurant serves traditional Shaanxi cuisine. An appetizer called *Ganquan doufu* (beancurd made of mung bean), *yangxue* (coagulated mutton blood), *mizi yougao*, like a doughnut without the whole, made of millet), *babao zheng nangua* (sweet steamed pumpkin with eight treasures), *hele* (noodles made of buckwheat), *huicai*—a variety of vegetables—potatoes, carrots, Chinese cabbage—thin sliced meat, and wide bean-starched noodles, simmered in spiced broth.

Qinren Mianzhuang
78 Dongyi Lu. Tel. 13572086622
秦人面庄 东仪路78号
Selection of hand-made noodles.

Suide Yangroumian
34 Taiyangmen Miao Men, Xiao Nanmenli. Tel. 83056804
绥德羊肉面 小南门里 太阳庙门34号
Special lamb and noodles from Suide county in Shaanxi province. Known for its millet wine and rice wine from Yulin county. Serves all sorts of lamb dishes.

The Tang Dynasty
39 Chang'an Lu. Tel. (029) 85261633
唐乐宫 长安路39号
Located south of the Bell Tower, opposite the Xi'an Hotel, the complex boasts a theatre restaurant with extensive banqueting facilities and authentic Cantonese restaurant. The theatre restaurant can comfortably seat 500 diners and is the only one of its kind in China. Whilst enjoying a menu which blends the best of East and West, diners are serenaded by musicians playing authentic Chinese classical instruments. Dinner is followed by an hour-long cultural show of traditional music, song and dance replicating the entertainment of the Tang court (see also page 43). For a hefty 410 yuan per person, you will be served 6 kinds of Chinese cuisine including dessert. The show runs from 7:00 to 9:40pm.

Baiyunzhang Jiaozi Restaurant
No. 364 Dong Dajie; Tel. 87212835, 87214438
白云章 东大街364号
A branch of the well-known Laosunjia restaurant which serves Hui-style *jiaozi* (dumplings). Their specialty, a set of six different kinds of jiaozi including mutton, mushroom, and seafood, is recommended.

Defachang Jiaozi Restaurant

Bell and Drum Tower Square. Tel. 87214060

德发长 钟鼓楼广场

Located next to the Bell Tower on the square, this restaurant was originally established in 1936. There are dumplings with more than 5 different types of filling listed on the menu—however, they are not always all available. On the second floor, there is a minimum charge of 60 yuan to 200 yuan per person, and one can sample different types of dumplings steamed or boiled. The dumplings are shaped like frogs, gold fish, ducks, cicadas, penguins, rabbits, pigs, etc.

Tongshengxiang Paomo House

Bell and Drum Tower Square. Tel. 87217512

同盛祥 钟鼓楼广场

Tongshengxiang is well-known for its mutton and beef paomo. Customers take one or two medium size baked flatbreads, break them into small pieces and put the pieces into a big bowl. The bowl is taken to the kitchen where a very hot mutton or beef soup, and bean vermicelli, are poured over the broken pieces of flatbread. Small plate of chopped cilantro, pickled garlic, fresh garlic and chili sauce are provided as condiments. On the cleaner but pricier second floor, diners can enjoy a hot pot and a variety of small snack foods.

Qingyazhai Restaurant

384 Dong Dajie. Tel. 87281881

清雅斋 东大街384号

Another branch of Laosunjia, this Muslim restaurant is run entirely by Hui, or Chinese Muslims. It specializes in lamb and vegetable dishes. Especially good are lamb dumplings.

Shaanxi shadow puppet.

Muslim Quarter

A variety of enticing scents permeate the streets of the exotic Muslim Quarter—cumin and ziran, cardamom, garlic and ginger, pepper, and nutmeg. Popular dishes here include barbecued mutton kebabs, dumplings, fried buns stuffed with mutton, noodles, transparent bean-starch noodles, and Muslim breads. There are also numerous stalls selling a wide variety of spices, breads and sweets. Try persimmon cake (shizi bing), steamed glutinous rice (zeng gao) layered with dates, walnuts, honey and red bean paste. There are also hawkers selling rainbows of dried fruits, roasted chestnuts, melon seeds, delicious peanut and sesame candies, crystal rice cakes (shuijing gao) and green mung bean cakes. The bigger and better known restaurants are located on Beiyuanmen Street, which you enter when you pass under the gate of the Drum Tower. The street comes alive in the evening as tables are placed outside in front of the shop fronts and white capped Muslim cooks turn kebabs on the pit under naked light bulbs and shout out to passersby. To get away from the tourists, try one of the restaurants on the surrounding streets.

Yixianglou Restaurant

5 Miao Houjie (In the Muslim Quarter—walk north down North Gate Street (Beiyuanmen) to the corner of Xi Yang Street and turn left and walk west for about 10 minutes)

伊祥楼 庙后街5号

This small family eatery, away from the touristy restaurants in the centre of the Muslim Quarter, offers lamb skewers barbecued on charcoal (most restaurants here have upgraded to gas barbecue ranges). This is the best place to try roujiamo, a 'Muslim hamburger' with bits of barbecued lamb stuffed in flat-baked bread—only available in the evening. During the day try suantang shuijiao, dumplings in a sour spicy soup, and liangpi, transparent noodles made from mung beans and served in a sauce.

TEA HOUSES AND COFFEE SHOPS

Xian Zong Lin

238 Dong Dajie. Tel. (029) 87270599
1 Bei Dajie. Tel. (029) 87214104
仙踪林 东大街238号；北大街1号
Opening Hours: 9:00 am–1:00 am

This clean and bright small restaurant serves excellent pearl milk tea and a wide variety of other hot and cold tea drinks made with tropical fruits and other flavourings.

Kcoffee

52 Nan Dajie. Tel. (029)87280981
Opening Hours: 8:00–12:00 midnight

肯德基 南大街52号

Part of the Kentucky Fried Chicken empire, Kcoffee serves freshly brewed coffee, expresso, latte, cappuccino, and fruit and regular teas. Tiramisu, cheese cake, black forest cake and cappuccino cake are also available. Located one block from the Bell Tower, this is a clean and comfortable place for a break.

Su Xin Chafang

61 Xiao Zhai Xilu, less than 200 metres east of the Oriental Hotel

Tel. 85225977

Opening hours: 10:00am–1:00am

素心茶房 小寨西路61号

This peaceful tea house is run by a Buddhist monk, Master Fa Qing, who is also a self-taught artist and designer. Sit on a tatami mat at a small table and sample chrysanthemum tea made from flowers brought from the Master's own garden or one of the other Chinese teas available. The water used here to brew tea comes from the nearby Qin Mountains. Also try some of the simple snacks: rose or tea roasted pumpkin seeds, pomegranate and fresh dates. Su Xin Chafang provides an escape from the bustling life outside. "The city is too busy and people need quiet," says Master Fa Qing, "so I brought the solitude of the Buddha to the city."

YAN'AN

Wuqi Dajiudian

Opposite Beiguan Yanzhonggou. Tel. (0911) 2139720

吴起大酒店 北关延中沟对面

This excellent restaurant serves traditional and authentic Shaanxi dishes. The typical Shaanxi dishes include *huangmo* (a slightly sweet steamed millet cake), *you momo* (fried doughnut made of millet), *yougao* (fried sweet and chewy-like cake made of glutinous flour), *kucai tudou* (wild vegetable mixed in mashed potatoes), *niurou liangfen* (bean-starch noodle sautéed with beef), *qiaomian hele* (buckwheat noodles). And don't forget to order a small kettle of its *mijiu*, a milky, sweet millet wine.

Yan'an Binguan

56 Yan'an Street. Tel. (0911) 2113122

延安宾馆 延安市大街56号

The restaurant offers an inexpensive, but varied Chinese style breakfast. Also serves Shaanxi, Cantonese and Sichuan cuisine.

Yan'an Tourism Mansion

Yan'anshi Zhongxinjie Shizi. Tel. (0911) 2138666

延安旅游大厦 中心街十字

Cantonese and Shaanxi cuisine served in a clean and quiet environment.

SHOPS

Shaanxi Sheng Xiangcun Hualang (Peasants Painting Gallery)
18 Hua Jue Xiang, The Drum Tower. Tel. 87212442
陕西省乡村画廊 鼓楼里化觉巷18号
Peasant paintings by Ding Jitang, the person who introduced art into Huxian villages, and other peasant painters.

Wenbaozhai Store
5 Yanta Lu. Tel. 85532380
文宝斋旅游购物中心 雁塔路中段5号

Xi'an Special Arts & Crafts Factory
210 Huancheng Xilu Beiduan. Tel. 88622045
西安市特种工艺美术厂 环城西路北段210号

Xi'an Guwan Shichang (Xi'an Antique Market)
Located at the northwest corner of Zhuque Dajie and Erhuan Lu. Old books, paintings, photographs, jades, brass, cameras, and knick knacks of all sorts.
西安古玩市场 朱雀大街和二环路西北角

Chenghuang Miao Market (Temple of the City God)
The market is situated in front of the City God Temple, about a 10 minute walk west of the Drum Tower. It sells opera costumes, red drums from Ansai, embroidery thread and yarn, all sorts of utensils, mahjong sets, and hundreds of other daily use items.
城隍庙市场 城隍庙前

Century Ginwa Plaza
Between the Bell Tower and Drum Tower. Tel. 87631700
世纪金花 鼓楼和钟楼之间
An underground modern and clean shopping center selling name brand goods. Coffee shops and an excellent supermarket selling Japanese foodstuffs and other food products from around the world. Fresh milk, yogurt, cheeses, breakfast cereals, sushi, soft drinks, biscuits, and fresh baked breads and pastries.

Foreign Languages Bookstore
349 Dong Dajie. Tel. 87219872
English language books on China.
陕西省外文书店 东大街349号

MISCELLANEOUS

Bank of China
157 Jiefang Lu.
中国银行陕西分行 解放路157号

Bank of China
3 Nanguan Zhengjie
中国银行西安分行　南关正街3号

Long-distance Telecommunication Office
28 Xixin Jie.
西安长途电讯局　西新街28号

Post Office
1 Bei Dajie (opposite the Bell Tower)
西安市邮政局　北大街1号

Xi'an Tourism Complaint Office
4th Floor, H3 Xi Dajie Hongfu Daxia. Tel. 87630166
西安市旅游局信息中心　西门宏府安定广场4号楼4单元401室

Shaanxi Province Tourism Complaint Office
Chang'an Beilu. Tel. 85261437
陕西省旅游局办公室　长安北路

Xi'an Taxi Complaint Office
17 Ximenwai Renmin Dongcun. Tel. 88624509; fax 88610314
西安市出租车管理处　西门外人民东村17号
To complain about taxi misconduct.

Foreign Affairs Office, People's Government of Shaanxi Province
272 Jiefang Lu. Tel. 87442949
陕西省人民政府外事办公室　解放路272号

Shaanxi Provincial Hospital
256 Youyi Xilu Tel. 85251331-ext. 2283
For foreigners: 85251439; Emergency: 85241709
陕西省医院　友谊西路256号

Fourth Army Medical University Hospital
17 Changle Xi Lu. Tel. 83374114; Emergency: 83375539
第四军医大学医院　长乐西路17号

Division of Aliens and Entry-Exit Administration of the Xi'an Municipal Public Security Bureau
138 Xi Dajie. Tel. 87275934
公安局出入境管理处　西大街138号
Visa extensions can be processed here.

USEFUL WEBSITES

www.travelchinaguide.com/cityguides/shaanxi/ Travel information about major cities and sites in Shaanxi province

www.asia-hotels.com Easy to navigate and user friendly website for travellers in Asia.

www.cnta.com The domain of the China National Tourism Authority, with basic information on practicalities, hotels, restaurants, shopping, attractions and festivals.

www.cnto.org The official site of the China National Tourism Office based in the US.

www.china-travel-guide.com A useful site compiled by renowned author Ruth Lor Malloy. For travellers who want current, grass roots information about visiting the major cities and travelling off the road in China.

www.lonelyplanet.com The popular site for up-to-date information. Regular contributions from travellers on the road.

www.odysseypublications.com An on-line library of the much-acclaimed Odyssey Books and Travel Guides. Odyssey fans tend to be adventurous travellers with a literary bent.

NEWS SITES

For general news information on China, including Beijing and Shanghai, take a look at the following sites:

www.chinadaily.com.cn Online version of China's only English daily national newspaper. Features national and business news, as well as weather and sport.

www.china.org.cn/english Authorized state portal with daily updates of general and business news. Contains topical features and a travel guide section.

www.cnd.org Topical news and an extensive historical archive from 1644 to the present as well as an extensive photo library covering most places you are likely to visit.

http://english.peopledaily.com.cn/home.shtml English version of the main Communist Party daily with official views on the economy and politics as well as current headlines, topical features and city weather.

http://www.einnews.com/china/ Part of the European Internet News global network. Extensive general and business news, with links to travel-related sites.

www.sinolinx.com A collection of China-related headlines swept from numerous Internet sites.

www.xinhua.org News from China's official news agency.

www.scmp.com The on-line edition of the *South China Morning Post*, Hong Kong's English language newspaper, bringing you daily news and business updates.

BUSINESS-RELATED SITES

Some of the following sites may be of interest to the business traveller.

www.ccpit.org Trade and associated matters from the China Council for the Promotion of International Trade.

www.chinalaws.com Useful information on doing business with legal perspectives.

www.chinabiz.org Comprehensive online daily full of business oriented news, with numerous links to news and entertainment sites.

www.chinabusiness-press.com Government-approved China business magazine, with links to numerous Chinese companies.

www.chinaonline.com Business-focused US news site.

www.chinapages.com Up-to-date business news and information on Chinese companies.

www.english.mofcom.gov.cn/ Topical business information from the Ministry of Commerce.

www.sinofile.net Multi-sector business news based on a wide range of Chinese press reports and special business features.

www.sinonews.com Highlights news on business and investment opportunities.

www.sinosource.com Offers a China business directory.

www.stats.gov.cn/english Official statistics from the National Bureau of Statistics on all aspects of the economy and society.

TRAVEL ARRANGEMENTS

A number of tour operators and experts are listed below. These are a small selection of the many companies based in the USA, the United Kingdom, Australia, China and Hong Kong who offer comprehensive travel arrangements, in particular in China, and about whom clients report positive news.

Abercrombie & Kent (Hong Kong) Ltd.
19/F, Tesbury Centre, 28 Queen's Road East, Wanchai, Hong Kong
Tel. (852) 2865-7818; fax (852) 2866-0556
E-mail: hatherly@abercrombiekent.com.hk, pmacleod@abercrombiekent.com.hk

Audley Travel Ltd
6, Willows Gate, Stratton Audley, Oxfordshire, OX27 9AU, UK
Fax: (01869) 276 214
E-mail: mail@audleytravel.com; www.audleytravel.com

China International Travel Service (CITS)
2/F, 212 Sutter Street, San Francisco, CA 94108, USA
Tel. (415) 398-6627; Toll-free (800) 332-2831; fax (415) 398 6669
Suite 303, US CTS Building, 119 S. Atlantic Blvd, Monterey Park, CA 91754, USA
Tel. (626) 457-8668; fax (626) 457-8955

4/F, CTS House, 78-83 Connaught Road Central.
Tel. (852) 2853-2888; fax (852) 2541 9777

China International Travel Service (Xi'an branch)
48 Chang'an Beilu. Tel. 85262066; fax 85263959
E-mail: zhaolicheng2002@yahoo.com; www.citsxa.com
中国国际旅行社西安分社　长安北路48号

Geographic Expeditions
1008 General Kennedy Avenue, PO Box 29902
San Francisco, CA 94129-0902 USA
Tel. 415-922-0448; Toll Free: 800-777-8183; fax 415-346-5535
E-mail: info@geoex.com; www.geoex.com

Grand Circle Corporation
347 Congress Street, Boston MA 02210, USA
Tel. 1-800-321-2835; E-mail: poreilly@gct.com; www.gct.com

Helen Wong's Tours
Level 17, Town Hall House, 456 Kent Street, Sydney, Australia 2000
Tel. (02) 9267 7833; fax (02) 9267 7717
E-mail: info@helenwongstours.com; www.helenwongstours.com

Peregrine Adventures
258 Lonsdale Street, Melbourne, Vic 3000, Australia
Tel. (03) 9663 8611; fax (03) 9663 8618
E-mail: websales@peregrine.net.au; www.peregrineadventures.com

Regent Holidays (UK) Limited
15 John Street, Bristol, BS1 2HR, England. Tel. (0117) 921-1711; fax 925-4866
E-mail: regent@regent-holidays.co.uk; www.regent-holidays.co.uk

Saga Holidays Ltd.
The Saga Building, Enbrook Park, Folkestone, Kent CT20 3SE, UK
Tel. 0800 414 525; services.sales@saga.co.uk; www.saga.co.uk

Shaanxi China Travel Service
103 Chang'an Beilu. Tel. 85269464; fax 85261821
陕西省中国旅行社　长安北路103号

Shaanxi China Youth Travel Service
21 Nan Erhuan Xiduan, Huarong Guoji Shangwu Daxia Bldg. A, 6/F, B–E
Tel. 85256415; fax 85256409
陕西中青年国际旅行社　南二环西段21号 华融国际商务大厦A座6层B–E

Silk Road Travel Management Ltd

16/F Chinachem Century Tower, 178 Gloucester Road, Wanchai, Hong Kong
Tel. (852) 2736 8828; fax (852) 2736 8000
E-mail: travel@the-silk-road.com; www.the-silk-road.com

Steppes East

51 Castle Street, Cirencester, GL7 1QD, United Kingdom
Tel. 01285 651010; fax 01285 885888
E-mail: sales@steppeseast.co.uk; www.steppeseast.com.uk

TRAVCOA

2424 SE Bristol Street, Suite 310, Newport Beach, CA 92660, USA
Tel. (949) 476-2800; email: requests@travcoa.com; www.travcoa.com

Travelsphere Limited

Compass House, Rockingham Road, Market Harborough, Leicestershire, LE16 7QD, UK
Tel: (0870) 240 2426; email: telesales@travelsphere.co.uk; www.travelsphere.co.uk

Wild Wall

Whilst not currently offering tours of Shaanxi's Wall we are listing this company, not least because founder William Lindesay wrote the essay starting on page 276. This idiosyncratic British researcher offers Great Wall culture weekends and Wild Wall weekends based at either of his farmhouses, both located within 2.5 hours drive from Beijing. Trips include Lindesay's personal guidance and storytelling, accommodation in renovated yet traditional farmhouses, all meals and return transportation from Beijing, with hotel or airport pickups. For details please enquire to www.wildwall.com.

AIRLINES

China Northwest Airlines Booking Office (direct to Beijing)
296 Xishaomen (outside west gate). Tel. 88792299
中国西北民航售票处 西稍门296号

Bangkok Airways (direct to Bangkok)
48 Keji Road, Xi'an High-tech Zone, Pioneering Square Tower B, Room 105
Tel: 88375575; 88375660; www.bangkokair.com
曼谷航空 开发区科技路48号 创业广场B座105室

Dragonair Booking Office (direct to Hong Kong, Shanghai)
Lobby, Sheraton Xi'an Hotel, 12 Fenghao Lu. Tel. 84260390; fax. 84203097
www.dragonair.com 港龙航空公司 西安喜来登酒店 丰镐路12号

China Eastern Xibei Airlines (direct to Shanghai, Hong Kong)
Xishaomen, Laodong Nanlu (opposite the CAAC building). Tel: 88792299
中国东方航空西北公司 西稍门劳动南路 (民航大厦对面)

INDEX

N

O

P